CADOGAN
gourmet guides

lazy days out
across the channel

Cadogan Books plc
London House, Parkgate Road,
London SW11 4NQ, UK

Distributed in the USA by
The Globe Pequot Press
6 Business Park Road, PO Box 833, Old Saybrook,
Connecticut 06475–0833

Copyright © Nick Rider 1996
Illustrations © Charles Shearer 1996
Book, cover and map design by Animage
Cover photography and illustration by Horacio Monteverde
Maps © Cadogan Guides, drawn by Animage and Map Creation Ltd

Series editor: Rachel Fielding
Editing: Linda McQueen

Additional editing and proof-reading
    cookery: Jane Middleton
    French language: Jacqueline Chnéour

DTP: Linda McQueen and Kicca Tommasi
Production: Rupert Wheeler Book Production Services
Printed and bound in the UK by Redwood Books Ltd , Trowbridge

ISBN 1–86011–071–1
A catalogue record for this book is available from the British Library

Please help us keep this guide up to date

Every effort has been made to ensure the accuracy of the information in this book at the time of going to press. However, standards in restaurants and practical details such as opening times and, in particular, prices are liable to change. We would be delighted to receive any comments concerning existing entries or indeed any sugestions for inclusion in future editions or companion volumes. Significant contributions will be acknowledged in the next edition, and authors of the best letters will receive a copy of the Cadogan Guide of their choice.

The Author Prior to the Award of his Booker/Nobel etc.

Nick Rider's first experience of French food was a *crêpe* with jam from a stand in Brittany when he was six years old, made by a man with a beard in baggy brown shorts. Its impact has never been forgotten. More recently, he lived in Barcelona for ten years, and has travelled widely in Spain, France, Italy and Mexico, as well as writing, among other things, a Ph.D on Spanish history, a general index of movies, and articles on food, travel, history, music and art and design. He writes regularly for the London *Time Out* restaurant guide and was editor of the 1995 *Time Out Paris Guide.*

Acknowledgements

Sincere thanks must go, first and foremost, to all the restaurateurs mentioned in this book, for their hospitality, helpfulness, skills, and, of course, fine food, and for generously sharing their recipes. My appreciation, too, to all the shopowners, museum staff, farmers, foodproducers and others mentioned in this book, for always responding well to sometimes tedious questioning from dumb foreigners. Warmest and very special gratitude is due from the publishers and myself to the representatives of the various Comités Départementaux du Tourisme and other local authorities for indispensable assistance, and for combining in the process unfailing courtesy, professionalism, interest in and knowledge of their area, and friendliness: Diana Hounslow of the CDT Pas-de-Calais, and Isabelle Leclercq of the Comité Régional Nord-Pas-de-Calais; Anne-France Rouxel of the CDT de la Somme; Philippe Rabany of the CDT-Seine-Maritime; Isabelle Heudier and Jacques Leprieur of the CDT de la Manche; and Gilles Clémente of the CDT-Eure and Arnelle Le Goff of the CDT-Calvados. To Chantal Atamian of the Office de Tourisme and Martine Bailleux of the Musée Louis-Philippe in Eu, and M. Paul Dechamps, Conservateur of the Palais Bénédictine in Fécamp, extra thanks for making visits there particularly enjoyable. In Britain, I have to thank Elizabeth Powell of the Maison de la France in London, and Diana Bailey at P&O Ferries.

Many thanks also to Jean-Christophe Novelli of the Four Seasons Hotel, London, and native of Arras, for his interest, enthusiasm and helpful suggestions; Andrew and Deirdre Solomon for Saint-Malo; Jenni Muir; Josephine Thomas and Lenny Cameron; Philippa Perry; and Aymeric de Salvert. To Neil Norman and Susanne McMillan, for letting us use their Norman mansion. To my editors at Cadogan, Rachel Fielding and Linda McQueen, for their concern, amiability, unflappability and patience. And most of all to Ethel for eating her way round with me, making the whole trip more enjoyable, identifying things I didn't even notice, and for everything.

Contents

Introduction

In 1768 Laurence Sterne, after meeting someone who said that 'they had been in France', marvelled that simply moving oneself a short distance should entitle all and sundry to make such an apparently imposing statement, and was spurred to go on a trip himself, recorded in his Sentimental Journey. That very night he dined in Calais on a fricasséd chicken, and declared that from then on he could state with the best that he, too, had incontrovertibly been in France.

Visiting France has always been bound up with eating. In the Middle Ages English soldiers, taking a break from pillaging the Artois countryside, were among the first British travellers horrified to discover the range of things that French peasants ate, and decided to call them all 'Frogs' as a result. By the last century, on the other hand, France was established as the unchallenged international paragon in anything and everything to do with the pleasures of the table, the lofty standard and pinnacle of refinement against which all other cuisines were judged.

The very idea of a 'restaurant' is a French invention; on another level, special foods from cabbages and strong, meaty sausages to gourmet cheeses, *foie gras* and fine wines are among the most prized products of their home regions, often the best-known and most genuinely appreciated of the features that make up their distinctive local identities. Among visitors, especially the British, the French preoccupation with fine food has long produced mixed reactions: some have looked on *cuisine française* with suspicion as over-fancified, and romanticised the simpler fare back home, while, for the more sybaritic, France and its restaurants became places of luscious pilgrimage. France can attract for many reasons—its superb cathedrals and architecture, its instantly distinctive street life, its sensuous tradition of great art, its still remarkably natural, unpavemented countryside—but for foreigners and the French themselves *la vie française* is also a culture to be enjoyed through the taste buds.

In the last few years it has been widely suggested, in any number of magazine features, that French cuisine may no longer merit its traditional exalted status and esteem. Restaurants in France, it is said, fail to justify their high prices, the waiters are haughty and unhelpful, and the cooks rest smugly on their laurels trotting out the same dishes year after year with a distinct air of routine. As standards have improved elsewhere, the argument goes, the French culinary world has sunk into complacency, and allowed its own to slip. Well, there are of course plenty of mediocre French restaurants, and indifferent waiters. On the whole, though, the level of French country and small-town restaurants—not, naturally, all of them, but compared with similar areas elsewhere in Europe—is still extremely high.

French provincial diners may sometimes be stick-in-the-mud when it comes to innovative dishes, but they are also extremely demanding with regard to quality. And when French restaurants are good, whether they're in the luxury range or quite modest, this quality depends on the observation of some basic essentials. One is that many French cooks simply take more pains—indeed, may be required to take—than their counterparts elsewhere, in the selection of ingredients, the development of their skills or the preparation of dishes, whether wholly traditional or more original. Another, fundamental factor is the sheer quality of the ingredients themselves, preferably local and used as near to source as possible, an authentic obsession in contemporary French cuisine. Freshness is everything, and, though conglomerates and agribusiness are expanding there as everywhere else, a sufficient part of French agriculture and the distribution system—in short, the much-decried ways of working of the traditional French farmer—is still geared to satisfying this overriding demand. Such ingredients simply taste exactly as they should taste, in immediate contrast to the bland specimens pulled out of freezer cabinets elsewhere, and the difference this makes is exhilarating, so that even dishes that are otherwise very simply prepared can be positively spectacular. As to service, far from the proverbial rudeness, it is on experience much easier to find places that offer a charming welcome, whether with the smooth, but not superior, courtesy of the traditional French restaurant or the warm *accueil* of a village *auberge*.

Since restaurants are not automatically good just because they are French, it pays to be selective, and this book is not a guide to the restaurants of northern France—of which there are hundreds, or thousands—but a selection. Each of the restaurants here is within easy distance of one of the Channel ports. There are some of the region's most prestigious chefs, such as Jean-Pierre Dargent in Arras or Roland Gauthier at Montreuil, and small-town, local favourites. Some are bustling, lively town restaurants and *brasseries*, others are lost in the countryside. All of them, though, can provide a wonderful meal that's a rare pleasure, and would make them worth a detour. Along the way, there are in each chapter plenty of other things to see and do, to make a foray into France into a complete day or weekend trip, according to the pace at which you wish to travel: famous sites such as Mont St-Michel, Monet's garden at Giverny or the cathedral in the city of Amiens, countryside to explore such as the valleys of Artois or the Norman Pays d'Auge, with farmhouse cider and cheese-makers hidden up tree-shrouded lanes, or the market in hip Trouville, with the chic resort of Deauville still keeping the Jazz Age somewhat alive alongside it. All are equally part of the complex reality of France, a country that likes to proclaim its modernity with one hand while clinging limpet-like to its traditions with the other, a combination for which anyone who enjoys looking at the world from beside a restaurant table can only be continually grateful.

A Note on Phone Numbers

The eight-digit telephone numbers given in the chapters of this book are for dialling currently from within France. It is often advisable to book in advance, however, and for dialling from abroad France's international country code is 33.

From October 18th 1996 France will be divided into five regions, each of which will have a two-digit area code to be placed before the eight-digit number. Paris will be 01; for the purposes of this book, chapters 1–7, being Picardy and Flanders, will be 03, and chapters 8–20, in Normandy, will take the code 02. When dialling from abroad, you should drop the 0 and just dial 00 33 3 or 00 33 2, followed by the eight-digit number.

Just across the Water

Thousands of people visit Calais from Britain every year, and thousands use it just as a supermarket, or as a place to be passed through as quickly as possible on the way to somewhere else, a big modern city that even its warmest admirers rarely describe as beautiful. Many who do want to linger and explore are not sure where else to head for. It's an area that's at once familiar, and yet has curiously few known landmarks. Immediately west of Calais there is a beautiful, sweeping coastline of dunes, cliffs, wind-blown coarse grass and long beaches, labelled the Côte d'Opale because of the sometimes iridescent, milky-green colour of its waters. And just south is Boulogne, a town of real charm and personality.

No longer the busiest of the Channel ports, Boulogne is the oldest; it was the main harbour for links with Roman Britain and, on the site of the Roman city, boasts the best-preserved medieval walled town in northern France. Today it's the most important fishing port in France, and has an ultra-modern aquarium/nautical theme park that's a great attraction for families. It's also an excellent place for shopping of the more

le Grand Cerf

pleasurable kind, with a fine, bustling street market and gourmet specialists—including one of France's very finest cheese emporia—as alternatives to the hypermarket hustle.

Only a few minutes from the Calais ferries and the Tunnel, in the town of Marquise, is Le Grand Cerf, an old coaching inn that has been welcoming travellers just off or on their way to the boat for two centuries. It is an unalloyed pleasure to come upon a restaurant where the finest standards are evident in every aspect of the food, and where a meal can leave you with the unshakeable conviction that it has justified the trip across by itself.

It also has a chef of the highest pedigree. Stéphane Pruvot previously worked under Michel Lorain at the Côte Saint-Jacques at Joigny in Burgundy, universally placed among the twenty or so best restaurants in the whole of France, and recipient of the highest possible accolades from the likes of Michelin and Gault-Millau. He has been at the Grand Cerf since 1991, but as yet those who travel around with the grand French guides in hand will not find it given much prominence in either of them. This cannot be any reflection on the unassuming Stéphane Pruvot's subtle dishes, but only an indication of the elephantine pace at which these institutions operate. Here is your chance to stay ahead of the crowd.

getting there

As an old mail coach inn, the Grand Cerf stands square on the Route Nationale 1, for centuries the main Paris–Calais road, which runs straight along the flank of the town of Marquise (where it's called avenue Ferber). From Calais or the Tunnel terminal take the A16 *autoroute* (for once, toll-free) south to exit 7, signposted to Marquise. Follow the signs into town and this will bring you directly on to the RN1, where you'll see the Grand Cerf on the left. This should take about 10–15 minutes. From Boulogne, leave the *autoroute* at exit 6, and the journey should be even shorter.

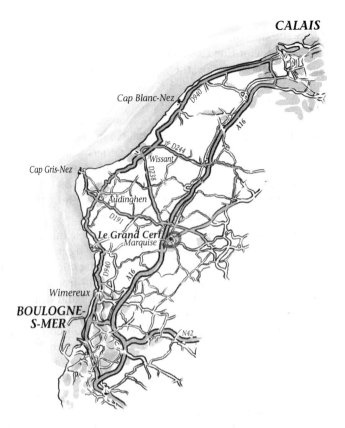

Le Grand Cerf

Le Grand Cerf, 34 avenue Ferber, 62250 Marquise, ☏ 21.87.55.05. Open Tues–Fri, noon–2pm, 7–9pm; Sat, noon–2pm, 7–9.30pm; Sun, noon–2pm. Closed Mon and 15 Aug–early Sept. Book in advance, esp. at weekends. Menus at 95F (2 courses), 125F, 160F, 200F, 320F; carte average 250F.

Built in 1795, the Grand Cerf is a stout, impressively solid-looking tile-roofed inn typical of the region, occupying the whole of a street corner. Despite its size it's compactly built around a courtyard, with two rows of tall shuttered windows on the outside, and an ample gateway where coaches once went in and out. It was the last stop for the Paris mail coaches to change horses on their way to Calais (or the first, in the opposite direction), and a plaque by a bench outside records that Victor Hugo sat on it on 2 September 1837, which seems improbably precise. Inside, the courtyard has now been made into a small garden, alongside which an ample, elegant hallway leads on to the comfortable dining rooms.

Stéphane Pruvot is a native of Calais, and some dishes are based on the region's traditional fare, such as beef braised in beer and cumin, a variation on the Flemish *carbonnade*. Others stand more within the general repertoire of modern French cuisine, but with a similar reliance on northern ingredients—local fish, lamb and vegetables. Throughout the menu, there is the same inventive use of herbs and seasonings.

The shorter menus certainly include their full share of fine dishes, such as a starter of a beautifully light gazpacho with diced prawns—a simple idea, and one that once you've tried it you can't believe no one else has tried—from the 95F/125F menu, or main courses of the beef in beer and cumin or duck fillet with a *foie gras* sauce from the 160F list. But if you're visiting the place as a treat you'll regret it if you don't go for the six-course 200F menu, or maybe take your pick from the *carte*. As each delicacy appears, you will find your anticipation never wavers.

The six-course menu might begin with a choice of rich hot *foie gras*, or a salad with a savoury mousse of peppers and sorbet of tomato and basil. Among the fish dishes, but only on the *carte*, is one of M. Pruvot's particular specialities, the wonderful filo pastry *aumônières*—parcels, literally 'beggars' purses'—of crab in shellfish essences. The sauce is heavily reduced but light and savoury, the touches of carrot, onions and garlic unusual with the crab. The meat can be equally spectacular—from the menu, perhaps the superb Boulonnais lamb *à la badiane* (in star anise). First savour the tenderness of the meat; and then let your palate appreciate the delicate aromas of the *badiane*, as much a sensation as a taste.

The 200F menu also offers a second fish course, perhaps a firm, mouthwatering herby monkfish; then there is a strictly local cheese-board, including a tangy Rollot. Desserts are delicate and pleasing to the eye: tiny pastry shells of raspberries and wild strawberries in vanilla, or a chocolate *délice* with a full-flavoured caramel ice-cream. Wines, and the smooth service, are entirely consummate with the food. And as, over coffee and *petits-fours*, you contentedly contemplate your return visit, you might also consider that, for cooking of this quality and refinement, prices even with current exchange rates, are still extremely reasonable.

Aumônières de Tourteaux en Fleur de Fila aux Essences de Crustacés

(Serves 4)

2 large crab, approx 600–700g/1½lb

1 tablespoon olive oil

2 onions, chopped

2 carrots, sliced

1 tablespoon Cognac

1 bouquet garni

2 cloves garlic, finely chopped

1 tablespoon tomato purée

100g/4oz unsalted butter

4 sheets filo pastry

Cook the crabs in a large pan of boiling salted water for 7 minutes. Drain and leave to cool, then twist off the claws and legs and extract the meat from them. Remove the apron flap from the body and pull the meat from the shell, discarding the soft gills from around the edge. Season the crab meat and set aside. Fry the crab shells in the olive oil for 5–6 minutes. Add the onions and carrots and sweat for 3–4 minutes, then raise the heat, pour in the Cognac and flambé. When the flames have died down, add 2 litres/1¾ pints of water, the bouquet garni, garlic and tomato purée. Simmer for 45 minutes, skimming frequently. Strain the stock through a fine sieve into a clean pan and set aside.

Melt 25g/¾oz of the butter. Lay out one sheet of filo pastry, brush with melted butter, and cut in half widthways. Place a quarter of the crab meat in the centre of one half and fold the pastry around it, to resemble a flower bud. Place on top of the remaining half-sheet and fold that as if forming petals. Repeat this process with the remaining pastry and crab. Place the parcels on a lightly oiled baking sheet, and bake in an oven preheated to 190°C/375°F (gas mark 5) for about 10 minutes or until golden. Meanwhile, make the sauce. Boil the stock until reduced to about 4 tablespoons. Dice the remaining butter and whisk it into the stock a few pieces at a time to give a glossy sauce. Season to taste.

To serve, pour the sauce around each crab parcel.

touring around

If, instead of turning into Marquise, you take the road west at exit 7 from the *autoroute*, you will come to a fork, from which one road leads to Cap Gris-Nez and the other, the D238, runs north up to the little town of **Wissant**, seemingly half-swallowed up amid the sand dunes. The name comes from the old Flemish for 'White Sand', and is apt: in front and on either side is a vast expanse of white beach and dunes stretching away for miles, a magnet for sand-yachters and windsurfers from all over Europe. Wissant has a claim to be almost as old a Channel port as Boulogne, for it is asserted that Caesar used it for his second invasion of Britain in 54 BC; it was an important port in the early Middle Ages, and Thomas à Becket passed through here in 1170 on his last journey back to Canterbury. By the 16th century, however, the harbour had entirely silted up. Since then the fishermen of Wissant have had to drag their distinctive little boats, called *flobarts*, back and forth across the beach. Not so many locals work in fishing today, but a few still haul their *flobarts* to and from the sea with tractors, and keep them in their back gardens the rest of the time. The town also has a clutch of hotels, and *crêperies*, *moules-frites* stands and little bars for the sand-yachters and anyone else who passes by.

The view along the beach at Wissant is framed at either end by the two capes, **Cap Blanc-Nez** to the east and the much taller **Cap Gris-Nez** to the west, their white chalk cliffs a perfect mirror to the Kent cliffs seen across the Channel. From Wissant there's a great walk to Cap Gris-Nez, either along the beach (for most of the way) or the GR coastal footpath, over dunes, grassy cliffs and bits and pieces of German blockhouses, which are scattered all along this coast. Alternatively, a more leisurely route is by car on the Boulogne road from Wissant. At the Cape there's a lighthouse, the Channel shipping control station with its thicket of aerials, grand views, especially on a bright, windy day, and, below, another sandy beach. At Audinghen, where the Cape road rejoins the main Boulogne road, there's a small museum, the **Musée du Mur de l'Atlantique** in a German blockhouse (*open April–Sept daily 9am–7pm; Oct–Mar daily 9am–noon, 2–6pm; adm 25F; 12F 8–15s; free under-8s*), the main exhibits of which are two of the huge guns installed there to bombard Dover.

If you arrive in **Boulogne** on a Wednesday or Saturday morning, make straight for the Grande Rue, the main street, and just on one side of it, presided over by the church of St-Nicolas, is place Dalton, site of one of the best traditional markets in this part of France. There are plenty of stands offering fine cheeses, terrines and a kaleidoscope of herbs, fresh flowers and pot plants; this being the north, it's also good for sweets, biscuits and chocolates, and vegetables such as carrots and chicory. Boulogne also has its hypermarkets, mostly near the *autoroute* or the N42 St-Omer road, but the main town-centre shopping area is just across the Grande Rue from the market, around rue Thiers and rue Victor-Hugo. Anyone with the remotest liking for cheese will want above all to make the pilgrimage to the legendary *fromagerie* of **Philippe Olivier** at 43 rue Thiers. It has around 300 varieties of cheese in stock at any one time, but both the shop and the caves beneath are surprisingly small, for M. Olivier believes that any change in scale could lead to a compromise in quality. All the cheeses—and the equally fine butter—are made by entirely non-industrial methods, and the range changes continually, for he is always researching into new varieties and artisan producers in France, Italy and elsewhere, even Britain.

If Boulogne has more character than most other Channel ports, it is in good part because it's more historic. Whatever the claims of Wissant, it is known with certainty that Caesar sailed on his first invasion of Britain in 55 BC from the mouth of the river Liane, and that after their conquest of Britain the following century the Romans built a fortress-town near its banks as their main base for communications with the new colony. After the fall of Rome Boulogne was semi-abandoned, but revived in the early Middle Ages as the seat of a line of independent Counts. Though not a Norman, Count Eustache II *As Grenons* ('Fine Moustaches') went with William the Conqueror to Hastings; his son, Godefroy de Bouillon, was one of the leaders of the First Crusade. In

1214 King Philippe Auguste of France succeeded in establishing his authority over Boulogne, and from then on it was the main bastion of French power in the north, against challenges from the Counts of Flanders and, later, England and Spain. The King gave Boulogne to his second son Philippe *Hurepel* ('Frizzy Hair'), who in between plotting to take over the crown himself substantially rebuilt the old town and gave it the present castle and ramparts, between 1227 and 1231. Louis XIV's fortress-builder extraordinary, Marshal Vauban, did some renovation work on the ramparts in the 1680s, but today large sections of the entirely intact walls remarkably still look much as they did in the 13th century, especially the Porte des Degrés on the west side.

To get to the **Haute-Ville**, walk straight up the hill of the Grande Rue. Before entering through Vauban's porte des Dunes, spare a glance for the plaque on the tower to the right dedicated to François Pilâtre de Rozier, an early adventurer in cross-Channel flight. Pilâtre made the world's first manned balloon flight in November 1783, two months after the Montgolfier brothers' first experiment with a duck, a sheep and a cockerel, and, 26 years old, was a superstar of his day. He attempted to cross the Channel in June 1785, but his balloon suddenly caught fire and plummeted into the ground near Wimereux. Beneath the ramparts to the left of the porte des Dunes is a broad esplanade with a very large, distinctly odd monument of a man in a fez on top of a pyramid. This is Auguste Mariette, father of French Egyptology, distinguished Boulonnais and only one of several engaging figures who gave Boulogne its independent and individual cultural and intellectual life in the last century.

Walk through the gate and you come to the heart of the old town, the place de la Résistance and, just beyond it, the **place Godefroy de Bouillon**, on the site of the crossroads that, as in all Roman military towns, formed the centre of Roman Boulogne. On the left are the neo-classical Palais de Justice and the **Hôtel de Ville**, attached to a massive stone belfry that's partly 12th-century and so a rare survivor from before the arrival of Philip Frizzy-Hair. On the right, in the place Godefroy de Bouillon, past a pleasant bar with tables outside, is the **Hôtel Desandrouins**, an elegant Louis XVI mansion that was used by Napoleon and Josephine as their residence during their extended stays in Boulogne while the Emperor sought the means to invade England.

The streets of the old town are narrow and cobbled, the tight ring of the ramparts creating an enclosed, hushed atmosphere. The **rue de Lille**, the most important street running off the place Godefroy de Bouillon, was also a main street, the *decumanus*, of the Roman town. Today, it contains some irresistible chocolate shops and *boulangeries*. At No.58 is the oldest house in Boulogne, built as an inn for 16th-century travellers. Above the gate there is a scallop shell, indicating that it was used by pilgrims on their way to Santiago de Compostela. Just across the street is the **cathedral**, the giant dome of which can be seen from miles around, but which close-up comes upon you almost by surprise. During the most radical phase of the French Revolution in 1793, the revolutionaries of Boulogne were not content with just desecrating their 12th-century Abbey Church, but actually destroyed it. So, in the 1820s the Catholic Church, reinstated and in truculent mood, decided to put the Godless to shame with this colossal edifice, taking as models the modest examples of St Peter's in Rome, the Paris Invalides and St Paul's in London. Completed in 1866, it's equally huge inside—the dome above all—but is impressive rather than beautiful.

At the end of rue de Lille is another gate and one of many points where there are steps up to the **ramparts**, a circuit of which is a special part of a meander around the Haute-Ville—the timeless streets of old Boulogne inside, and to the outside views over the rest of the town and out to sea. In the eastern corner is the well-preserved, monolithic castle of Philippe *Hurepel*, now the **Château-Musée** (*open 15 Sept–14 May, Mon, Wed–Sat 10am–12.30pm, 2.30–5pm, Sun 10am–12.30pm, 2.30–5.30pm; 15 May–14 Sept, Mon, Wed–Sat 9.30am–12.30pm, 1.30–6.00pm, Sun 9.30am–12.30pm, 2.30–6.00pm; closed Tues; adm 20F; 13F 13–18s; free under-12s*). The collection is a real hotch-potch, put together out of donations from a string of local private collectors and *savants* and so following their interests rather than any noticeable logic. There are, for example, Mummies and other Egyptian relics from the great Mariette, some very fine classic 18th-century porcelain, and, perhaps most astonishing to find, a remarkable collection of Inuit and Native American masks acquired by a local anthropologist, Alphonse Pinart, on an expedition to Alaska in 1871. The most interesting part of the castle itself, which can be seen towards the end as you go round, is the Salle de la Barbière, a fine vaulted Gothic hall.

From the Haute-Ville, walk back down the hill into the shopping streets of the new town, down the Grande Rue or the parallel rue Félix-Adam. At the river, turn right for a walk along the quays of the port, which are usually pretty busy. Unmissable at the end of the riverfront is the modernistic geometry of Boulogne's most innovative attraction, the curiously named **Nausicaá** 'sea experience museum' (*open 15 Sept–end May, Mon–Fri, 10am–6pm, Sat, Sun, holidays 10am–7pm; June–14 Sept, 10am–8pm daily; closed two weeks Jan; adm 50F; 35F 3–12s*). This all-modern aquarium has been a big hit since it opened in 1991, especially with British visitors. It succeeds in providing a wealth of ecological information about the sea in a very enjoyable form, through dynamic multi-media displays (with good provision for different languages). As well as all kinds of fish and sea creatures from across the world, there are theme-park-ride exhibits like the deck of a trawler in a storm, or a sealed 'tropical environment' in which to warm up in midwinter. It's also hands-on, with a tank where children can touch things like rays or skate, if not the sharks that are always among the main attractions. A tour around Nausicaá takes at least two hours, and there are good cafés and restaurants in which to take a break. If afterwards you need to catch some real sea air, just next to the museum is Boulogne's fairly clean but often under-used **beach**.

On the north side of Boulogne, just off the Calais road and ironically next to the main British war cemetery in the area, is another of the town's most visible landmarks, the **Colonne de la Grande-Armée**, one of the greatest monuments ever raised to a non-event. In 1803–4 Napoleon kept an army of 200,000 men encamped at Boulogne for months on end while he tried to work out a way of invading England, until he finally gave up the idea and marched them off to greater glory in Germany. The men, however, had had such a good time that they voted to erect a memorial to their stay, and all the officers chipped in to pay for this column, with statue of the Emperor on top, but only completed under Louis-Philippe in 1841. Today, it's possible to climb up the 263 steps inside (*open 9am–noon, 2–5pm Mon, Thurs–Sun, Oct–Mar; 9am–noon, 2–6pm Mon, Thurs–Sun, April–Sept; closed Tues, Wed; adm 20F*) for a panoramic view over Boulogne and the Côte d'Opale.

The First Town in France

It's such a common impression that there must be something to it: any number of people, having wandered across the Channel and come across St-Omer, describe it as the first real French small town within a short distance of the exits from Calais. It's not hard to see why: at its heart there is a broad, cobbled main square, with cafés around the sides and presided over by an imposing Hôtel de Ville, which hosts a vibrant weekly market; nearby, there are charming narrow streets that contain some beautiful *pâtisseries*, *charcuteries* and other individual shops. It also has a magnificent, oddly little-known Gothic cathedral, and an attractive museum with some real treasures housed in a fine 18th-century *hôtel particulier*.

The idea that St-Omer should epitomise all that is French might seem strange, since it has only been part of France since 1678, later than any other part of Artois. For much of its history the town was attached to Flanders, ruled successively by the Counts of Flanders, the Dukes of Burgundy and the Kings of Spain, all of them in endless warfare with the Kings of France. Like much of Flanders,

La Belle Époque

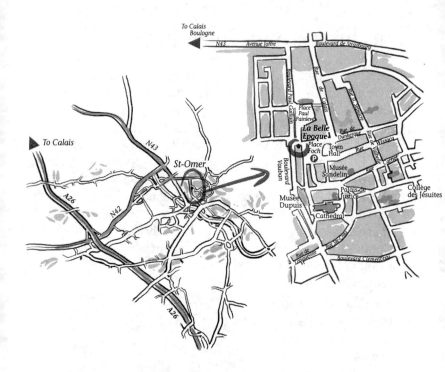

St-Omer was partly built on water, and just to the east there is an atmospheric, silent landscape of drained marshes, the Marais Audomarois, rich in wildlife, with a web of canals built up over centuries between reed beds and prolific vegetable gardens.

The produce from these marsh-gardens—leeks, chicory, cauliflowers—has always been among the staples of food in St-Omer. Others, typical of northern France and Flanders, are beef, rabbit, fish from the nearby ports, and beer (to drink and in cooking), and locals very noticeably share the region's love of chocolate and other things sweet. For fine versions of local dishes in St-Omer—plus others from a broader French range—you would have to look hard to do better than La Belle Epoque, an unassuming but very hospitable little restaurant just off the main square.

getting there

St-Omer is about three-quarters of an hour from Calais. Whether you come from there on the N43, or from Boulogne and the A26 *autoroute* via the N42, you will eventually reach the bypass around the town; follow signs for '*Centre-Ville*' to come on to a long straight road along the north side of St-Omer, avenue Joffre. After the Cedico hypermarket, look for a major road right, also signposted '*Centre-Ville*', boulevard Paul-Guillain. Take this road into town and you will come alongside a large square on your left, place Paul-Painlevé, where La Belle Epoque is actually in front of you, also slightly over to your left. Turn left in front of it to enter St-Omer's main square, place Foch, which is usually the best place to park, except on market days (Saturdays).

La Belle Epoque

Restaurant La Belle Epoque, place Paul-Painlevé, 62500 St-Omer,
℗ 21.38.22.93. Open Mar–Oct, daily, noon–3pm, 7–10.30pm; Nov–Feb,
Mon, Tues, Thurs–Sat, noon–3pm, 7–10.30pm, Wed, Sun, noon–3pm.
Menus at 72, 108, 140F; carte *average 150F.*

Mme Dacheville does everything in the kitchen at the Belle Epoque, while her husband looks after front-of-house. On some days, since he also has other work, she takes the orders, lays the tables and serves as well, but will still agree very amiably to provide quite complex dishes at short notice late in the evening. This kind of effort and dedication would inspire respect in itself, but on top she also manages to remain entirely charming and welcoming throughout, and, most important of all, the results of her cooking are excellent. There's no sign of anything being skimped under pressure. Moreover, she is used to the inability of British visitors to observe proper French hours (and the needs of those arriving late from or on their way to a ferry), and is willing to serve food well outside the customary local closing times. Those given above are more guidelines than strict timings; if the couple are there in mid-afternoon, she may well be able to cook something up for you.

The restaurant is small but neat and comfortable, with plenty of flowers, white linen and smart red plush bench seats, up a few steps from street level in a turn-of-the-century townhouse. Although the Belle Epoque's is essentially a one-woman band, the menu offers an ample choice. Apart from dishes based on local fare, the other speciality is fish, with a list of specials that changes according to whatever's fresh in that day, but which might feature monkfish, turbot or trout, from the River Hem, between St-Omer and Calais. There are also several varieties of grilled steaks, lamb and so on.

The set menus are generous, and impressive value. The 108F menu offers the classic Flemish *carbonnade de bœuf*, a fine, strong beef and beer stew for a chilly day, among the main courses, and perhaps lobster soup among the starters. But try the 140F *menu gastronomique*: the choice is difficult between the five alternatives for first course, but the Chavignol *gratinée* with a bacon salad is a very light, enjoyable start to the meal, the goat's cheese cooked just enough so that its flavour is not blunted. Second courses include rabbit with prunes and Armagnac, one of Mme Dacheville's prime specialities, and a variation of her own on a traditional local favourite. The rabbit is unusually meaty, and the sauce a delicious, rich mixture with all the right blend of savouriness, fruit and alcohol. Fish-eaters, on the other hand, might opt for an excellent *lotte à l'américaine*, monkfish cooked with tomatoes, garlic, shallots, brandy and white wine.

The wine list is sizeable for a small restaurant, with some quality bottles for around 90F. After the cheese, including a good local Maroilles, the highlight among the desserts must be the delectably sticky home-made chocolate mousse, one more example of the Belle Epoque's very attractive and likeable combination of home comfort and quality food. And, since Mme Dacheville is always prepared to be flexible when she can, you'll not be obliged to hurry over your coffee if you feel no great need to be getting along.

Lapin aux Pruneaux et à l'Armagnac

(Serves 4)

15 prunes, stoned
500ml/1 pint red wine
75g/3oz butter
1 rabbit, approx 1.5kg/3lb, jointed
1 tablespoon chopped thyme
3 shallots, chopped
2 bacon rashers, chopped
2–3 cloves garlic, roughly chopped
1 tablespoon Armagnac
1 tablespoon flour
500ml/1 pint white wine
4 tablespoons tomato purée
salt and pepper

Soak the prunes overnight in the red wine. The next day, heat the butter in a large pan, add the rabbit pieces, and brown on all sides. Remove from the pan, sprinkle with thyme and set aside. In the same pan, sweat the shallots, bacon and garlic, then return the rabbit pieces to the pan and flambé in the Armagnac.

When the flames have died down, stir in the flour and cook for 1 minute, then add the white wine, tomato purée and salt and pepper. Finally, add the prunes and their soaking liquid. Simmer gently for 1 hour or until the rabbit is tender, then adjust the seasoning and serve.

---

touring around

The main square, officially **place Foch**, is still very much the hub of St-Omer, which almost inevitably draws you back on any walk around the town. Like many town squares in Flanders and Artois it is strikingly large, built to accommodate the market. Today it looks a little as if it was created around the **Hôtel de Ville** which occupies one side, although it is in fact much older. The town hall was only built in the

1830s, in a standardly grand style for French public buildings, replacing a 14th-century Gothic town hall that had reached a state beyond repair. The biggest pavement cafés are on the south, higher side, with a balcony view over the rest of the square. It is busiest on Saturday mornings, when it's taken over by the **market** (there is also a smaller market on Wednesdays).

The stalls have all the many attractions of a French town market, plus some specific to St-Omer, notably fine chicory and other vegetables from the Marais, highly regarded because of the special qualities given by the rich soil of the drained marsh-gardens, which can produce several crops each year. In amongst the crowds mingling, comparing the qualities of fruit, there are also stalls with fresh herbs, or home-made biscuits, or piled up with whole arrays of northern cheeses such as the strong, under-appreciated Maroilles, as well as others with bric-à-brac from baby clothes to books.

St-Omer was founded in 637 by Audomar (later Saint Omer), a monk sent to evangelise the pagan population of this region of bogs and swamps. He also founded an abbey, St-Bertin, which remained a powerful influence in the town until its dissolution during the Revolution. In the early Middle Ages, St-Omer and Bruges were the two richest cities in Flanders, larger than Arras and many cities to the south; however, the position of St-Omer also put it square in the middle of the area chosen by France, England and, later, Spain as their prime battleground for nearly four centuries. When the town was finally secured for Louis XIV and France after a long siege in 1677, Marshal Vauban encased it in a massive set of new ramparts as part of his *pré carré* or 'square field', the line of forts built to protect the new frontier. They held the town like a clamp for two centuries.

If you leave the place Foch by the place Painlevé, past the Belle Epoque restaurant, you will come to St-Omer's main park, the **Jardin public**, which incorporates the only remaining section of Vauban's ramparts, a giant, monolithic screen of plain brick. The rest, remarkably, were entirely demolished during the 1880s and 1890s, and the only trace of them is the line of boulevards around the city centre. St-Omer is very proud of the *jardin public*, opened in 1894. It is a very attractively landscaped space, an atmospheric, rather wintry northern park with giant pines throwing deep shadows, and some deer at the centre that in autumn you can hear rutting through the trees.

Back in the place Foch, the little streets that run off the square between the cafés on the south side will take you into old St-Omer, mostly built in the 18th century, a small area but with a distinctive charm that, as they will say about this town, is very French. Especially attractive is the rue des Clouteries, opposite the Hôtel de Ville, an alley-like street with bakers offering superb fresh bread and a *charcuterie* window full of bulging red sausages. Here and in the other streets of the town centre the sweet tooth of northern France is catered for in a markedly high number of chocolate and cake shops. They are at their most spectacular in November and early December: like the Netherlands and much of the rest of northwest France, St-Omer celebrates St-Nicolas, 6 December, prior to Christmas, and during the run-up to the day *pâtisserie* windows are full of chocolate saints (who look like a medieval bishop, and not at all like Santa Claus) in all styles and sizes, and sometimes with coloured-icing surplices too. If you require more run-of-the-mill shopping, there are two **hypermarkets** in St-Omer, one, Cedico, on the road in from Calais, and the other, Mammouth, on the N42 south towards Lille.

At the opposite end from the main square rue des Clouteries leads into the rectangular **place Victor-Hugo**. To the right there is a rather endearingly over-grand Baroque fountain, the **Fontaine de Ste-Aldegonde**, put up by some local notables in 1757 to celebrate the birth of the Comte d'Artois, younger brother of Louis XVI and eventually Charles X, last Bourbon King of France. Leave the square to the left of the fountain, admiring its chubby cherubs on the way, and then turn left again, and you will come to St-Omer's greatest monument, the **cathedral**.

It was begun around 1200, on the site of three earlier churches, and completed 300 years later, and so falls squarely within the Gothic, the largest, grandest Gothic church anywhere in the Pas-de-Calais. Before going in, walk around the outside to get an idea of the monumental strength of the building: some of the lower, 13th-century sections are quite plain, similar to Romanesque, while the squared-off 15th-century tower is a work of elaborate, *Flamboyant* late Gothic. Most impressively sculptural of all is the *portail royal* outside the south transept, on the opposite side from place Victor-Hugo, flanked by two massive, soaring towers. Once inside, you are met by a forest of columns, and the cathedral appears all the larger because the transepts can seem as big as the nave. It has many treasures, perhaps finest of all the truly magnificent organ that fills the whole of the west end of the nave, a superb piece of baroque woodcarving from 1717 that manages to combine perfectly with its medieval surroundings. It is regularly used for concerts. In the north transept, look up to see a wonderful and very rare astrological clock from 1558—an illustration of Renaissance ideas of the world, and still in working order—beneath an intricate *Flamboyant*-Gothic rose window from the 1450s with fine glass that, because St-Omer cathedral does not actually face due east as it should, beautifully catches the evening light.

The streets to the east of the cathedral are a mixture of plainish, largely 19th-century buildings together with some much grander brick edifices from the era when St-Omer was an important city of the Spanish Netherlands and a major centre of the Catholic church. The local *lycée* on rue Gambetta was built behind the long and very solid Flemish-style façade of a former seminary, built in 1605. On the parallel rue St-Bertin, reached up a small side-street opposite the *lycée*, there is the similar **Ancien Collège des Jésuites**. A plaque outside records that this was built as the English College, a reminder of a time when in England to be found to have come on a mission 'from St-Omer' was something like being discovered with credentials from the KGB at the height of the Cold War, and liable to much bloodier penalties. In 1592, as measures against Catholics in England became ever more restrictive, English Jesuits sought help to found a new college to educate the sons of Catholic families on safe soil. It was the most important of several English colleges on Spanish territory, and was lavishly endowed by Philip II of Spain himself and many of the Spanish aristocracy. To English ministers it was a den of subversion, and indeed the Gunpowder Plot and diverse other conspiracies were almost certainly discussed within its walls. It remained an English college until 1762, when all Jesuits were expelled from France.

On the opposite side of rue St-Bertin, just back towards the centre of town, a small side courtyard contains the church of **St-Denis**, a very attractive work of simple, 13th-century early Gothic, one of the oldest of St-Omer's remaining churches. It has a *Last Supper* from 1523 attributed to Della Robbia, although this has been contested. Carry on through the little alley past the church to the rue Carnot, and then turn left to reach the **Musée Sandelin** (*open Tues, Wed, Sat, Sun, 10am–noon, 2–6pm; Thurs, Fri, 10am–noon, 2–5pm; adm 14F*). After its final absorption into France, St-Omer acquired its more Gallic appearance with a set of large *ancien régime* buildings, the finest of them this mansion, built for Marie-Josèphe Sandelin, Comtesse de Fruges, in 1777, a very elegant Louis-XVI *hôtel* entered through a grand courtyard. A prime attraction is the house itself, very well preserved, especially the delicate turquoise dining room laid with some of the fine blue local china that made St-Omer famous in the 18th century, and with some paintings from the same era, equally pretty in their chocolate-box way, such as a portrait of Madame de Pompadour by Nattier. The museum collection includes a very extensive display of other fine porcelain and ceramics, and more paintings, mostly Dutch and Flemish, notably the provocatively enigmatic *The Bawd* (*La Ribaude*) by Jan Steen, but its greatest possessions are local, and from the Middle Ages, the relics of local abbeys. Finest of all is the *Pied de*

musée de l'hôtel sandelin

Croix de St-Bertin, made as a stand for a crucifix at the end of the 12th century, a piece of extraordinary craftmanship in copper, bronze and enamel. A joint ticket (*18F; same opening times*) to the Sandelin also allows you to see another museum, the **Musée Henri-Dupuis**, near the cathedral. Its collection mainly features birds, shells and other items amassed by the local naturalist after whom it is named, and is a specialised taste, but it does have another special feature in the shape of a beautiful, painstakingly restored Flemish kitchen, dating from 1635.

For a complete change, between spring and autumn you can also add to the day with a boat trip through the canals of the **Marais Audomarois**. Three companies run tours; most accessible to casual travellers without bookings is **Isnor** (*℗ 21 39 15 15; tours April–June, Sept, Oct, Sat, Sun, hourly 11am, noon, 2–5pm; July–Aug, daily, 11am, noon, 2–6pm; adm 38F; 33F under-14s; free under-4s*), who use open boats (the closed launches of the other companies may be more convenient when the weather turns, but have much less charm). They are based in **Clairmarais**, on the east side of town; to get there, follow the road to the right of the railway station across the Aa river from central St-Omer. Tours last an hour, and commentaries on the flora, fauna and the many legends associated with this strange, flat, space are given in English if there are enough people who require it, although if not you may have to make do with an explanatory leaflet. Canals to drain the marshes, known by their Flemish name *watergangs*, began to be built in Audomar's time, and have been added to ever since. It's a different world of green and brown rushes, lilies and marsh flowers, immensely tranquil, inhabited by grebes, ducks and herons. During the day, there are also the *maraîchers*, the cultivators of the marsh allotments. Few now live full-time in the little houses that loom up along the banks, but they still take their produce to market in long, silent punt-like boats. On weekends, they also line the Clairmarais road with great ranks of cauliflowers, leeks and chicory, to be sold to drivers who come out from Lille or further afield to acquire these much-prized greens.

Luxury Under the Walls of Montreuil

The country just south of Boulogne has provided the first taste of France for many British travellers for a very long time. Its place-names can be familiar, and it might not seem an obvious place to look for the peace and timeless atmosphere associated with the French countryside. Away from the main routes, though, there are any number of quiet villages with farmers going about their business, and lush green valleys, producing local cheeses and meats. And, on a rock above the wooded valley of the Canche, there is Montreuil, called *sur-Mer* despite the absence of any sea, a historic walled town still contained within its ramparts as it was in the 16th century, and showing no inclination to outgrow them. It has always been near the route south, and receives its fair share of visitors, yet nothing

Auberge de la Grenouillère

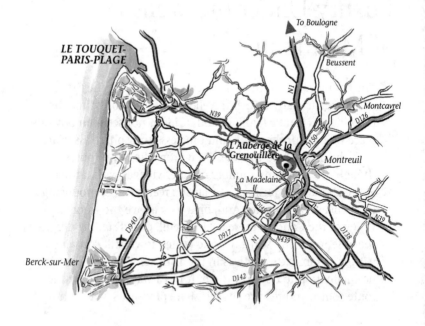

seems to disturb its placid pace and very refreshing small-town atmosphere.

Just outside Montreuil there is a superb restaurant in a quite ravishing location. The Auberge de la Grenouillère ('The Frog-gery') is in La Madelaine-sous-Montreuil, a village at the bottom of Montreuil's crag with a special view up to the town's remarkable ramparts. The restaurant occupies a beautifully restored old farmhouse by the River Canche, amid woods and lush meadows. Inside, award-winning chef Roland Gauthier creates endlessly inventive, richly enjoyable dishes based on seasonal, local ingredients. For a combination of pure pleasure, comfort and rural calm, it's hard to beat.

All the roads south, from Calais and Boulogne, Le Touquet or St-Omer, join up just north of Montreuil in the N1, which makes a wide loop around the town. Instead of staying on this road, take the turn into Montreuil, and carry on through the ramparts and the old town on to the Abbeville road. On the south side of Montreuil look for a sharp right turn signposted to La Madelaine-sous-Montreuil. In this village there is then another right turn, with a sign for the Auberge de la Grenouillère, which is at the very end of this lane.

L'Auberge de la Grenouillère

Auberge de la Grenouillère, La Madelaine-sous-Montreuil, 62170 Montreuil-sur-Mer, © 21.06.07.22. Open Sept–June, Mon, Thurs–Sun, noon–3.30pm, 7.15–9.30pm; July–Aug daily; closed Jan–mid-Feb. Book always. Menus at 150F (not available Sat evening, Sun lunch, public holidays), 190F, 260F, 380F; carte *average 330F.*

The winding lane that takes you down to the Grenouillère runs past the houses of the village, eventually petering out beside the bright waters of the Canche. There are trees all around, and fine horses in a little field beside the river. The restaurant is just to your left, in a traditional one-storey farmhouse, with red roofs and white walls, around a courtyard with tables, sunshades and flowers. It is quite exceptionally pretty, and just as lovely and very comfortable inside, with dark wooden beams, tiles, more flowers and white linen. In winter, there's also a log fire. The unique feature of the décor is that the walls of the 'Froggery' are covered in whimsical pictures of very human-looking frogs, illustrating one of La Fontaine's fables about a frog who wanted to be as big as an ox and ate so much he exploded, painted during the thirties by Frank Reynolds, once art director of Punch, a friend of the then owner.

Roland Gauthier, once at the Connaught Hotel in London, has been at the restaurant for 16 years, but throughout the concern shown for standards is so high that you might think it had newly opened. His cooking has won great praise, but there's no culinary grandstanding here: he still takes the orders himself, with quiet charm. The menus, which change monthly, are strictly seasonal, and also employ almost entirely local, '*du terroir*', ingredients. This means that in autumn they may heavily feature game and duck, as well as cod from local ports; at other times they might include more lamb, or mackerel, or river fish. Also, though he himself is originally from the Jura, Gauthier often presents versions of local northern dishes, such as the *caudière*, the classic fishermen's stew of the Pas-de-Calais, usually part of the 260F *menu de la mer*.

The pleasures begin with the appetisers, which on an autumn day might include some delectably creamy small leek pies. If it's among the starters on the five-course, 190F *menu du terroir* (the 150F menu is the same, without cheese) don't miss duck and pearl barley soup, a wonderfully smooth, fragrant flavour that lodges itself in the brain. Next you might choose warm venison pâté *en croûte*, very rich and gamey, but with delicate herby tastes and textures too. Seasonings and methods are complex, but one of the most outstanding qualities of his cooking is an exceptional combination of strong, very enjoyable flavours and others of great delicacy. A fricassée of rabbit with salsify and onions, for example, manages to be both succulently meaty and fragrant at the same time. Also, the reliance on the local *terroir*—and so no Mediterranean tomatoes, courgettes or other products out of season—means that you are presented with continuously surprising, delicious combinations of often-undervalued northern European products.

Cheeses are selected by Philippe Olivier of Boulogne, and there is an exhaustive, if expensive, wine cellar. Especially spectacular, though, are the desserts, another Gauthier forte. *Crème brûlée* comes with grilled oats, giving a new texture to an old standard; damson tarts are an explosion of fresh fruit in the mouth. Best of all, though, is the *croustade* of apples and cinnamon ice cream.

If the weather's suitable, go into the courtyard for coffee and *petits-fours*, among them some very rich, dark chocolate frogs, and watch the breeze in the trees. Afterwards, take a wander down the path alongside the soothing river. And, for a longer rural idyll, note that the Grenouillère now also has four well-equipped guest rooms, which need to be booked well in advance.

Glace à la Bière Ambrée

This simple dessert is made like custard but with beer instead of milk.

6 egg yolks
250g/9oz caster sugar
1 litre/1¾ pint beer

Beat the egg yolks and sugar together for 3–4 minutes. Bring half the beer to the boil and cool slightly, then gradually stir into the egg mixture. Return the mixture to the pan and cook very gently, stirring constantly, until it is thick enough to coat the back of the spoon. (Do not let it boil or it will curdle.) Add the remaining beer a little at a time and continue to stir until it thickens again. Pour into an ice-cream maker and freeze, or freeze in a shallow container, taking out and beating 2 or 3 times while half-frozen to remove ice crystals. Serve with speculoos or other crisp biscuits.

touring around

It's possible to get from Calais or Boulogne to Montreuil in not much over half an hour on the N1, unless you get stuck behind a line of trucks, but an incomparably more attractive route is the little D127 road which runs roughly parallel to it down the valley of the River Course, just inland. To get on to it, turn off the N1 in Samer on to the road to Desvres, and then, in a switchback section with great views north over the valley of the Liane, look for a tiny lane off to the right, with a sign to Bois-Julien, that disappears into the trees straight up a steep hill. At the top, follow the signs to Doudeauville, and you will come down into a green, narrow valley that is immediately so different from the semi-industrial small towns straggling south from Boulogne that it feels like a lost world. The river is a quick-flowing, burbling stream. Hunkered down alongside it there are villages of white, red-roofed one-storey cottages, surrounded by the trademark flowers of all the Artois valleys.

The Course has been discovered by a fair number of British travellers (there are very *gentils* little signs reminding you to drive on the right), but it manages to remain a genuinely rural, sleepy stretch of French countryside; villages with old-fashioned bars and other, hidden attractions are tucked away from view. On the left just before you enter **Beussent** from the north—and very easy to miss—is Les Chocolats de Beussent, a cottage industry producing high-quality hand-made chocolates. From Beussent village, a narrow lane runs across the river and then away from the Course into a wild branch valley that seems almost uninhabited; turn right and you will come to **Le Fond des Communes**, a farm where Eliane Leviel produces an excellent *chèvre*. She also offers tours of the farm from February to November, every day except Sundays.

Further south, just past Estréelles, the Course Valley road brings you back to the main N1. **Montreuil-sur-Mer** is just a little further south, the old *ville-haute* atop its impressively steep hill reached via a hairpin road that brings you up to the main gate, the **Porte de Boulogne**, in the town ramparts. Beyond the gate the road winds round again to the right, as it has since the last century to avoid one of Montreuil's most famous streets, the **Cavée St-Firmin**, a precipitous cobbled incline, lined with quaint white houses with roofs each at a different level, which used to cause havoc among the carriages and carts that had to negotiate it.

It is believed that the site of Montreuil was already occupied in Roman times, though the town was actually founded in the 7th century by monks. It grew to be of particular interest to the region's warriors, and the first fortifications appeared 200 years later. It's not hard to see why, for the crag on which the *ville-haute* stands has a commanding view in every direction, and especially along the Valley of the Canche. It was also an important port, which is why, against all visible evidence, it still retains the title '*sur-Mer*'. The harbour was one of the wealthiest in northern Europe during the 13th century, trading in grains, wines and wool, but the Canche had already begun to silt up and by 1400 was virtually impassable. Today, if you look from Montreuil out towards the sea, now 15km away, across the fields and thick woods where the port's traffic once came and went, you can only marvel at the capacity of this stretch of coast to shift and change.

For centuries, Montreuil's position as a harbour and fortress gave it a torrid and violent history. Its greatest catastrophe came during the wars between Francis I of France and the Holy Roman Emperor Charles V. In 1537 an Imperial army besieged Montreuil and destroyed virtually the entire town. After it was recovered, Francis I ordered it rebuilt in a radically different manner, abandoning the old lower town alongside the now-useless river and retreating to the *ville-haute* on top of the hill, to be surrounded by the ramparts that are now Montreuil's most exceptional feature. The townspeople were required to take part in the building work, which continued off and on for over a hundred years. In the 16th century, though, as the French frontier moved away to the east and the sea receded further to the west, Montreuil was allowed to slip back into being a very quiet backwater, which is why most of the town, remarkably, is still contained within the walls begun in the 1540s. It was still a stop for the Paris–Calais mail coaches, and as such was visited by Victor Hugo, who set part of *Les Misérables* here, as the town where Jean Valjean briefly achieves peace and prosperity under the name of M. Madeleine, and even becomes mayor.

If you arrive in Montreuil on a Saturday morning, carry on straight along the main street past the centre to the south side of the *ville-haute* and the place Charles-de-Gaulle, commonly called the Grande-Place, a wide, rambling square that's the site of the weekly **market**. This is a real small-town country market, with stalls in no apparent order offering excellent local vegetables, fresh herbs, CDs, very good, strong cheese and terrines, farm eggs, *Lion King* sets and shoelaces. Around the square there are several bars and cafés, bustling with shouted conversations on market days, tranquil again after the stalls have packed up. Overlooking the scene from one side of the square, perhaps with little admiration, is Field Marshal Haig, atop a horse, a statue placed here in commemoration of the fact that during the First World War little Montreuil was the headquarters of the British Army in France. One of the main buildings they used was the one behind him, since converted into a rather odd-looking theatre. Haig himself stayed at the Château de Beaurepaire (not open to visitors), in the village of St-Nicolas, just south of the town. He was a familiar figure in the countryside around Montreuil, for he used to exercise by going riding every morning, always accompanied by several officers and a troop of lancers, and preceded by another horseman carrying a Union Jack.

When the market finishes it's probably time to go down through the gate in the ramparts on one side of the Grande-Place to the Grenouillère for lunch. Afterwards, or before lunch if it isn't market day, head back into the rest of Montreuil north of the square. The intertwining streets and squares of the old town are small-scale and have enormous charm. As a town upon a hill it has a noticeably airy feel, an impression helped by its mostly whitewashed or light grey stucco buildings. The little white cottages in the older streets sometimes look as if they should be in a fishing town, perhaps some kind of hangover from when it was *sur-Mer*. The main streets can sometimes be busy in a small-town way, such as when the *lycée* lets out and crowds of children mill around waiting for buses waiting to take them back to surrounding villages. At other times they can be deserted.

The main through street of Montreuil, rue Pierre Ledent, runs through the west side of the *ville-haute*. Just off it is the **place Darnetal**, a very pretty square (also the site of the tourist office) with lime trees and an engagingly twee fountain in the middle. The two 16th-century half-timbered houses across rue Ledent are the oldest in the town, and may even be survivors from before 1537. From place Darnetal a little street connects with the main square, **place Gambetta**.

Montreuil has a curious range of churches. **St-Saulve** on place Gambetta is the largest, a fine Gothic pile, but which only half survived the great sack of 1537. The 15th-century main façade and nave are both beautiful, but the choir and the transepts were all destroyed, leaving it only half its previous size, and the sections rebuilt or added at different times since look like no more than attempts to put a brave face upon it. Inside, though, its battered state can make it strangely atmospheric. Across the square is the **Chapelle de l'Hôtel-Dieu**, a building often not open to the public, but this does not matter much since its main features are all on the outside. The hospital it serves is 15th-century, but the chapel was built in the 1870s by Clovis Normand, a local architect and Gothic revivalist of the school of Viollet-le-Duc, and is a pure medievalist fantasy, with a mass of luxuriantly sculpted Flamboyant-Gothic details.

Go down the street to the right of the Hôtel-Dieu and you come to another quiet little square, with the **Chapelle de Ste-Austreberthe**, a simple, whitewashed late medieval church. From there, rue Porte Becquerelle and then rue de Paon, to the right, will take you to the most picturesque area of all in Montreuil, with the little cobbled alleys of **Clape-en-Bas** and **Clape-en-Haut**, huddled against the ramparts. The tiled roofs of the cottages that lean against each other up the steep streets seem almost to be about to touch the ground, and each door is painted in a different colour. Ungraciously, the names of the streets mean roughly Lower Drain and Upper Drain, referring to the gutters, the remains of open sewers, that still run down the middle of them. They are of course the stuff of postcards, and several of the houses are used as craft workshops, or bars, during the summer season, which keeps the area lively, but on other days they might be as slow-moving as the rest of the town.

Mid-afternoon, when shadows are beginning to be more noticeable, is a good time to approach Montreuil's particular attraction, the walk around the **ramparts**, which are accessible from many streets in the town. They form an unbroken loop, and the circuit seems to accentuate the smallness of Montreuil, confined upon its hill. They extend for three kilometres, and the full walk takes about an hour, but it's never strenuous, and along the way there are plenty of places to stop. And, despite the walls' original purpose, they are wonderfully peaceful, overgrown with grass and ivy along the top, with at some points a sheer drop beneath you. All around the views are superb, and invite you to keep looking: inwards, over the streets of Montreuil; northwards, over lower Montreuil and the Canche; westwards, towards the sea. By the Porte de Boulogne, rebuilt in the 1820s, you look down over lush flowerbeds by the roadside, which soften the town walls' naturally forbidding glare.

In the northwest corner of the ramparts, beyond an especially attractive, grassy area, a little bridge leads to the **Citadelle** (*open Mon, Wed–Sun, 9am–noon, 2–6pm; closed Tues and all of Oct; adm 10F; 6F under-14s*). Tour commentaries, on cassette, are available in English. It was built, still more than the rest of Montreuil, to dominate the approaches along the Canche, and so has a still better view. Since it was attacked, damaged, rebuilt and added to over centuries, different parts of it vary in age enormously, from the first Montreuil of the 9th century, through two massive towers built for Philippe Auguste, and up to the 17th century with an entrance by the ever-present Marshal Vauban. There is also the Tour de la Reine Berthe, where one of France's least distinguished kings, Philippe Ier, is supposed to have confined his Dutch Queen Berthe in 1091 after he had repudiated her to marry another, Bertrade de Montfort.

After exploring old Montreuil, if you still have time, follow the N39 road west towards the sea and two utterly different towns. **Etaples**, on the north side of the mouth of the Canche, is very much a working, quite rough-and-ready fishing port. To the south, meanwhile, is the eccentrically glitzy resort of **Le Touquet**, an artificial town created in the 1890s as a rival to Deauville and other fashionable spots further south, and long especially successful with British high society. Today, its Art Deco architecture, casino and giant grand hotels still give it a vaguely Noël Coward air, but it also still has some cachet, with some very giant houses to be glimpsed among the pines that surround the town, and all the fine shops that go with a French conception of luxury. More mundanely, its long promenade and sandy beach are fun places to get in touch with a traditional idea of the seaside, and watch the sun go down in the evening over the Channel.

On the Back Roads of Artois

The countryside inland in the Pas-de-Calais, east of the main roads south, can seem plain, an open expanse of rolling downs with few trees and giant fields patrolled by lonely tractors, and always wind-blasted when the winter weather sets in. Explore a little, though, and you find that the downland is divided by a string of sheltered, mellow valleys, some open, some steep-sided, lined by groves of trees and with fast-flowing rivers that divide and meet again, in some places forming babbling becks and waterfalls and in others placid, near lake-sized ponds. The landscape, instead of bleak, suddenly seems abundant and richly varied.

Get away from the main roads into this area, known as the Sept Vallées, and you also come upon villages of neat, white-washed cottages with red-tiled roofs and brilliantly coloured flowers around their doors, and so peaceful and quiet they seem lost to the world. Each has its individual quirks and features—a tumbledown château glimpsed through trees, or a bizarrely shaped church porch. And, like any other part of rural France, the region has its traditions and special foods—especially cheeses, *charcuterie* and unusual liqueurs—and along the valleys there are many craft workshops and food producers that open to casual visitors.

This area was also for centuries part of Europe's greatest battle-ground, fought over time and again by France, England, Spain and other powers. Its towns and villages have been conquered and re-taken many times, and this past is reflected in historic buildings found by market squares, or in battlefields such as Agincourt, still visible amid the rural quiet.

Roads wind up and around hills through the Artois valleys, interconnected by tiny, often sunken lanes, making them ideal for anyone who likes just wandering and taking each

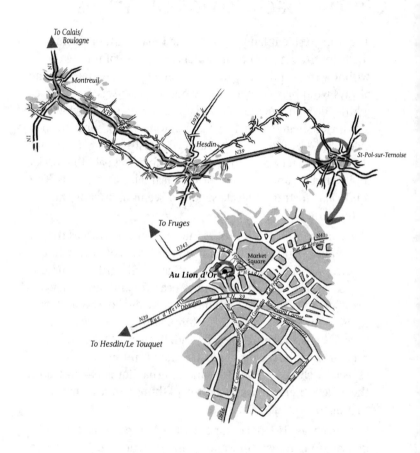

place as they find them. For thorough orientation, local tourist offices have plenty of literature on the Seven Valleys, including lists of most traditional food and craft outlets. And, as a focus when exploring, an excellent place to aim for is the Lion d'Or in St-Pol-sur-Ternoise, a traditional small-town inn long renowned as a showcase for the region's produce and cuisine.

To reach the Seven Valleys area from Calais or Boulogne, take the N1 south to Montreuil, and turn left on to the N39, signposted for Hesdin, which continues to St-Pol-sur-Ternoise. When you approach St-Pol from Hesdin, a turn off to the left takes you into the town. This leads you into a one-way system that actually avoids the main street, rue d'Hesdin, but if you follow it through it will take you in a loop around and back to the north of this street, on to rue de Fruges, where you can turn into rue d'Hesdin, or simply park in the former market square and walk around the corner. The Lion d'Or is right there on the north side of rue d'Hesdin, easily identifiable by its two imposing lions above the entrance.

Au Lion d'Or

Hôtel-Restaurant au Lion d'Or, 74 rue d'Hesdin, 62130 St-Pol-sur-Ternoise, ℂ 21.03.10.44. Open noon–2.30pm, 7–9pm daily. Book weekends. Menus at 88F, 118F, 188F; buffet and salad menu average 40F.

The Lion d'Or is a stout, 19th-century coaching inn, a Logis de France hotel, which through thick and thin has managed to conserve its two regal wooden golden lions that jut out over the street and give it a distinct touch of grandeur. Its reputation was established over many years by former owner Michel Théret, who first began its policy of using predominantly local ingredients and highlighting local dishes. He has recently retired, but Mme Théret is still present, and very little has changed. The bar past the entrance has a comfortably inhabited look that sets a cosy tone, happily combining some rather plush seats, plain wood panelling, a fireplace that's still used in winter, and lots of flowers. The dining room, similarly, is unfussily *rustique*, with oak beams, country scenes and yet more flowers around the diners, locals in for lunch and usually a few British people passing through. The menu is extremely flexible, for as well as the three set menus anyone looking for a quick meal can choose from a brasserie-type menu of dishes that can be ordered singly, from *hors-d'œuvres*, omelettes, assorted *charcuterie* or a range of generous mixed salads to specialities such as local sausages and brains, cooked *à la meunière*.

If you're in no hurry, though, have at least the 118F menu, if not the four-course *Menu Plaisir et Forme*. The mid-range menu includes an interesting choice of starters, such as a light but strongly cheesy *tartelette de fromage* beneath a crunchy, golden gratin, or mussels and cockles with one of the region's favourite vegetables, leeks. To follow, ham on the bone braised in two different beers, with a juicy gravy, is a local favourite that's a long-established house speciality, while for a very rich, powerful alternative there's also *tête de veau* in a *gribiche* sauce, made with hard-boiled eggs, oil, vinegar, capers and herbs. Some non-regional dishes are on offer: fish, usually cod or sole, in mint essences is a more recent speciality, and there are also good steaks.

After the main course, it's tempting to wander away from the set menus—despite the home-made *pâtisserie* they offer—to try some of the full page of other desserts (those served hot need to be ordered with the main meal), such as berries in a wine- and egg-yolk *sabayon*, or crêpes flambéd in beer. There's also a fair choice of wines, and a very extensive aperitif and liqueur list, to help you linger longer in the easy-going, country atmosphere of this hotel.

Filets de Soles à la Fleur de Menthe

(Serves 4)

1 litre/1¾ pint fish stock
500ml/16fl oz milk
1 slice lemon
4 sole fillets

For the sauce:
35g/1½oz unsalted butter
35g/1½oz plain flour
250ml/8fl oz milk
125ml/4fl oz fish stock
125ml/4fl oz lemon juice
50ml/4 tablespoons mint extract
50g/2oz crème fraîche
salt and pepper

For the garnish:

4 sprigs mint

4 lemon wedges

chopped parsley

Put the fish stock, milk and lemon slice into a large shallow pan (or a roasting tin) and bring to the boil. Reduce to a simmer, add the sole fillets and poach for 8–10 minutes, until tender. Remove from the pan, place in a serving dish and keep warm.

For the sauce, melt the butter in a pan, stir in the flour and cook gently for 1–2 minutes. Gradually add the milk, fish stock and lemon juice, then cook, stirring constantly, until it boils and thickens. Add the mint extract, crème fraîche and salt and pepper to taste.

Pour the sauce over the fish and garnish with the mint, lemon and parsley.

---

touring around

The valley of the Canche, running inland from Le Touquet past Montreuil, is the largest of the Artois valleys and the area's main artery. From Montreuil the N39 road towards Hesdin runs parallel to the river, rolling up and down hills along the wooded banks through a line of relatively lively villages, but several of which have their particular attractions. The Canche here is quite wide and slow-moving, and at **Brimeux** forms several large, slightly mysterious-looking ponds surrounded by willows and birches, and much-loved by local anglers (permits are required, obtainable from the town hall). In **Lespinoy** look out on the south side of the road for the **Atelier de Claire**, the workshop of Claire Rouch, who produces very pretty hand-painted furniture using original 18th-century techniques, and will work to order.

Everywhere there is colour, for the villagers of Artois are known for their love of flowers, and virtually every house has bunches of geraniums, hydrangeas and wild flowers around their window sills. Further east along the Canche in **Bouin-Plumoison**—the name *'plumoison'* comes from 'goose-pluckers', a reference to the villagers' early occupation—there is the **Musée de l'Abeille d'Opale** (*open*

15 June–15 Sept, Sat, Sun, public holidays, 3–6pm ; adm 20F), which will tell you everything you ever might want to know about honey and beekeeping, through a video (in French) and a tour of their hives. The museum is private, part of a company called Therry-Apiculture (with longer opening hours than the museum), who produce both honey and *hydromel*, fermented honey, otherwise known as mead. Billed here as 'the drink of the Gauls', it has been made in this area for centuries, and recently undergone something of a revival.

Beyond Bouin the road approaches **Hesdin**, the main town of the Seven Valleys and once a 'new town', transplanted from its original location a few kilometres to the east in 1554 on the orders of the Emperor Charles V. The great Franco-Spanish wars that long dominated the life of Flanders and Artois began when Charles fortuitously inherited both Spain and Burgundy, so that his territories effectively surrounded France. For the next century and a half, every French king and minister took it as their aim to break this ring around them, a goal finally achieved between 1640 and 1680 by Richelieu, Mazarin and Louis XIV. A hundred years earlier, though, the great Charles carried all before him, and in 1553, after their French garrisons had obstructed his troops once too often, he ordered that both Thérouanne to the north and the first Hesdin, a historic and wealthy town, be razed down to the last brick, and a new Hesdin created to the west.

Hesdin today is a very attractive little town, at the meeting-point of the Canche and Ternoise valleys. The main square, the place d'Armes, which seems almost too big for

La Canche

the town, is dominated by a grand, very Flemish-looking brick **town hall**, fronted by a magnificently sculpted two-level Baroque stone porch from 1629. At the top there is a fleur-de-lys, added in the 18th century, but the coat-of-arms at the centre of the balcony is that of Spain, flanked by those of Hesdin and Artois. Nearby is the large church of **Notre-Dame**, built between 1565 and 1585 in the style of a Flemish *Hallekerk*, as a rectangular hall instead of in the shape of a cross. Its brick façade is mainly very late Gothic, but it has an impressive Renaissance-style stone porch, surmounted, again, by the Spanish Habsburg arms.

Next to the church is the river, which runs through the middle of the town under little hump-backed bridges, sometimes disappearing under buildings and then re-emerging beside the winding, cobbled streets. In rue Daniel Lereuil at No.11 is the birthplace of the Abbé Prévost, born in 1697, famously un-devout and misbehaving priest and author of *Manon Lescaut*. Hesdin is busiest on Thursdays, when farmers from around the valleys descend on the square for the area's most important and vigorous **market**. The town is also known for two kinds of food in particular, a moreish crunchy chocolate called a *Panne Hesdinoise*, in the shape of an Artois roof tile, and *charcuterie*, often made with beer and honey, which can be found at the **Charcuterie Gervois** on the square. And, after wandering through the streets of Hesdin, you can also walk all the way around it along a lovely footpath lined with beeches, the **Tour-de-Chaussée**, created in the 17th century by travelling merchants to avoid passing through the town and paying the dues it was entitled to charge.

East of Hesdin, the main road runs straight towards St-Pol. On the way, pay at least some respect to tiny **Vieil-Hesdin**, site of what was until it incurred Charles V's wrath, one of the region's richest towns. It encompassed a famously palatial castle, the ruins of which are still visible, and the 'Park of Marvels', a giant pleasure garden created at the beginning of the 14th century by Richard, Count of Artois. Stretching all the way to the Ternoise, and landscaped to create all kinds of visual tricks, it contained exotic beasts, elaborate fountains, bizarre statues and even jokes such as bridges that gave way when you trod on them, and was renowned throughout Europe. The Dukes of

Burgundy frequently used it for extravagant entertaining, but later it, too, was obliterated on the Emperor's orders, and only the name of the village of Le Parcq remains to commemorate it.

St-Pol-sur-Ternoise itself is a plain town, badly damaged twice the last time Artois was a battlefield, in both 1940 and 1944. Much of it has been rebuilt quite simply, so that the Lion d'Or is now one of its most imposing older buildings, despite the fact that it too is a historic town, once the seat of a powerful line of medieval counts. After lunch, leave town on the D343 to the northwest, signposted to **Anvin**, along the Ternoise, at times a quite broad, misty valley. The rambling village of Anvin and, further west, **Blangy-sur-Ternoise** both have fine, but quite different 16th-century churches, the former late-Gothic, the second more eclectic. Blangy is also the place where Henry V of England and his army crossed the Ternoise in October 1415, on their way to **Azincourt**, better known in English spelt with a 'g', where they would defeat a French force five times larger in one rain-soaked day. It's now reached by turning north on to the little D104 road in Blangy.

In Azincourt there is a small **museum** (*open April–Oct, daily, 9am–6pm; Nov–Mar, daily, 2–6pm; adm 10F; free under-12s*), which tells the story of the battle effectively with the aid of a video made with much help from Kenneth Branagh's *Henry V*, and it's a good idea to visit it before walking or driving to the battleground. This museum (like the large stand-up figures of medieval knights around the village) is an all-local initiative, and especially welcoming. At the battlefield of Agincourt itself, remarkably, but perhaps due to its compact size, it's possible to recognise the outlines of what happened there nearly six hundred years ago more easily than at the sites of much more recent events. The forests either side of the field, which hemmed in the French army and made it impossible for them to use most of their strength, have gone, but the track is still there along which carts ran, keeping the English archers supplied with arrows as they poured them into the French knights sliding and falling in the mud; it is now the road past the neighbouring village of Maisoncelle.

From Azincourt take the main D928 road south towards Hesdin, then turn off right on to yet another tiny lane to **Fressin**, known to students of French literature as the long-time home of Georges Bernanos and the background to many of his novels. Also, in among the trees just to the west, beyond the end of the village's long main street, there are the romantic ruins of a castle that was once the seat of the Créquy, one of the grandest families of Artois from the Middle Ages right up until the *ancien régime*, and servants at different times of both the Kings of France and the Dukes of Burgundy. Fressin has one of the finest of the Valley churches, **St-Martin**, most unusual because its interior is entirely washed down in white. Especially beautiful is the funeral chapel of the Créquys, first built by a widow, Jeanne de Roye, for her husband and two others of the clan who died at Agincourt, and with some superb latticework Gothic carving. The rest of the church is actually later, with almost English-style columns added by a 16th-century Créquy who was ambassador to England.

As you leave the church, also, not far away down the hill is the **Caveau Le Vieux Chais**, a fine wine merchant's run by the Glaçon family for four generations, and an excellent place to buy as an alternative to the Calais hypermarkets, with a particularly good range of Bordeaux (wines are sold by the 12-bottle case). Near the entrance to the giant *caves* there's a photo of M. Paul Glaçon shaking hands with Gérard Depardieu, a man who's known to know a few things about wine.

North of Fressin the road winds on up to **Créquy** village, at the head of the Créquoise, perhaps the most idyllic of all the Seven Valleys. The valley sides wind and dip and are very green, while the river sparkles and rushes along the roadside and past the village churches and flowerbeds. Just outside Créquy there is a farm that produces a unique cheese, Sire de Créquy, named after a 13th-century Créquy, Raoul, who went off to the Crusades, was captured and believed lost forever, and then returned to claim his 'widow' on the day she was due to remarry (this story is also re-enacted in a cute pageant in Fressin in early July). Visitors can take a small tour of the cheese cellars and have meals at the farm (by reservation) as well as tasting and buying. Sire de Créquy is a variation on the region's traditional Rollot, a pungent, spicy, strong cheese with an orange rind and a short life.

The attractions of the valley are not only to do with the scenery or food-tasting. A little way downriver in **Torcy** there is a piano bar and cabaret, Le Baladin, an original combination of nightspot and village crêperie, which livens up every weekend. For a complete contrast, in the very tiny village of **Boubers-les-Hesmond**, up a side valley to the west, there is a tiny bar that looks as if it may well not have changed a jot since about 1890, run by a little old lady. Don't expect her, though, to have any new-fangled things like sandwiches, for it's more like a bar in which to watch the cows go by over a glass of *rouge*.

From the top of the valley, you reach Boubers via **Royon**, an exceptionally pretty village with the river right through the middle of it and a very fine *Flamboyant*-Gothic church from the 1540s. Back in the main Créquoise valley, the road eventually winds down to **Loison-sur-Créquoise**, sole home of another special product, Perlé de Groseille or de Framboise, which could be called redcurrant or raspberry champagne. Simple fruit wines are another thing that have long been made by local farmers for their own consumption, and at the **Maison du Perlé**, easy to find by the roadside, Hubert Delomel has refined the traditional recipes to produce a drink that's fruity but also light, refreshing and quite subtle. They also have ciders, preserves and cider *eau-de-vie*, which cannot be called Calvados because it's too strong, as well as offering tours and even bikes to hire to ride through the surrounding woods. Below Loison, the Créquoise runs into the Canche and the road meets the D113, which to the right will take you back to Montreuil along a leafier, emptier route than the N39 on the south side of the valley.

The Pleasures of the Grand-Place

France's northern region has a jewel of a city, Arras. Built to hold markets, its three great squares, among them the Grand-Place, one of the largest in all Europe, are an interlocking, harmonious ensemble of medieval and 16th-century buildings. The capital of Artois, and always French-speaking, Arras nevertheless long looked eastward for its political allegiance, towards Flanders, and the squares and several parts of the old city have a distinctly Flemish look to them. Nearby, others have a more classical, linear French elegance.

Restored with astonishing success after the First World War, the centre of Arras is full of unusual features. Beneath the squares is a labyrinth of cellars and tunnels, used over the years as chalk mines, wine stores, refuse dumps or refuges. Above, Arras still has a giant, sprawling market of a kind that you might no longer expect to find in a city so near an industrial area, and also shops that are both individual and opulent. And in the squares themselves, soberly beautiful on a winter's day or more noisy and animated when the sun is out or the market is in session, there is a relaxed, appealing atmosphere in the cafés and restaurants beneath the arcades.

the Grand Place

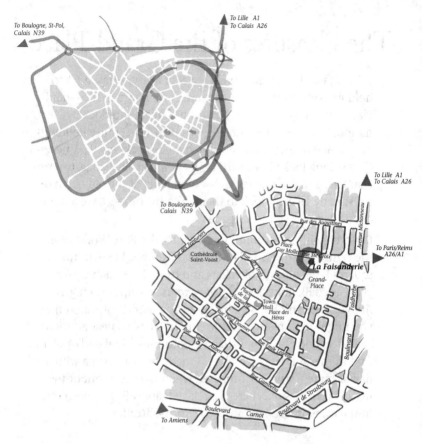

Arras also has another very special hedonistic attraction in La
Faisanderie, situated in a house and its cellar on the Grand-
Place itself. Jean-Pierre Dargent is one of the premier chefs of
northern France. Greatly admired by other chefs, he has been
here for over eight years, but remains continually creative.

getting there

Whichever direction you approach Arras from by road, you will
inevitably meet up with the ring of boulevards that runs around
the city centre. If you come from Calais via Le Touquet and St-Pol
on the N39, turn left and follow the boulevards round clockwise

until, at a wide junction, you see a sign to the right for Grand-Place (if you come in from the A26 *autoroute*, you will see this junction very shortly after coming on to the boulevards). This turning will take you very abruptly into the great expanse of the square, where La Faisanderie is almost directly in front of you in the opposite corner. It's often possible to park in the square itself, and, if not, in the car park beneath it.

La Faisanderie

La Faisanderie, 45 Grand-Place, 62000 Arras, © 21.48.20.76. Open Tues–Sat noon–2pm, 7–9.30pm; Sun noon–2pm. Closed two weeks Feb–Mar and three weeks Aug. Book always. Menus at 185F, 285F, 395F; children's menu 80F; carte *average 400F.*

You enter the Faisanderie via a hallway with classic, pastel-shaded French bourgeois décor. To eat, you usually go down a wide spiral staircase into an elegantly restored, airy barrel-roofed cellar, one of the caves beneath the square, with bare brick walls that give it a light, modern feel, and colour provided by paintings (for sale), and an abundance of flowers. The restaurant used to be a stable, but you would never know it. Front-of-house, the staff have all the professionalism that you would expect in a restaurant at this level, and the atmosphere is immediately relaxing.

Like his friend Roland Gauthier in Montreuil, Jean-Pierre Dargent is originally from another part of France entirely—the Haute-Pyrénées, in the far southwest—but in the pursuit of perfect local freshness he also uses predominantly northern ingredients, and produces spectacular versions of traditional northern French dishes. The menu is another that changes frequently, with the seasons. An ebullient man, he's also prepared to be flexible: each course on the main 185F menu is individually priced, in case you want only a sample of his food (although it would be hard to stay at just one dish), and there is a children's menu for junior gourmets. In the vast wine list, as well as French bottles, there are actually a few international wines, plus traditional beers from small local breweries.

The culinary innovations can be seen right away in the appetisers. He likes to experiment, and they change every day; one example might be a little dish of mushrooms with a mustard sauce and cracked wheat. While you're savouring the subtle flavours, the bread cart arrives, with six different fresh breads all made at the restaurant.

For first courses, there are so many different dishes that might appear on the menu that it's hard to cite specifics: there might be a *millefeuille* of cabbage leaves with smoked salmon and cumin, or oysters grilled in a shallot butter. Potatoes and mussels together are a wonderfully creamy dish, the potatoes whipped rather than mashed and almost infused with seafood flavour. If it's the season, though, try a tart of cep mushrooms and walnuts in a *marinade forestière*, which covers a whole range of rich, brown, lasting flavours. Among main courses, roast rib of veal with a Picard *andouille* and carrots is a stout, comforting but also very subtle dish, with a rich, thick sauce. Fish dishes are just as delicious: an ideally fresh brill comes lightly char-grilled with a delicate but succulent crab tart, and a gentle, fragrant seafood sauce that complements them perfectly.

If you were tempted to come in just for one course, though, it might be dessert. A *crêpe à la bière* with cream custard is decadently enjoyable, the beer adding a slight tang to the light custard filling. And then, apparently one of the more simple possibilities, there's a lemon mousse ice-cream *à la crème de thé*. Tea custard doesn't quite explain it: this is nectar, and as you finish this superb meal you can only wonder where you might discover the magic formula.

Chartreuse de Faisan au Chou

(Serves 4)

In this recipe the partridge exists solely to flavour the cabbage and is discarded after cooking.

1 large green cabbage, finely chopped
200g/7oz belly of pork or bacon
2 tablespoons goose fat
1 old partridge
1 garlic sausage

1 bouquet garni
1 teaspoon juniper berries
1 carrot
1 onion
1 litre/1¾ pints game or beef stock
1 pheasant
100g/4oz turnips, cut into matchsticks
100g/4oz carrots, cut into matchsticks
150g/5oz green beans, trimmed

For the veal stuffing:
225g/8oz veal, minced
125g/5oz unsalted butter
2 eggs
freshly grated nutmeg

Blanch the cabbage in boiling water for a few minutes, then drain and refresh under cold running water. Blanch the pork or bacon joint and drain well. Heat half the goose fat in a frying pan and brown the partridge on all sides. Place half the cabbage in a large heavy pan, put the partridge, bacon and sausage on top along with the bouquet garni, juniper berries, whole carrot and onion, then top with the remaining cabbage. Season well with salt and pepper, then dot with the remaining goose fat.

Pour the stock into the pan in which the partridge was browned and bring to the boil, stirring to scrape up the sediment from the base of the pan. Pour the stock over the cabbage and cover with a circle of greased greaseproof paper and the pan lid. Cook over a low heat for 1½–2 hours, removing the sausage and pork half way through the cooking time. Slice the sausage. Cut half the pork into strips and dice the rest. When the cabbage is done, drain well, reserving the cooking liquid.

To make the stuffing, put all the ingredients in a food processor and blend well, adding nutmeg, salt and pepper to taste.

Roast the pheasant until almost cooked, then quarter. Cook the turnips, carrots and beans until just tender, then drain and refresh under cold water. Generously butter a charlotte mould and arrange the vegetables alternately around the sides and over the base, interspersing them with a few slices of *sausage and strips of pork. Coat with a thin layer of veal stuffing. Put half the cabbage in the mould and top with the pheasant pieces, the diced bacon and the remaining sausage. Cover with the remaining cabbage, press down well and cover with the remaining veal stuffing and a piece of greased greaseproof paper. Place the mould in a bain marie and cook in an oven preheated to 180°C/350°F (gas mark 4) for 40 minutes. Leave to stand for 5 minutes, then turn out on to a serving platter.*

Pour the cooking liquid from the cabbage into a pan and boil until reduced to a syrupy consistency. Dice the butter and whisk into the sauce a few pieces at a time. Adjust the seasoning and serve the sauce with the chartreuse.

touring around

When you first enter the **Grand-Place**, you are immediately knocked back by its size; the far sides seem almost to recede into the distance. It is lined by Flemish-style houses all four storeys high, with curving gables. Their first floors jut out over the pavement, supported by slender stone columns, creating arcades that once sheltered market traders and their wares. From the corner of the square furthest from the main traffic entrance a little street connects through into the place des Héros, better known as the **Petit-Place** and accordingly more intimate, though dominated by the soaring Gothic town hall. Behind the hall is the third square, the plainer **place de la Vacquerie**.

A market was first recorded on the site of the Grand-Place in the year 828. The size of the square is an indication of just how important Arras was during its Golden Age, in the 14th and 15th centuries. Merchants from all over the continent came to buy and sell here, and Arras tapestries—such as the 'arras' behind which Polonius is hiding when he is stabbed in *Hamlet*—were prized luxuries as far away as Byzantium. The Grand-Place at this time was not only home to great markets, but was also used for jousts.

The *places* today look very much as they have done for the last few hundred years, yet a great deal is actually a reconstruction, still more impressive than the rebuilt St-Malo, and perhaps the greatest of all the restoration projects carried out in France following this century's wars. During the First World War, Arras had the terrible misfortune of actually becoming part of the front line, and was incessantly pounded by German artillery—photographs in the town hall vividly reveal the extent of the devastation. As the dust settled, though, the decision was taken to rebuild it exactly as it had been, to the extent of recovering individual bricks from the rubble and returning them to their exact former location. The result is extraordinarily effective.

The houses of the *places* are aligned with such simple harmony that at first sight they can appear quite uniform, but this impression rapidly disappears. Some have brick façades, others stone, and the spirals and other decoration on their gables are endlessly varied. Look above the arcades and you see all sorts of fascinating details: a mermaid, on No.11 in the Petit-Place; three kings, in rue de la Taillerie between the two squares; a cauldron, probably once a shop sign, at No.32, Grand-Place. The oldest house in Arras is No.47, Grand-Place, conveniently making a corner with the Faisanderie and now the Trois Luppars hotel, a wonderful semi-Gothic townhouse from 1467 with a watch-tower in the middle of its distinctive stepped-gable roof.

The best times to see the *places* are on Wednesday and especially Saturday mornings, when they regain their original function and some of their 14th-century bustle with one of the largest **markets** in all of France. It no longer fills the whole of all three squares, but is still huge, and enormously varied. Food, real farm products and even live animals can be found in Vacquerie and the Petit-Place, where the countryside comes into the city. In the Grand-Place you might come across clothes, tableware, antiques or old buttons.

There are also interesting permanent shops around the squares. On the corner of the Petit-Place and Taillerie is the *fromagerie* of Jean-Claude Leclercq, a master cheesemaker with a wonderful selection of local cheeses. Even if you're not interested in buying, take a look in the windows of the Cotellerie Caudron on place de la Vacquerie, far more than a cutlery shop. In the 1960s Louis Caudron succeeded in re-establishing the formula for the dye used in the Arras blue porcelain the making of which was the city's staple industry during the 18th century, and which had been lost. His company is now the sole manufacturer, and the shop has shelves and shelves of tableware in this light, pretty style. A little clutch of interesting souvenir and odd-ments shops can also be found by walking on past the Cotellerie, and across rue Paul Doumer.

The grandest piece of post-war reconstruction in Arras is the town hall, the **Hôtel de Ville**, between the two smaller squares (and also containing the tourist office). It is one of the finest pieces of civil Gothic architecture in Europe: grandest of all is the main central section, built very quickly between 1502 and 1506 in a *Flamboyant* style with elaborate traceries and pinnacles and a peppering of tiny dormer windows in the roof. The giant belfry behind it was built separately and took much longer, between 1462 and 1554. Both had to be painstakingly restored during the 1920s.

From the basement a lift can take you up—with some steps at the end—to the top of the **belfry** (*open Mon–Sat, 10am–noon, 2–6pm; Sun, holidays, 10am–noon, 3–6.30pm; adm 15F; 5F under-14s*) for a panoramic view. When you come down, you're also allowed to wander around the town hall whenever meetings are not in progress. Inside, no real attempt was made to duplicate the pre-1914 décor, but the very 20s-style substitutes give the place an engaging charm. The Salle des Mariages has murals with Isadora Duncanesque Grecian maidens on the subject of 'spring'; the beautiful main hall has still larger murals by the artist Hoffbauer, on life in Arras in the 15th century.

From the basement of the Hôtel de Ville you can also begin a tour of the **Boves**, the bizarre catacomb of tunnels that extends through the chalk beneath Arras (*opening times, adm same as for belfry*). Some tunnels existed here in Roman times, and many more were opened up during the Middle Ages. They extend downwards through three levels, and without a guide you would easily get lost. Until 1982 everyone in Arras had right of access to them, but since then the bottom levels have been closed for safety, except for the tour groups. They have been used for all kinds of different purposes. Their temperature and humidity makes them perfect for storing wine, and many Arras porcelain merchants routinely threw all their damaged stock down them. During the Revolutionary Terror of the 1790s, Catholics held secret services here. The caverns were greatly extended in 1916–17 by British troops, who used them as a safe means of getting to the trenches just east of Arras. Tours last about 30–45 minutes, and guides make great efforts for English-speakers.

From the town hall, walk across place de la Vacquerie, past the Cotellerie Caudron, and turn right at rue Paul Doumer to find the **Musée** des Beaux-Arts (*open April–Sept, Mon, Wed–Sat, 10am–noon, 2–6pm; Oct–Mar, Mon, Wed–Sat, 10am–noon, 2–5pm; Sun, 10am–noon, 3–6pm; closed Tues; adm 13.50F*). It occupies the former Benedictine Abbey of St-Vaast, which somewhat surprisingly is a giant neoclassical edifice, vast by name and vast by nature, completed in 1783. The abbey was founded in the 7th century, and St-Vaast was one of the most important institutions in Arras throughout its history. In the 1740s, however it was decided to knock its early-medieval buildings down and replace them with this all-new abbey. The museum collection is mixed, with a sizeable amount of unexceptional paintings. There is a beautiful collection of fine 18th-century Arras and Tournai porcelain, and several landscapes by Corot, who often painted in Arras. The museum's greatest artefacts, though, are its medieval sculptures. The 1446 tomb sculpture of Guillaume Lefranchois, a Canon of Béthune, is extraordinary, and can still shock: it's a decomposing skeleton, a classic product of the anguished late-medieval mind. Completely different is the 14th-century *Head of a Woman*, believed also to be from a tomb, a face so serenely beautiful it seems timeless. The museum has, though, only one Arras tapestry—there are very few still in existence—St-Vaast and the Bear, with a delightfully worked, almost abstract background.

Alongside the museum is the **cathedral**, in a similar neoclassical style. If the Cardinal de Rohan did not like Arras' antique abbey, he was no more taken with the Gothic abbey church, and in the 1770s work on a new one was begun by Constant d'Ivry, one of the most important architects of the day. Unfinished at the time of the Revolution, it was completed in 1833, and then had to be rebuilt after 1918. It's a huge building, plain and white and frankly unwelcoming.

To enter another piece of 18th-century Arras, cross rue Paul Doumer from the Musée des Beaux-Arts and veer to the left to come to the **place du Théâtre**, with several fine buildings such as the 1738 Hôtel de Guines, on the rue des Jongleurs into the square, and the gracious theatre, from 1786. And just off the square is the former home of one of the rising personalities of Arras at that time, in the street now named after him, **rue Maximilien-Robespierre**. Robespierre lived in this house in the late 1780s while he was establishing his reputation as a ferocious advocate, before going off to use his talents on a wider stage. Arras has never known quite what to do with its most famous son, or his house, for being the home town of a man widely credited with the invention of modern totalitarianism is not easy to handle. A few incorrigible Stalinists campaign to have the house opened as a museum, but for the moment it's tightly shuttered up, and seems less well cared-for than most other buildings in the city.

Another 18th-century addition to Arras is the **Basse-Ville**, which you come to if you carry on through the place du Théâtre and veer to the right. The product of an early foray into town planning, begun in the 1750s, it has streets intersecting in a grid, centred on place Victor-Hugo, a wide octagonal square with a pyramid in the middle, an idea quintessentially of the Enlightenment era. From there, if you continue roughly in the same direction, you will eventually come to the boulevards around the line of Marshal Vauban's ramparts, built in the 1660s and demolished in the last century. In the southwest corner, however, to the left, is his **Citadelle**, still in use by the French military.

Towards the northwest, on the other hand, the boulevard leads up to the only surviving part of Arras' walls, the **Bastion des Chouettes**, now landscaped into a tranquil park. Mid-way between the Bastion and the Citadelle on the outer side of the boulevard is the First World War **British Cemetery** for Arras, one of the largest of so many in the area. It contains over 2600 graves, and around the walls there are the names of nearly 40,000 men with no known grave, in lists that go on and on until it's impossible to take any more.

Even those without any special interest in the Great War, or in anything military, might appreciate a trip out to **Vimy Ridge**, north of Arras off the N17 Lens road. Taken by the Canadian army in 1917, it is now the Canadian National Memorial, ceded in perpetuity. It really is a small piece of Canada: everything is rigorously bilingual (in a Canadian-official, not French, way), and the free guided tours are given by Canadian students (*tours April–Nov daily, 10am–6pm*). Some of the trenches, terrifyingly close together, and grassed-over craters have been preserved, and from the peak of the ridge, by the sombre 1936 memorial, you can well appreciate why it was considered strategic, for it has a view eastwards for miles over France's traditional industrial heartland, from this distance surprisingly green.

Land, Sea and Sky

Seventy miles south of Calais there is a special, misty landscape of sand flats, water, dunes, salt marshes, giant skies and unbreakable stillness that is one of the least populated, least developed areas anywhere on the coast of France. The Bay of the Somme is a broad arc where at low tide the sea recedes for miles, and the placid channels, sandbanks and expanses of coarse grass, rushes and marsh lavender present an ever-changing, subtle mix of colours fading into the horizon. It's a landscape for lovers of the horizontal: borders between earth, sea and sky are often hard to distinguish, and the light in the Bay has an opaque quality celebrated by writers from Jules Verne to Colette, and by painters such as Degas and Seurat. The Bay is also exceptionally rich in birdlife, and birdwatchers and walkers are among those most appreciative of this rare natural environment.

The quiet little towns around the Bay can sometimes seem lost in the immensity of the landscape, and left behind by history as they have been by the tide. They include, though, some of the oldest towns in France. St-Valery-sur-Somme, the largest, stands on a site occupied since the Stone Age, on one of a few rocky outcrops around the Bay. Locals believe William the Conqueror's enemy Harold of Wessex was

Le Relais Guillaume de Normandy

imprisoned here, and the Conqueror himself passed through in 1066. Later, St-Valery became a fishing port, a weekend retreat for the Amiens bourgeois and, briefly, a military camp. Nowadays, the main qualities of the ancient town are a sleepy tranquillity and an idiosyncratic charm.

The traditional food of Picardy is a sturdy country cuisine, centred, naturally, around the local products: in the Bay of the Somme particularly, duck in season, and fish and shellfish caught offshore—shrimps, mussels, sole and *lieu* (pollack). Most celebrated of all local produce is the lamb from sheep grazed on the salt marshes (the *prés-salés*), which has an individual flavour. Much use is also made of ham and other pork products, rabbit, and northern vegetables such as leeks, carrots, greens and potatoes. In almost perverse contrast to their Norman neighbours, Picards make very little use of butter.

A good place to sample some of this cuisine—not widely known, even in France—in refined form amid engagingly eccentric surroundings is the Relais Guillaume de Normandy in St-Valery. A Logis hotel installed in a fancifully ornate turn-of-the-century mansion, it has an excellent view of the Bay, so you can contemplate the horizon from a table.

getting there

The coast road south from Calais and Boulogne via Le Touquet, the D940, runs directly to the Bay of the Somme. If you are travelling on the main N1 inland via Montreuil, turn right at Nouvion on to the D111, to join the D940 at Noyelles-sur-Mer, at the eastern end of the bay. From the first roundabout on the D940 signposted to St-Valery, 4km past Noyelles, follow the signs into the town and you will come on to the road along the quays alongside the river.

At place Guillaume le Conquérant, site of the tourist office, the road briefly divides in a one-way system, westbound traffic continuing around the quays; at place des Pilotes, the market square, the

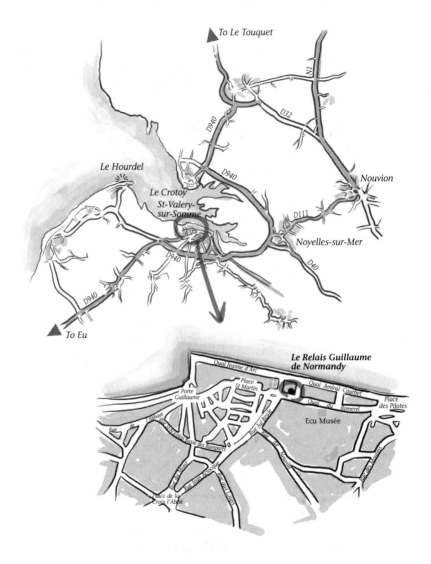

two halves are reunited, and continue on the other side of the square into the quai du Romerel, the main street of town. Halfway along on the right is the imposing entrance, with arched sign above thick hedges, of the Guillaume de Normandy. It has its own parking in the grounds. Coming from Dieppe or Eu, leave the D940 at the roundabout west of the town, and come on to quai du Romerel from the opposite direction; St-Valery is so small that it's very hard to get lost.

Le Relais Guillaume de Normandy

Le Relais Guillaume de Normandy, 46 Quai du Romerel, 80230 St-Valery-sur-Somme, © 22.60.82.36. Open Sept–June, Mon, Wed–Sun, noon–1.15pm, 6.45–8.15pm; July–Aug, daily, noon–1.15pm, 6.45–8.15pm. Book weekends. Menus at 87F, 128F, 165F, 205F; children's menu 50F; carte average 180F.

As you come down the gravel drive into the garden of the Guillaume de Normandy you see in front of you a large, elaborate house in a style that could be called a mixture of neo-Gothic, Art Nouveau and Norman/Picard traditional. Several storeys high and oddly tall for its width, topped off with steep roofs that in parts are almost pagoda-like, it has an undeniable fairy-tale, gingerbread-house look to it, especially the tower up one side. Local legend has long held that the house was built at the turn of the century for an English lord who set up his French mistress here, and maintained trysts with her every weekend. However, Francis Crimet, co-owner with chef Thierry Dupré, assures us, disappointingly, that the first owner was in fact an Amiens textile magnate, whose weekend pursuits were as far as anyone knows entirely of the respectable kind.

Much of the interior is as *fin-de-siècle*-ornate as the façade. The main dining room has red and gold fittings and flock wallpaper, well maintained if now appealingly aged. Beautiful during the day, though, is the dining room, overlooking the Bay through large windows. Inside, it is light and pretty, and decorated with flowers; outside is the quai Courbet, the quiet promenade along the harbour front, and beyond that the channels and misty distances of the Somme, with a few boats bobbing up and down or beached on the sand.

In each of the different menus there is a combination of local dishes and others from a more general French culinary repertoire. To make a real meal of it, go for the 165F menu and start with the *assiette de fruits de mer*, which among other delights features *crevettes roses et grises*, prawns and Somme Bay shrimps. The 87F menu includes one of the region's standards, the *ficelle picarde*: a savoury crêpe stuffed with ham, mushrooms and onions, covered in a cheese sauce, and put into the oven to form a *gratin*. A good winter warmer, this is the kind of simple, satisfying dish that's all the more enjoyable when done well, and it's especially good here, with a light sauce.

Among the main courses, all the menus offer the local lamb in different forms. The special qualities of *pré-salé* lamb are immediately apparent: the meat, very tender, has a lighter texture and flavour than most lamb, with a distinctive, slightly salty taste. Also, since it already has a high salt content, it needs very little seasoning. In the 87F menu it comes as a *navarin d'agneau*, a juicy stew served with a positively English range of vegetables that remind you you're in the north—potatoes, carrots, beans and cabbage; but go for the *carte* or the more expensive menus to try the rich *confit d'agneau*, or the impressive rack of *pré-salé* lamb. The Relais' other great *mussels* speciality is beautifully fresh fish, the range changing according to the season's catch: from simple *moules* and *frites* to skate simmered in a delicately garlicky *crème d'ail doux*.

One last highlight is the cheese trolley: it's no special advertisement for northern French cheeses, but has an excellent selection from other parts of the country, and for once has more variety than the list of desserts. There's especially good St-Nectaire and Reblochon—much stronger and tangier than the slightly weedy cheese that is sometimes given under that name—as well as Brie, Camembert and Livarot that are all worth savouring.

Rouleaux de Soles à la Purée de Champignons et Fumet de Safran

(Serves 4)

400g/14oz button mushrooms, very finely chopped
4 shallots, very finely chopped
50g/2oz unsalted butter
2 sole, approx 600–800g/1¼–1¾lb, filleted
4 large lettuce leaves, blanched for 10 seconds, then drained and refreshed
500ml/1 pint fish stock (made from the sole trimmings)
200ml/7fl oz whipping cream
pinch of saffron
salt and pepper

Sweat the mushrooms and three-quarters of the shallots in the butter until very soft, then season and remove from the heat. Season the fish fillets, then lay them on a board, skin-side up, and place some of the mushroom mixture in the centre of each one. Roll up the fillets around the stuffing, then wrap them 2 at a time in a lettuce leaf. Steam the parcels for about 10 minutes or until tender.

Meanwhile make the sauce. Put the fish stock in a pan with the remaining shallot and boil until reduced to a syrupy consistency. Add the cream and saffron and cook gently until thickened. Season to taste.

To serve, pour the sauce on to 4 warmed serving plates and place the sole parcels on top. Serve with seasonal vegetables such as honey-glazed carrots, lightly cooked spinach, broccoli or cauliflower florets or a mousseline of celery or carrot.

touring around

St-Valery-sur-Somme consists of two halves, the old **Haute-Ville** on its hill, and the port beneath it to the east. The harbour is a very low-key affair; there are no docks or breakwaters, only a long quay winding round the shoreline from the end of the Somme Canal, alongside which a surprising number of fishing boats and small pleasure craft are moored in line. For several hours each day they will just rest on the sand, and the only water to be seen is a shallow channel running out of the canal. The quayside is a beguiling place to walk along, with a little gentle, unhurried activity usually in progress, and a few characterful bars with outside tables for taking in the scene.

The quay runs into place des Pilotes, which fills up with the main **market** on Sunday mornings, and a slightly smaller one on Wednesdays, with especially spectacular displays of mussels and Somme Bay shrimps, known as *sauterelles*. West of the square, the road is closed to vehicles, and becomes the quai Amiral Courbet, a tree-lined walkway where on Sunday evenings a large part of the town promenades up and down in positively Mediterranean fashion beside the water- or sand-side, whichever it may be. Alongside it there are a few quite grand turn-of-the-century houses, of which the Guillaume de Normandy is by some way the most extravagant.

At the eastern end of the quays, by the Somme Canal, stands the **Entrepôt des Sels**, a large 1736 salt warehouse built when salt was a Royal monopoly. It sports a plaque indicating that William the Conqueror sailed from this spot on his way to Hastings in 1066. St-Valery was then in the midst of one of its periods of greatest activity. The rocky hill on which the old town stands was settled in the Neolithic era, and was used as a port by the Romans. In 611, an Irish monk called Walrick or Valerius (Saint Valery) came here, and founded an abbey which for some centuries was one of the most prestigious in the region. The town also became a stronghold. As the Bayeux Tapestry vividly recounts, a few years before 1066 Harold of Wessex, sent on a mission to Normandy by Edward the Confessor, was shipwrecked on the French coast and held to ransom by Count Guy de Ponthieu, until the Count's powerful neighbour William of Normandy demanded his release. This was the first step in Harold's supposed debt of honour to William, made so much of in the tapestry. St-Valery was a prime possession of the Counts of Ponthieu, and it is believed that Harold was held here; just past the western end of the quays are the remains of an ancient tower, the **Tour Harold**, where he was allegedly imprisoned.

The little old town of St-Valery, the **Haute-Ville**, is one of the most charming and atmospheric of French walled towns. On market days the port area can sometimes get vaguely busy; the old town scarcely ever. Its main entrance is the 16th-century **Porte de Nevers** at the end of quai du Romerel, named after a family of local lords, some of whom still lived in the house above the gate until quite recently. It was badly damaged the last time St-Valery became a battle zone, in May 1940, but has been finely restored. The steep cobbled street beyond the gate leads to the **Eglise St-Martin**, an impressive church that conforms to none of the architectural rules: it has two complete naves of almost equal size, having had to be rebuilt several times after wars, fires and other catastrophes. The exterior, mostly from 1558, has some great gargoyles, and is made of stone and black flint in an eye-catching chessboard pattern typical of the Picardy coast. In the narrow streets near the church there are several houses in the same style. Next to the church is the **place St-Martin**, with a sheer drop on one side down to the quays, and a wonderful view over the Bay.

Because St-Valery peaked so early as a military stronghold, no one ever saw a need to undertake any systematic renovation of its fortifications, and parts of its medieval walls are among the oldest still standing. The rough-brick **Porte Guillaume**, the western entrance to the Haute-Ville, now with flowers growing out of its towers, is definitely old enough to have been here when Duke William paid his visits. Joan of Arc was also brought through the gate as a prisoner in 1430, on her way to be handed over to the English in Rouen. Beyond the Porte Guillaume the town is delightfully rural, and chickens and other animals scratch about in the gardens of many of the houses. A little way past the gate are the walls of the old abbey, demolished after the Revolution, and which now contain a luxurious private house. From there, a track leads through fields to the **Chapelle des Marins**, a 19th-century chapel in chessboard style built over the tomb of Saint Valery. Just beneath it, there is a spring associated with the Saint called the Source de la Fidelité, although the water is now murky enough to deter all but the most desperate pilgrims.

St-Valery also has an engagingly personal folk museum, the **Ecomusée Picarvie** (*open Sept–May, Mon, Wed–Sun, 2–7pm, June–Aug daily; adm 20F, 5F under-12s*), in the lower town at 5 quai du Romerel. This is the work of an Abbeville builder, M. Paul Longuein, who over many years amassed a collection of over 6000 items related to traditional crafts and every other aspect of life in the Picardy countryside, from tools, toys and cider presses to a whole schoolroom and shop interiors.

For exploring the Bay of the Somme outside St-Valery, there are alternatives to walking or driving. Railway enthusiasts and many others drool over the **Chemin de Fer de la Baie de Somme**, a genuine 1900s narrow-gauge steam railway that runs from Le Crotoy through Noyelles and St-Valery to Cayeux. The trains chug around the Bay at a very leisurely pace every Sunday and some other days from April to September, and virtually every day in July and August, with three trains each afternoon. In St-Valery, the little station is right at the Canal end of the quays. Cycles can be hired from a shop in the old town, almost opposite the church, and there is a centre on the quays offering kayaks, for getting around even at low tide. The north side of the Bay, where the sand is firmer, is popular for sandyachting.

Before trying any **walks** in the Bay, an essential first step is to get the current tide table from the St-Valery tourist office: the sea may often be lost to view, but can also return with surprising speed. The office also has a booklet of walks in the area. An easy, popular if muddy walk at low tide is simply to follow the well-marked path from the end of the quays, past the little resort development at Cap Hornu and through the salt marshes (called *mollières*) towards the mouth of the Bay. The full distance is nearly 10km, but you can always go part of the way and turn back. The patterns of the channels and swathes of grasses and marsh flowers are infinitely variable; at times there's a strong sea wind; at others, the stillness is impenetrable. The birds to be seen include virtually every kind of European wetland and wading bird, but especially oystercatchers, avocets, wild geese and ducks.

The path eventually comes to an end at **Le Hourdel**, a quite phenomenally calm little fishing village with a noticeably remote feel to it, and a lighthouse, a quay, a few boats and, for most of the day, no water. Past Le Hourdel the nature of the coast changes rapidly, from the marshy, placid bay to an endless bar of shingle and mounting waves along the edge of the sea. If you have a car or bike, take the narrow coast route down to Cayeux, the *Route Blanche*, a mysterious-looking road between heather-clad dunes of brilliant white sand that often seem to threaten to envelop it completely. The shingle beach is usually deserted. Lost in the dunes is the curious little seaside village of **Brighton-les-Pins**, which once hoped to attract droves of English tourists with its name, and now looks a bit like a French town out of a Sam Shepherd story. Beyond it is **Cayeux**, famous as a fishing port since the Middle Ages and which became a holiday resort in the 1900s. It has a long, rolling bank of a shingle and sand beach, with an old-fashioned seafront alongside that except in August seems far too big for the town. Just south of Cayeux is another area of marsh that forms the bird reserve of **Hable d'Ault**, which is of interest more to experienced than to casual birdwatchers.

Alternatively, take the road east from St-Valery, past Noyelles and more views over the *mollières* to the north side of the bay. **Le Crotoy** is known in French history as the place where Joan of Arc was first imprisoned after her capture by the Burgundians in 1430, but also enjoyed a certain fashionable vogue at the end of the last century as a summer resort. Colette extolled the virtues of its light and giant skies, Seurat came to paint, Toulouse-Lautrec visited and the Caudron brothers carried out some of the first experiments in French aviation on the sands. One of its first and most regular visitors was Jules Verne, who came here from Amiens virtually every summer; while here he spent a lot of time with the inventor and experimenter in sub-marining Jacques-François Conseil, who provided much of the inspiration for *Twenty Thousand Leagues Under the Sea*.

Anyone who is not a regular birdwatcher and yet wishes to see some of the birdlife of the Bay of the Somme should make above all for the wildlife reserve of **Marquenterre** (*open April–11 Nov daily; 12 Nov–Mar, Sat, Sun, holidays only; timings April–Sept 9.30am–7pm, last admission 5.30pm, Oct–Mar 10am–5pm, last admission 3.30pm; adm 45F; 37F under-16s; binocular hire extra*), north of Le Crotoy. One of the most beautiful areas around the Bay, this 2300-hectare stretch of marsh, lake and dunes is extremely well-organized for novice visitors without their own equipment, with a clear path, the *parcours d'initiation*, with good viewpoints from which you can see plenty of duck, geese, herons, waders and with luck polecats and wild boar. It takes about an hour, or more. Those who wish to can also follow longer paths into the reserve to look for rarer species such as storks and spoonbill. Attached to Marquenterre there is also a centre that offers pony-trekking through the dunes (*for information call © 22.25.03.06*).

Amiens:
the Cathedral
and the Canals

Amiens, capital of Picardy, is
a sizeable, historic city with a
substantial modern sprawl
and a charming and attractive
heart. It was badly scarred in
both world wars, but in the
middle of town there are still
small, atmospheric streets and
squares along the banks of the
River Somme, where the Roman
city was founded in the 1st century BC. It also has fine shops, a
large student population, and a
sparky street, café and night life.
There is one of the best of

Amiens Cathedral

France's regional museums. And presiding over everything is
one of the greatest works of humanity, France's largest cathedral, described by John Ruskin as the most perfect creation of
medieval Christianity in northern Europe.

It is, though, Amiens' natural setting that makes it such an
engaging place to explore. In the 1470s, when it was one of
the most important merchant cities in Europe, Louis XI of
France called it 'my little Venice', and the reasons why are as
evident today. The Somme divides around a string of narrow
islands, connected by footbridges and lined by old, steep-
roofed houses with many-coloured façades that lean and bend.
Just to the east the river runs through hundreds of manmade
canals between drained marsh-gardens, the Hortillonages,

7

which bring a stretch of silent, watery countryside right into the centre of the city. The produce from the dark, heavy soil of these allotments is a special feature of Amienois cooking. And there is nowhere better to try it than La Couronne, a long-established local favourite where Philippe Gravier skilfully prepares fine-quality, complex dishes based on a mix of classic French cuisine and Picard traditions.

Amiens has a fairly complicated road system, but if you come by car aim for *Centre-Ville* and the ring of boulevards, which as usual run around the core of town. Street parking in the centre is limited to 1 hour 40 minutes for 10F, but note that outside the boulevards parking is free, so try and leave your car along or behind the boulevards on the south side, near the Cirque Municipal and the Mail Albert 1er. From there, it's an easy walk up rue de la République to the centre of town. To go directly to La Couronne, carry on to the end of République and then up rue des Sergents to get on to rue St-Leu. La Couronne is a little way up on the right, past the church.

La Couronne

Restaurant La Couronne, 64, rue St-Leu, 80000 Amiens, © 22.91.88.57.
Open Mon–Fri, Sun, noon–2pm, 7–9.30pm. Closed Sat and 15 July–14 Aug.
Book Fri, Sun. Menus at 92, 130F; carte average 220F.

In Amiens La Couronne is known as the best place to go to find classic *cuisine française*. A little conservative perhaps, but of unfailingly consistent quality. Much has been said lately about the supposed decline of this kind of French restaurant, of conservatism leading to complacency and a falling-off of standards. Classic cuisine, though, can still be highly satisfying, and can still surprise you.

The restaurant is snugly comfortable, with stained glass in the windows made by an Amiens glassmaker. All the proper niceties are observed, such as the very enjoyable, delicate salmon appetisers, and service is very courteous, without being stuffy. The set menus change regularly, but might feature some of the dishes from the carte, fish in classic sauces, duck, another Picard staple, or maybe other local specialities such as *flamiche aux poireaux* (a leek quiche). Here it's worth it, though, to go for the *carte*.

Immediately recognisable throughout is the fine use of high-quality local vegetables, fruits, and herbs. A fricassée of scallops with *girolles* mushrooms is a wonderful combination of seafood and woodland flavours, with succulent scallops cooked to exactly the right point. Home-made terrines, mostly made with duck and other poultry, are outstanding, strong and rich but with complex, subtle aromas there as well. For a main course, there may be breast of lamb *au jus de thym*, where the delicate thyme gravy sets off the excellent-quality meat, or beautifully fresh baked turbot, simply cooked with grains of mustard.

As befits a traditional restaurant, La Couronne also has a very comprehensive wine list, with quality bottles from all the French regions (but naturally nowhere else). Cheese is another high point, with particularly good, spicy Maroilles and Rollot, from Picardy rather than further north. The classic desserts such as a bitter chocolate fondant with *crème anglaise*, hazelnut parfait, *crème brûlée* with brown sugar or a *cassis* sorbet may be familiar, but they're beautifully done—especially the wonderfully thick, pure chocolate—and hugely enjoyable.

Ballotine de Canard au Torchon

(Serves 10)

This dish must be prepared 48 hours in advance.

1 Barbary duck, approx 3.3kg/7lb 5oz
200g/7oz uncooked duck foie gras (optional)
100g/4oz lean veal
250g/9oz lean pork
2 eggs
pinch of nutmeg
1 celery stick, chopped
1 carrot, chopped
1 onion, chopped
1 bay leaf
a few peppercorns
2 sprigs thyme
salt and pepper

For the marinade:

100g/4oz bacon strips
100g/4oz ham (optional)
100ml/4fl oz Cognac
4 tablespoons port

Combine all the ingredients for the marinade and set aside. Bone the duck, taking care not to tear the skin (a delicate operation which a butcher could do for you). Remove all the meat from the skin. Thinly slice one of the breasts and leave in the marinade for about 6 hours.

Put the duck carcass, in a large pan, add the celery, carrot, onion, bay leaf, peppercorns and thyme and cover generously with cold water. Bring just to the boil, then simmer for 3 hours, stirring frequently. Strain the stock.

Meanwhile, mince the other duck breast and the legs with the veal and pork. Mix with the eggs and season very lightly with nutmeg, salt and pepper. Chill this stuffing until needed.

Lay out the duck skin on a damp cloth such as a tea towel or a piece of muslin and spread it with a thin layer of stuffing. Lay on top a row of bacon strips, then the slices of marinated duck breast, then a row of foie gras pieces. Cover with a second layer of stuffing.

Carefully roll the skin around the mixture, keeping the cloth round the skin, to form a sausage shape. Tie tightly at each end and in 2 or 3 places along the middle as for a roast. Weigh to calculate the cooking time.

Poach the ballotine very gently in the duck stock for 30 minutes per 450g/ 1 lb. Do not let the stock boil or the ballotine may burst. Remove the ballotine from the pan and refrigerate for 24 hours.

Remove the cloth and string and slice the ballotine. Serve as a first course with salad and some aspic, and with a light wine such as a red Sancerre.

---

touring around

If you do begin a visit to Amiens by leaving your car on the southern boulevards, near Mail Albert 1er, you will immediately notice the Cirque Municipal, an odd drum-like building with many ornate 19th-century details which today is most often used for concerts, but is inseparably associated with one of Amiens' most celebrated residents,

Jules Verne. He was actually born in Nantes, but his wife Honorine was *Amienoise*, and after they moved here in 1871 he became an institution in the city for over thirty years. Verne was not the kind of local author who stays in his study and only emerges for the odd book-signing; instead, he busied himself with every aspect of local life, served on the city council, and in 1889 badgered his fellow-councillors into giving Amiens one of the world's few permanent circus-halls. In front of it there is a plaque that records that from the same spot, place Longueville, the great man had also made a flight in a balloon, in 1873. Just east of here at 44 boulevard Jules Verne, parallel to the main boulevard, is the house where he died in 1905, although the **Maison Jules Verne** (*open Tues–Sat, 9.30am–noon, 2–6pm; adm 15F; 5F under-18s*), where he actually lived during most of his time in Amiens, is just around the corner at 2 rue Charles Dubois.

From the Circus cross the main boulevard and walk up rue de la République to reach the **Musée de Picardie** (*open 10am–12.30pm, 2–6pm Tues–Sun; adm 20F; 10F under-18s*). The grandest building in Amiens after the cathedral, it's a Second-Empire wedding cake of a museum, immediately comparable to the Paris Opera, opened by Napoleon III in 1867 and with a large 'N' for Napoleon and 'E' for his Empress Eugénie built into the front. Inside it is still more imposing, with a giant main staircase and a vast Grand Salon with murals by the Symbolist artist Puvis de Chavannes. They present a fanciful vision of the prehistoric Picards, but their monumental size, style and curious stillness are very impressive, and they influenced Gauguin and many later artists. Also, even if you don't feel like a coffee, don't fail to visit the cafeteria, a neo-Gothic, neo-Byzantine extravaganza.

The museum houses an impressive collection of local treasures. There are a great many fine Roman artefacts, many from excavations of the first Amiens, Samarobriva or 'Bridge-over-the-Somme', which in the second century AD was the most important city in northern Gaul, twice the size of Paris. There are several rooms of wonderful medieval sculptures in wood and stone, mostly from Picardy and other parts of northern France; look out for the exquisitely modelled series of bas-reliefs on the Life of Christ, from around 1500. Most extraordinary, though, and unique, are the *Puys*, paintings offered to the Cathedral of Amiens during the 16th century by the Fraternity of Notre-Dame, an association of local merchants. It was the custom for each master of the Fraternity to commission one painting, and the results are a panorama of Amiens and its burghers over more than a century. The artists were anonymous, but the paintings are superb—the *Vierge au Palmier* from 1520, for example, presents a vision of the city akin to Brueghel. In front of the Virgin forming the centrepiece of each picture are arrayed the members of the Fraternity and their wives, all of whom look as if they could drive a very hard bargain.

Beyond the Puys there are also several fine works by more familiar, 'named' artists—El Greco, Salvator Rosa, Frans Hals and other Dutch masters, Fragonard and Boucher. The more modern sections are not so eye-catching, but the museum does have one great recent addition in *Wall Drawing 711*, a rotunda on the ground floor painted in 1992 by the American artist Sol LeWitt in a whole spectrum of colours in complex geometrical patterns.

Opposite the museum there is an elegant Louis XV *hôtel particulier* that now houses the Prefecture of Picardy, and immediately nearby there are several more fine, varied older buildings. As you continue towards the city centre, though, the architecture becomes more plainly modern and uniform. Much of old Amiens, however, was destroyed in only two days, 18th and 19th May 1940. German bombers rained incendiaries on the city; the cathedral and many larger stone buildings emerged remarkably undamaged, but most of the old wooden houses in the centre went up like torches. Post-war, much of the city centre was rebuilt in a simple, unobtrusive modern style according to a plan by the architect Pierre Dufau.

République ends at rue des Trois Cailloux, to the right, heart of the main shopping area. To the left, the pedestrianised rue Delambre leads to the very large **Hôtel de Ville**, rebuilt after the war, with a square in front remodelled in the last few years to an innovative, locally controversial design by the Catalan architect Joan Roig, with some intriguing inclined fountains. Walk around the Hôtel de Ville and you come to a survivor of the fires, the solid 15th-century belfry, **Le Beffroi**, once, as it looks, a prison. Close by there is a glass-walled market hall, **Les Halles du Beffroi** (*open shop hours*). This is not the most atmospheric of markets, but it's a great place to find high-quality food and produce, especially at the beautiful stand of Daniel Quentin, a master cheese merchant or *maître fromager affineur*.

From there, walk back past the Beffroi and across a few more streets to approach the cathedral (in front of which is the main tourist office). You could of course continue inside, but for the moment turn downhill on rue Flatters and, after crossing a small canal, turn right down the little rue des Rinchevaux to reach the riverside district and the **place du Don**, a likeably attractive cobbled square with 16th-century houses on three sides, some original and some restored, and the river on the other. Virtually every house contains an antique shop, a restaurant or a bar with pavement tables, and this is a major centre of Amiens' summer evening- and night-life. Just off the square at 67 rue du Don is the tiny shop of Jean-Pierre Facquier, only remaining maker of the traditional Amiens puppets, the *Cabotans*, at the centre of which is always Lafleur, a roguish, Mr Punch figure in a red suit, considered the archetypal Amiens and Picard character.

Across the road from the square to the right, looking towards the river, is place Parmentier, where on Thursday and Saturday mornings the vegetable and fruit growers of the Hortillonages tie up their boats packed with produce to sell direct, in one of France's most special **markets**. Look to the left, next to the pont de la Dodane bridge, and you see a man standing in midriver, which never fails to entertain kids. This is actually a sculpture by the German artist Balkenhol, and if you look back at the place du Don you'll see two more of his strangely life-like figures, a man and a woman, on either side.

And across the river is Amiens' engaging 'little Venice', the canalside quarter of **St-Leu**. This was formerly the weavers' and dyers' district, and the ne'er-do-well proletarian Lafleur is always seen as a native of St-Leu. St-Leu's houses are endlessly varied: original half-timbered, stucco or plain brick, and with woodwork painted in greens, blues, ochres and reds, among many. One at least, 56 rue des Marissons, is only about two metres wide. And as you wander round—the only way to do it—you'll also find individual craft and antique shops, especially on rue Motte and in the gallery behind rue de la Dodane.

Immediately after lunch is the best time to visit the water gardens of the **Hortillonages**. To get to the landing-point, follow the signs along the river bank to the right from place du Don, cross the boulevard Beauvillé bridge, and the entrance is on the right. Tours of some of the over 50km of channels are run by the association of allotment holders in their traditional long black punts, fitted with silent motors that are electric in order not to damage the canal banks. They run every afternoon during the season (*tours April–Oct daily, from 2pm; adm 28F; 21F, 11–18s; 13F under-11s*), but note that they depend on demand, and the last tour may leave at times between 3 and 7pm. The trip lasts about an hour.

Vegetable plots on land drained from the Somme were known here in Roman times, and have been extended ever since. As in the Marais of St-Omer, this green, wet maze has given rise to its own legends, and has been used as a place of refuge, most recently by Resistance fighters in the Second World War. At the turn of the century, nearly a thousand people lived on the Hortillonages, a separate community. Only a handful do so now, but many people work the plots, or just use them as a weekend retreat. As you travel almost at water level around the apparently endless, silent canals, you see some plots that are neat gardens, with clipped hedges and even garden gnomes; others are distinctly reminiscent of a mangrove swamp. There are birds everywhere, and on some plots also goats, kept to keep down the fast-growing marsh grass. It has a wonderful serenity, with its own fresh, still air.

This leaves till last the **cathedral**, up on its hill above the place du Don. For many it is the greatest of all Gothic cathedrals. Ruskin called the staggering west façade, with its hundreds of figures of saints, apostles and biblical scenes, 'the Bible in stone'. It entranced him particularly because he saw in it the perfect example of his idea of the medieval unity of art and craft, and indeed in the small roundels around the base of the three portals, portraying virtues and vices, or the course of the seasons, you can see every element of 13th-century life represented: men working in the fields, or cooking fish over an open fire. The central statue of Jesus, the *Beau Dieu*, has in legend always been said to have been sculpted directly from a vision of Christ, and is extremely beautiful.

When your neck can no longer stand craning up at the west façade, walk around the outside of the cathedral to take in its elaborate buttresses and gargoyles before going inside. It has to be said that from the outside, especially from a distance, it can look odd: it seems too tall for its length, and has a strange, slender spire, the Flèche, made of wood clad in lead, which dates from 1529. Inside, though, Amiens cathedral soars like no other. Vaults and columns seem to reach for the sky, and high windows give the nave a special luminosity. It was begun in 1220, after Amiens had acquired the head of John the Baptist, brought here in dubious circumstances after the Fourth Crusade (it can still be seen, in the cathedral treasury). Most of it was built within 50 years, which gives it an unusual unity of style. Also, very unusually for a medieval building, it has a known first architect, Robert de Luzarches, who died in about 1225, and whose name is only recorded because it is written in the centre of the great 'Labyrinth' in the cathedral's intricate tiled floor.

Amiens cathedral has many treasures, and it is only possible to mention a few of them here. If the façade is the Bible in stone, the stalls of the choir are the Bible in wood, carved by Amiens craftsmen between 1508 and 1522. The outside walls of the choir, in the Ambulatory, are just as impressive. Two series of scenes in polychrome painted stone from the early 16th century depict the life of John the Baptist on one side, and Saint Firmin, credited with having brought Christianity to Amiens, on the other. The detail and the colour of each scene are extraordinary, and, once again, they give a vivid picture of life at the time as much as of their subject matter. And, before you leave, look up to the three great rose windows. Much of their glass is no longer the original, but they are still breathtaking, more glass and light than stone. Afterwards, walk back down to the quai Bélu for a drink, and a great view of the cathedral from across the river.

The Lost Town of Eu

Hôtel restaurant de la Gare

The valley of the river Bresle marks the northeast border of Normandy, a long, straight cleft lined with stretches of thick woodland. It has not been a real frontier between states since the 13th century, but it remains a significant dividing line: in food, in agriculture—between the grain fields of Picardy and the Norman pastures and orchards—and in the historical memory of the people. And, straddling the Bresle, there is the traditional main gateway to Normandy, the little town of Eu.

Today this town with its oddly monosyllabic name has a noticeably out-of-the-way feel, and is not very well known even in the rest of France. It's a relaxed, charming French provincial town, its life centred on a main square that fills up with a market on some days and flocks of chattering *lycéens* on others. Eu, though, has also cropped up in the history of both France and the British Isles a remarkable number of times and in a curious variety of circumstances, and hosted a whole gallery of heroes and villains. This past has left Eu with a range

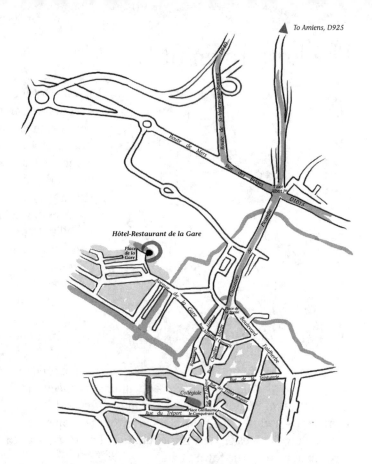

To Amiens, D925

Route de Mers

Rue des Hêtres

Route de St-Valéry-sur-Somme

D1015

Place Albert 1er

Hôtel-Restaurant de la Gare

Place de la Gare

Avenue de la Gare

Place de la Bresle

Boulevard Faidherbe

Rue de la Teinturerie

Collégiale

Place Guillaume le-Conquérant

Rue du Tréport

of historic buildings, some hidden away, some of undeniable grandeur, exceptional for such a small, ordinary town. Inland from the town is the Forêt d'Eu, a long swath of wild virgin forest, ideal for walking, and containing within it an unexcavated Gallo-Roman city. Towards the sea is the traditional beach town of Le Tréport.

And Eu also has an exceptional restaurant, as unobtrusive and as idiosyncratic as the whole town. The Hôtel-Restaurant de la Gare is easy to miss, but the food and hospitality make it worth a stopover in Eu.

If you come into Eu from St-Valery-sur-Somme (D940) or the main Calais/Boulogne road via Abbeville (D925), you will first arrive at a large roundabout, the place Albert Ier. Carry straight on down the south exit, the Chaussée de Picardie (signposted '*Centre Ville*') to another roundabout, the place de la Bresle, and take the boulevard Hélène, which leads off the exit to the right. About 50m down on the right is the avenue de la Gare, which, as you might expect, leads to the station and the Hôtel-Restaurant de la Gare.

From Dieppe, on the D925, you will also come to a large round-about, place Charles-de-Gaulle, on the south side of town. Take the left exit, boulevard Victor-Hugo, following the signs for '*Centre Ville*'. At the next roundabout the right exit will lead you into place Guillaume-le-Conquérant, the centre of town, dominated by the church of the Collégiale in front of you. Go round the square and take the street down the hill to the right of the church, rue de l'Abbaye, which leads straight into rue Charles-Morin. Second on the left on this street is rue Adjudant-Deparis, which leads directly on to avenue de la Gare.

L'Hôtel-Restaurant de la Gare

Hôtel-Restaurant de la Gare, 20 place de la Gare, 76260 Eu,
© 35.86.16.64. Open Mon–Sat noon–2pm, 7.30–9.30pm; Sun noon–2pm.
Closed usually two or more weeks in Aug, check in advance. Book weekends.
Menus at 85F (Mon–Fri only), 130F, 220F; carte average 230F.

A few trains still stop at Eu, even though most of the station has now been taken over by an insurance company office. The Hôtel de la Gare, naturally enough, is alongside it, a plainish brick building with mansard roof much like many other small station hotels put up around France at the end of the last century. Inside, the bar, to the right of the entrance and catering to a steady flow of locals, has a collection of modern designer lamps in the form of feet and other strange shapes, piles of old magazines and some unusually comfortable furniture, indicating a quirky individuality you don't necessarily expect in a small-town restaurant. The distinctive taste of Jean-Claude and Marie-

Françoise Maine, owners since 1972, is just as present in the hotel upstairs, in yellow staircases, blue walls and stylish red Hollywood/Art Deco carpets that give it a post-modern look.

The dining room is something else again: large and ornate to the point of being baroque, in apple green, with classic *bourgeois* mouldings in the first section and a magnificent, sinuous Art Nouveau fireplace and window frames in the larger end room. It's also very comfortable, and around the walls there's plenty of odd bric-à-brac and an eccentric collection of paintings, especially old portraits of stolid local burghers, to add to the interest while you're thinking about your meal.

This cheerfully eclectic décor is only part of the place's original charm. Jean-Claude Maine, tall, wiry and sporting an ample grey walrus moustache, takes the orders, ambling from table to table and chatting with the clientèle, many of them local regulars, and service throughout has a warm, nicely personal touch instead of the formality found in many a classic French *restaurant bourgeois*, without ceasing to be attentive and efficient. The cooking of chef Emmanuel Auvray, meanwhile, would not be out of place in a major metropolitan eating house. It's rooted in French and local tradition, with a fine use of butter to introduce you to Normandy. There are two main menus at 130F, one '*du pêcheur*', all fish and seafood, and the other '*du boucher*', all meat, with four courses in each. Menus and the *carte* are changed completely with each season, providing a wonderfully varied and tempting choice (at an equally exceptional price).

The Maines and Auvray stress the importance of taste, rather than any complexity for its own sake, in their cuisine, and finely marked flavours, whether strong or subtle, are as immediately apparent in all the hotel's dishes as the outstanding quality of every ingredient. A first course from the '*du boucher*' menu might be *rémoulade de langue de veau à la moutarde de Meaux*, tongue shredded in celeriac with a mustard sauce; beautifully light and fresh, it's at first deceptively bland, until the wonderfully meaty but smooth taste of the tongue leaves you with a perfumed, almost wistful aftertaste. To follow, try one of the lamb dishes, perfect-quality meat with rich but complex sauces and marinades. Alternatively, a fixture on the menu throughout most of the year is *faux-filet à la moelle*, a superb steak with juicy marrow.

To go with this meal you couldn't do better than the Crozes-Hermitage at 105F, a great example of one of the best of the current Rhône reds. The fish menu, for its part, might offer delights such as mussels and cauliflower cooked in butter and aromatic herbs, and sea bass *à la crème de badiane*, in a light star-anise cream sauce.

mussels

The same attention to ingredients, flavour and every other detail is seen in the cheese course—including a strong Camembert that's just as striking as some of the more unusual cheeses—and the desserts, especially the delicious iced nougat with a raspberry coulis. It's a meal that stays in the mind, with refined but flavoursome, very enjoyable food that can appeal even to anyone who suspects quality French cooking of being over-fancified. Afterwards, if you don't have to drive anywhere, try one of Jean-Claude Maine's selection of Calvados, another excellent welcome to Normandy, especially the superbly fragrant Hors d'Age.

Gigot d'Agneau Mariné au Gamay

(Serves 8)

1 leg of lamb, approx 3kg/6 ½lb
100g/4oz of butter

For the marinade:
500ml/1 pint Gamay wine
4 tablespoons red wine vinegar
2 tablespoons Cognac
1 head garlic, peeled and roughly chopped
100g/4oz carrots, chopped
200g/8oz onions, chopped
100g/4oz shallots, chopped
1 tablespoon chopped thyme
1 bay leaf
salt and pepper

Bone the leg of lamb and then tie it with string. Mix together all the ingredients for the marinade, add the meat, together with the bones, then cover and marinate in the fridge for 48 hours.

Melt half the butter in a roasting tin on top of the stove, add the lamb and brown well on all sides. Transfer to an oven preheated to 200°C/400°F (gas mark 6) and roast for 45 minutes/1 hour. When the lamb is cooked, the juices should run out slightly pink when the meat is pierced with a skewer.

Remove the meat from the tin and keep warm. Pour off most of the fat from the pan then add the marinade and bring to boil on top of the stove, stirring to scrape up the sediment. Simmer until the sauce has reduced to a syrupy consistency, then strain into a saucepan. Heat gently. Dice the remaining butter and whisk into the sauce a few pieces at a time. Taste and season, if necessary.

Slice the lamb and pour a little sauce over each serving. Creamy dauphinoise potatoes and finely shredded green beans and carrots make good accompaniments.

---

touring around

The first settlement of Eu appeared on a shelf of land above the Bresle, where the Château d'Eu and the church of the Collégiale stand today. The history of Eu really begins, though, in the 10th century, when the recently established Dukes of Normandy built a castle here as the furthest defensive bastion of their new territories. It was also a port, with access to the sea along the Bresle. In 1050, William the Conqueror brought Matilda, daughter of the Count of Flanders, to the castle of Eu to marry him. Apparently she was none too keen on the match, and only submitted to it after William dragged her around her chambers by her hair. An abbey was also founded near the castle, and the town of Eu grew up around the two. It has the oldest municipal charter of any town in Normandy, granted in 1151.

The town's central square, occupied by an excellent market on Wednesday and, especially, Friday mornings, is appropriately called place Guillaume-le-Conquérant. It is dominated, however, by a great church dedicated to a more permanent resident of Eu, who was not

Norman but Irish. This was St Laurence O'Toole, for centuries the only officially canonized Irish saint (since St Patrick, St Kevin and many others had never been formally recognized by the Vatican). He was Archbishop of Dublin at the time of the first Anglo-Norman invasion of Ireland in 1169, and in 1180 was sent to England by the Irish lords to intercede with Henry II. The King refused to see him, and went off to Normandy; Laurence, old and sick, followed after him, but only got as far as the abbey at Eu, where he died, and the rest, as they say, is history. He had supposedly stopped the day before on the crest just north of Eu, where the 19th-century **Chapelle St-Laurent** now stands out against the sky, and, looking down, said, 'There I will take my rest'; he was also said to have raised seven people from the dead, and his canonisation was begun very quickly, in part because of the papacy's own arguments with Henry II. Laurence's shrine at Eu immediately became an important pilgrimage centre, and remained so throughout the Middle Ages. More recently, Eu has sought to revive its Irish links, and in a garden on the north side of the church there is now a Celtic cross in stone from St Laurence's birthplace in County Kildare, donated by a contemporary Dublin archbishop.

Laurence's church, officially Notre-Dame-et-St-Laurent but better known locally as the **Collégiale**, was begun as a pilgrimage church in 1186, replacing the much smaller earlier church of the abbey, and first completed a hundred years later. Like many French churches battered by the Revolution it was restored during the last century by the great Gothic revivalist Eugène Viollet-le-Duc, who said that he had seen churches that were bigger or taller, but none that was more beautiful. Most of the nave is the original from the end of the 12th century; the choir and the apse, in contrast, are an extravagant work of *Flamboyant* Gothic, built after a major fire in 1426, and especially spectacular from the outside. Even so, the different styles do harmonise, and the building is wonderfully light.

The Collégiale has some very fine baroque woodwork, especially the grand 1614 organ above the nave, and the statue of Our Lady of Eu in the Lady Chapel behind the choir. Its greatest treasure, though, is in a small chapel off to the right of the choir, an exquisite 16th-century *Entombment of Christ* in polychrome stone. The modelling and colour

of the eight figures around the dead Christ are superb, with a mysterious stillness suspended in time: look only at their marvellously expressive hands. Like much else in Eu, it is curiously little-known; it is believed to have been made in Burgundy, and no one knows how it got here.

In the later Middle Ages, Eu was also another of the places where Joan of Arc was held on her way to her trial in Rouen, in 1430. Very little of the medieval town can now be seen, though, because it, and William the Conqueror's castle, were burnt wholesale in 1475 on the orders of King Louis XI of France to prevent them falling into the hands of the English, leaving only the abbey and some churches intact. If, however, you walk from the south side of place Guillaume up Eu's traditional main thoroughfare, rue Paul Bignon, you enter an area of little, winding streets built during a revival in the town's fortunes in the 16th and 17th centuries, with many fine Louis XIII-style merchants' houses in brick, with the occasional more elaborate ornamental detail. Rue Bignon, a charming narrow street that changes width several times along its route, also contains some great food shops, and Eu's tourist office.

Overlooking a tiny square that seems virtually unchanged since the 1660s on rue du Collège, which runs away from the main square just left of rue Bignon, is the **Chapelle du Collège des Jésuites** (*open mid-Mar–early Nov, Mon–Sat, 10am–noon, 2–6.30pm; adm free*). This was built following Eu's next intervention in history, in the French Wars of Religion of 1560–93. The title of Count of Eu had been passed around between several aristocratic dynasties, and in 1570 the then Countess, Catherine de Clèves, married Henri, Duc de Guise, known as *le Balafré* ('Scarface'), the foremost standard-bearer of intransigent Catholicism and a perennial conspirator who played a significant part in the St Bartholomew's Day Massacre of Protestants in Paris in 1572. Guise decided to make Eu a powerhouse of the Counter-Reformation, and founded a Jesuit college here (alongside the chapel, and now the main *lycée*) in 1582. His wife Catherine was notorious for her '*galanteries*' with a string of lovers, from servants to gentlemen, some of whom were murdered on Guise's orders; nevertheless, she shared his religious ideas, and after he himself was assassinated by agents of King Henri III in 1588 she developed something of a cult to his memory. Reconciled to the former-Protestant Bourbon King Henri IV, she lived to a great age, becoming known for her good works, and commissioned the chapel in Eu to be built between 1613 and 1624.

As in many other Jesuit churches built around that time, its design is clearly based on the mother church of the order, the Gesù in Rome, only in brick and stone instead of marble, and with decoration that's similarly a mix of Italian Renaissance and more local influences. The fine carving on the façade was the work of some local sculptors, the brothers Anguier. Inside, the most prominent features by far are two giant, bombastic but very finely sculpted Baroque memorial tombs in marble, made for Catherine de Clèves in 1627, one for herself and one for her husband. The latter is actually another empty tomb, since after his assassination Henri III had ordered that the Duke's remains be burnt and scattered in the Loire, to prevent them becoming a focus for his followers.

Thanks to the Guises and their successors, there were once so many churches and religious foundations in Eu that in 1650 the Mayor complained that they blocked off many of the town's streets. Most were demolished after the Revolution. Near the southern end of rue Bignon, though, on the corner of rue Ste-Anne and rue Clemenceau, there is still the **Hôpital Ste-Anne**, now the tax office, built in 1664 as an almshouse for orphan girls. Also, if from there you return back across the place Guillaume and take rue de l'Abbaye downhill beside the Collégiale—conveniently, if it's time for lunch, towards the Hôtel de la Gare—you will pass on the right the beautiful **Hôtel-Dieu**, a convent and hospital from 1654, built around three sides of a garden courtyard in a happy combination of Norman half-timbering and more august Louis XIII-style architecture.

The Guises were also responsible for the other building that with the Collégiale makes up the grand centrepiece of the town, facing the church across the broad place d'Orléans, the French-Renaissance-style **Château d'Eu**, begun on the site of the earlier castle in 1578. What we see today represents only a part of the vast palace with four sides around a great courtyard that they had planned to create for themselves, for they were only able partially to complete one wing before *le Balafré* was murdered. In 1660 the château passed to Mademoiselle de Montpensier, known as '*La Grande Mademoiselle*', cousin of Louis XIV, who was confined here by the Sun King to prevent her intriguing against him. It was she who first made it habitable, and added the elegant Le-Nôtre style French garden which forms the main part of the delightful park that sweeps away on its western side. The Château d'Eu is most associated, though, with Louis-Philippe of Orléans, who inherited it, together with the title of Count of Eu, in 1821.

Louis-Philippe loved Eu; not only did he amply restore his château and the crypt of the Collégiale, he also had the Bresle Canal built, restoring the town's access to the sea for the first time in centuries, in part in order that he could sail up it in his yacht. Moreover, it continued to be his favourite residence after the revolution of July 1830 catapulted him into power as France's 'Citizen King', considered an archetype of respectable virtues and famous for never going out without his umbrella. Eu became for a while the virtual summer capital of France, and a new, rather barracks-like building, the **Pavillon des Ministres**, was put up next to the Collégiale to accommodate the members of the government who were obliged to decamp here for several weeks each year. In September 1843, Queen Victoria and Prince Albert arrived at the château, for a week of picnics, parades, concerts and other entertainments. This was the first time a British monarch had set foot in France since Henry VIII's meeting with François Ier at the Field of the Cloth of Gold in 1520, a fact that enables Eu to claim the title of 'Birthplace of the *Entente Cordiale*'. The visit had tremendous impact. Each day's events were followed with rapt attention by the local population, and in the following year every third girl born in Eu was named Victoria, Victoire or Victorine.

After Louis-Philippe was himself deposed by another revolution in 1848 Eu fell back into its more usual obscurity, but in the 1870s the Republic returned the château to the king's grandson the Comte de Paris, pretender to the French throne, who again restored the house and gardens. Since 1964 it has belonged to the town, and part of it is now the Mairie, while the rest is the **Château d'Eu-Musée Louis-Philippe** (*open 10am–noon, 2–6pm Mon, Wed–Sun, 15 Mar–end Oct; Closed Tues; adm 20F; 6F under-12s*). Maintaining such a large monument is a heavy burden for a small town, and sections of it have an engagingly tumbledown quality, but it is again individual, full of unusual details, and a notable effort has been made to label everything in English. Some rooms still have the ornate 17th-century décor of the *Grande Mademoiselle*, and there is a brilliantly coloured firescreen embroidered with glass beads by the lady herself; others were redecorated in the 1870s for the Comte de Paris by Viollet-le-Duc, in his last commission before his death, with fascinating, multicoloured designs almost on the borderline between Gothic revival and Art Nouveau. Most of the rooms on view, though, are as they were left by Louis-Philippe. He was an undemonstrative king, and his palace is accordingly cosy. He was also a man of his time, who installed in his château one of the earliest running-water systems, driven by millwheels on the canal, and one of the most eye-catching rooms is a bathroom with some giant Heath Robinsonesque brass plumbing. Many of the more moveable treasures of the château have been lost over the years, but there are still many souvenirs of the British visits, including paintings of events during those weeks that were done at breakneck speed by Winterhalter and other artists in order that they could be shown to the royal couple before their departure.

The park of the château is, mostly, a tranquil formal garden; for a contrast, and a change from sightseeing, escape the town into the **Forêt d'Eu**, a wild, atmospheric expanse of deciduous forest of the kind that once covered much of northern Europe but which is now sadly rare, and home to a range of wildlife that includes deer and wild boar.

There are easy paths into the woods from the Beaumont road, off the D49 south, and from near St-Pierre-en-Val, off the D1314 to Neufchâtel. For a guide to these and longer routes, ask for a walking map at the tourist office, which also organises walks led by foresters that end at a *carcahoux* or traditional woodcutters' hut deep in the woods, with a drink and maybe an opportunity to pick and cook the forest's prized wild mushrooms. Just inside the forest at **Bois-l'Abbé** there is a major Roman site that is almost a new discovery. The existence of Roman remains in the area has been vaguely known since the 18th century, but only recently has a preliminary dig been undertaken to determine whether full-scale excavations may be justified; they have already unearthed, though, a mass of ceramics and an amphitheatre with a capacity of 4–6000, indicating a Gallo-Roman city of considerable size. The dig is not yet open to the public, but tours are organised by the tourist office, which also include the finds from the excavations stored in the Hôtel-Dieu.

For a little sea air, leave Eu in the opposite direction for **Le Tréport**, which has a pretty if well-commercialised harbour and a long shingle beach, where Prince Albert took healthy exercise during his stay here by swimming at seven in the morning. Le Tréport has several grand seaside-style houses and hotels from its late-19th-century heyday, as well as the inevitable casino, and still fills up with the crowds on summer weekends. **Mers-les-Bains**, on the Picardy side of the Bresle, has a better, sandy beach.

Deep in France

Long, rolling ridges rise and fall between steep-sided valleys in the Pays de Bray, the long rift that runs from just below Dieppe diagonally southeast towards Beauvais and Paris. It's a geological oddity, known as the Boutonnière or 'Buttonhole'— a cleft of clay and sandstone between two great slabs of chalk—which has created a pocket of hilly, often lush land-scape in between the flat and frankly monotonous plateaux of Caux and Picardy.

The clay soil makes excellent pasture, and the region's sheep and its brown and white dairy cattle are often its most visible inhabitants. This is the home of Neufchâtel cheese, by far the oldest of the classic Normandy cheeses, already known before William the Conqueror first set foot in England. Since the coming of railways in the 1850s, the fortunes of the Pays de Bray have depended on an expanding market in Paris. In 1850, in Gournay-en-Bray in the south of the main Bray valley, an enterprising local businessman called Charles Gervais with a

Mesnières-en-Bray

shop in Paris began to manufacture the Petit-Suisse, supposedly invented in a happy collaboration between an itinerant Swiss farmhand and a Norman milkmaid. The Bray valleys are also known for their duck, geese and the products made from them, and also, not surprisingly, for their apples. Yet the overall impression is not one of an area given over to large-scale agribusiness. Instead the farms, between hedgerows, are small and discreet, often built in a distinctive brick-chalet style with low-hanging roofs against the weather. Nor, despite its range of traditional produce, is this a part of Normandy where agri-tourism is intensively developed. The local tourist authorities have adopted the slogan for the Pays de Bray of '*Normand tout simplement*', 'simply Norman', perhaps a shy way of admitting that its farmhouse-speciality food producers and other attractions are engagingly low-key rather than postcard–pretty.

The Pays de Bray was also once a border area, the eastern frontier of the independent Duchy of Normandy. It was settled relatively late, much of it in the 12th century, and many of the villages have small, plain Romanesque churches from that time. The towns, similarly small-scale, mostly grew up as markets for the surrounding farms. An exception is Forges-les-Eaux, right at the centre of the Pays de Bray, which has a rather grander past as a spa, 'discovered' in the 17th century. And at the centre of Forges is the Hôtel de la Paix, a classic small-town Logis hotel, where M. Rémy Michel has won an enviable reputation throughout the valleys with his rich and satisfying traditional Norman cooking.

getting there

All roads into Forges-les-Eaux converge on the main square, place de la République, and the smaller place Brévière that runs off it to one side. The Hôtel de la Paix nearly overlooks the latter. If you come into Forges from Neufchâtel and the north, on the D1314,

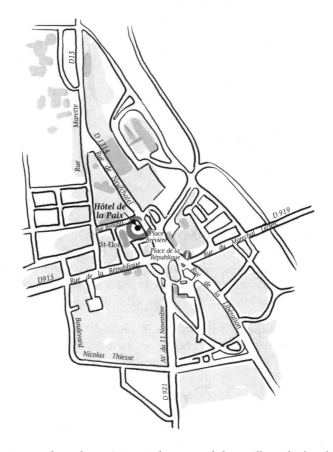

you pass through a quiet part of town, and then will see the hotel on your right on the same road just before you enter the square.

Entering from Dieppe or Rouen on the D915 you have a grander introduction to Forges-les-Eaux, passing the casino and the lake on the river Andelle. When you arrive in the square, turn left and the hotel is on the left. The Paris (also D915) and Amiens (D919) roads also enter the square, on the side more or less opposite from La Paix. The hotel has its own entrance to a public car park, at the back.

L'Hôtel de la Paix

*Hôtel-Restaurant de la Paix, 15 rue de Neufchâtel, 76440 Forges-les-Eaux,
✆ 35.90.51.22. Open Oct–May, Tues–Sat noon–2pm, 7.15–9.30pm, Sun
noon–2pm; June–Sept, Mon 7.15–9.30pm, Tues–Sun noon–2pm,
7.15–9.30pm. Book weekends. Menus at 75F, 90F, 120F, 162F; children's
menu 52F; carte average 140F.*

Come into the restaurant at the Hôtel de la Paix,
especially at the weekend, and you feel you are
entering *la France profonde*, the 'deep France' that all
French politicians claim to communicate with regularly. M. Michel reckons—and this is a considered
observation, not a casual remark—that in the 18 years since
he took over the hotel 80% of the inhabitants of Forges-les-Eaux and
vicinity have eaten there at some point, and many return at least once
a month. There are whole family groups, young couples, big men in
denims, ladies with their little dogs and every other element of local
society around the tables, all being fed with efficient familiarity.

As usual in the French countryside, the décor is not self-consciously
rustic: the dining-room is bright and comfortable, substantially renovated like the hotel, and ornamented with local painted ceramics.
Front-of-house is presided over by Mme Régine
Michel, and service is provided by a teenage staff
who are nevertheless already schooled in the traditional arts of French waitering, *comme il faut*. The local
clientèle know what they like from their culinary roots, and
M. Michel's cooking is firmly based in the classic regional repertoire—
plenty of duck, ham, chicken and steaks, fish such as cod, sole and
salmon, and cream, cheese and cider sauces. This does not
mean, though, that he is not creative, and dishes
such as his salmon *quenelles* (dumplings) *La Paix*
or *suprême de barbue* (brill) *au cidre* are skilful variations on traditional styles and ingredients.

A feature of the restaurant which regulars swear by is its range of four exceptional set menus, handily labelled A to D. They change a little from time to time, but each offers an excellent and generous choice of quality Norman cooking at very reasonable prices, with four alternatives for each course. The B menu (90F) includes compôte of rabbit among the starters, and *poulet au cidre* or cod in a *duglerée* (shallots, white wine, tomato and parsley) sauce to follow, but try the C (120F) for the meaty but subtle home-made terrine of *canard Rouennais* or the delicate salmon pâté. Main courses on the same menu include a flavour-rich *magret de canard aux cerises à l'aigre doux*, a *côte de veau* in a mushroom and cream sauce that's an exemplary version of a great French restaurant standard, and a prime-quality *faux-filet* steak.

All but the A menu include a cheese course: considering where you are you have to try the Neufchâtel, and the well-aged example at the hotel is a powerful demonstration of how good it can be, salty but with finely toned flavours. Just as excellent is the Camembert. After that, finish off with a dessert, maybe one of the fine range of fruit-based dishes, whether a traditional Norman *tarte aux pommes*, served hot, sorbets, or a *jalousie aux fraises*.

Another aspect of the Hôtel de la Paix that Rémy Michel suggests, modestly, has perhaps made its reputation more than any other is its excellent cellar, well above the norm for a small-town hotel. There's nothing on the wine list that isn't French—the very idea!—but there is a fine representation of classic French regions, especially Bordeaux. You can if you wish venture into grand bottles such as a 1986 Amiral de Beychevelle Haut-Médoc, for 246F, or Premier Cru red Burgundies for over 300F; even if you stay at the more accessible end with wines like the St-Nicolas de Bourgueil from the Loire (80F), you'll find they've been well and carefully selected.

Délice de Barbue au Cidre

(Serves 4)

1 brill, approx 1.2–1.5kg/2¾–3¼lb
1 onion, chopped
1 carrot, chopped
50g/2fl oz butter
1 bouquet garni
1 tablespoon flour
1 shallot, finely chopped
100ml/4fl oz cider
1 tablespoon Calvados
300ml/ ½ pint crème fraîche
1 egg yolk
chopped mixed herbs such as tarragon, chervil and parsley, to garnish
salt and pepper

Fillet the brill, reserving the trimmings to make stock. Sweat the onion, carrot and fish trimmings in half the butter, then add the bouquet garni and 500ml/1 pint water. Simmer for 15 minutes, skimming to remove scum, then strain the stock through a fine sieve and set aside.

Melt the remaining butter in a pan, stir in the flour and cook for 1–2 minutes, until lightly coloured. Gradually stir in the stock, then simmer for 10 minutes, stirring from time to time.

Scatter the chopped shallot over a buttered gratin dish, arrange the brill fillets on top and season. Pour the cider over the fish and cook in an oven preheated to 180°C/350°F (gas mark 4) for 15–20 minutes, until tender. Remove the fish, place in a serving dish and keep warm.

Strain the cooking liquid into a pan and boil until reduced to a scant tablespoon. Add the Calvados and boil until reduced by half, then stir in the sauce and all except 1 tablespoon of the cream. Simmer until reduced and thickened, then mix together the egg yolk and the remaining cream and pour a little of the sauce into it, stirring well. Pour this mixture into the sauce and heat gently until thickened but do not allow it to boil. Season to taste, then strain over the fish and serve garnished with the herbs.

touring around

Neufchâtel-en-Bray, at the junction of the roads from Dieppe and from Calais via Eu, is the traditional capital of the Pays de Bray, although no longer its largest town. It's also one of the best places to buy Neufchâtel cheese, especially at the **market**, which every Saturday crams both the square around the church of Notre-Dame, halfway up the hill of the Grande-Rue, and the place du 11 Novembre, further up the hill. Try and get there in good time, for many stalls start packing up at 12.30pm; the best cheese displays are generally inside the covered market in place du 11 Novembre. In addition to the local cheese you can find fine *chèvre*, as well as the usual stalls offering excellent terrines, spit-roasted chickens, and a huge number of leather jackets.

Neufchâtel cheese is mentioned in a document from 1035, and some was already being shipped to England in its current form in the 16th century, but it only gained its *appellation contrôlée* in 1977. It still comes entirely from local farms, for there are no large-scale producers, and has a drier, powdery texture than the better-known Normandy cheeses. Neufchâtel is made in a variety of shapes, cylindrical (*bondes*), rectangles (*briquettes* and *carrés*) and, most distinctively, hearts (*cœurs*). This doesn't affect the flavour, which depends on whether it's *jeune* (up to twelve days old), *demi-affiné* (one to three weeks) or *affiné* (one to three months), the last of which has a pretty gnarled look to it. The story goes that the heart shape was first made by Norman milkmaids during the Hundred Years' War, in an effort to 'soften the hearts' of the depraved English soldiery.

When the market is not in session Neufchâtel is a quiet country town where the sound of a passing van echoes in the clean valley air. The church of **Notre-Dame**, at the hub of one of the market squares, was begun in 1126, and has a fine 13th-century Gothic choir. Like much of the town, though, the church was severely damaged by German bombing in 1940, and a good deal of the present building is a reconstruction. Luckily its most beautiful possession was unharmed: a delicate 16th-century carved *Entombment of Christ*, in one of the side chapels. Down the Grande-Rue at the foot of the hill, in a pretty 16th-century house, there is a charming local museum, the **Musée**

Mathon-Durand (*open 16 Sept–June, Sat, Sun, 3–6pm; July–15 Sept, Tues–Sun, 3–6pm; adm 10F, 5F under-16s*), dedicated to rural traditions and crafts, and housing an 1837 cider press.

South of Neufchâtel the D1314 valley road, though crossed by the A28 autoroute, immediately re-enters open downland. European regulations mean that it's now difficult to visit farms to see cheese being made, but there are several around the area that offer their Neufchâtel cheeses for direct sale, indicated on the tourist offices' leaflet *Route du Fromage de Neufchâtel*. Local offices also have information on the occasional cheese and other produce markets held on farms in addition to the regular town markets, plus a little book of recipes (expensive at 30F) for cooking with Neufchâtel. One place that is organised for visitors is Alex Brianchon's **Ferme des Fontaines**, six kilometres south of Neufchâtel just north of the turning for Nesle-Hodeng. Mme Brianchon, as well as selling her fine Neufchâtel, gives tours around the farm's *caves*, with a demonstration of cheese-making (*by reservation April–Oct, daily, 10–11.30am; adm 10F, © 35.93.08.68*).

From here meander on southwards along tiny lanes and through villages like **Mesnil-Mauger**, where massive old farmhouses and a tumble-down château stand between small cottages, all with an air of quaint remoteness. This will bring you into **Forges-les-Eaux** on the north side, from where it looks just like another plain country town, its market held on Thursdays in the central squares. A walk down rue de la République after lunch will reveal its smarter aspect.

The town's hot springs, the *Eaux*, were discovered in the 16th century, but they were not widely known until 1633, when Louis XIII, his queen, Anne of Austria, and Cardinal Richelieu arrived here together to try the waters. In the last century, however, when the most famous waterholes of Europe were doing their best business, the town was largely forgotten. The spa was only redeveloped in the 1950s, when the bulky modern **Grand Casino** was built amid neat gardens on a hillside on the western side of town, above a formal French park along the River Andelle, which here widens into two pretty lakes with pedalos for hire. Walk through the park and you will come to the **Bois d'Epinay**, an unspoilt forest with well-marked paths where you could wander for miles.

While the spa was declining in the last century, one business that was thriving in Forges was the manufacture of painted earthenware using local clay, introduced by an Englishman, George Wood, in 1797. A good collection of the decorative Forges pottery is on show in the **Musée de la Faïence**, above the tourist office on the main square (*for details, enquire at tourist office*); the industry too fell into decline early this century, but there have been recent attempts to revive it.

The most interesting museum in the area, though, is a wonderful 'farm-museum', the **Ferme de Bray**, well-signposted on the D915 Dieppe road, about six kilometres from Forges near the village of Sommery (*open Easter–Christmas, Sat, Sun, public holidays, 2–6pm; July–Aug, daily, 2–6pm; adm 15F, free under-15s*). Its owner Patrice Perrier, an engaging combination of Norman farmer and middle-aged hippy, has a document in his possession showing that his family have been on this property since 1452. The main farmhouse is 16th-century, and nearby there's a 15th-century watermill, a *laiterie* (dairy) built and altered from 1400 to 1800, and a 15th-century brick bread-oven and 17th-century horse-driven cider press, both still regularly in use. It all seems implausibly ancient, especially since no conscious effort has ever been made to bring it all together. An explanatory leaflet is provided in English. The farm also has *chambres-d'hôtes*, trout fishing, meals (for groups) and courses in such things as cider-making and restoring the local wattle-and-daub-style buildings, cleverly orientated towards urbanites who buy up old properties and find that they're crumbling away. This is no synthetic heritage site, but a fascinating repository of rural traditions, and very amiably run. A series of special events is held through the season, culminating in the *Fête du Cidre* in November, when the cider press is set in motion; there's also a farmers' market.

From Sommery, anyone going on south should backtrack towards Forges-les-Eaux for the roads to Rouen or Paris; otherwise, continue on a circuit northwards on the same road, the D915. Back to the north of Neufchâtel—and only open in the afternoons, so visiting requires planning—is the Pays de Bray's grandest monument, the Renaissance château of **Mesnières-en-Bray** (*guided tours only, Easter–13 July and Sept–Oct, Sat, Sun and public holidays, 2–6.30pm; 14 July–Aug, daily 2–6.30pm; adm 20F*). It was built between 1520 and 1550 for the De

Boissay family. The white and grey exterior is dramatic and imposing, especially if you approach it as once intended, coming upon the main façade on the little road from the D915 via Fresles, rather than on the D1 from Neufchâtel. It has massive round drum towers with pinnacle tops on either side, steeply raked roofs and ornamented dormer windows in the main building; a superb peacock-tail-shaped staircase, added in the 18th century was designed to be ridden up on horseback.

The interior, on the other hand, is very much a mixed bag, and anyone used to a more organised kind of stately home should be aware of what to expect. Mesnières' last aristocratic owners, the De Biencourts, reclaimed it after the Revolution but then ruined themselves restoring it, and in 1835 they sold it to a Catholic order as an orphanage. Today, most of it is an agricultural college and school, still run by the same order. Parts of it are beautiful, especially the Galerie des Cerfs (stags), with seven life-sized statues of stags installed by a hunting-mad *seigneur* in 1660, and the superb small original chapel, with some magnificent Renaissance stained glass and Baroque woodwork. Other rooms have the shabby look of a distinctly under-heated boarding school, and there is a huge, gloomy neo-Gothic additional chapel, built on for the orphanage in the 1860s, where one can well imagine rows of crop-headed little boys sitting in silence wondering if it would ever stop raining in their lives. The guided tours, given by sweet but harassed students, take you indiscriminately round all of them (in French only; a leaflet is provided in English).

Alternatively, look to the left along the D915 road going north and you'll see the **Forêt d'Eawy**, 20kms of dense and beautiful beech forest. Several roads run into the forest, and tourist offices have maps of the many foot- and bridle paths such as the Allée des Limousins, a renowned 14km track that's a riders' favourite. A number of places in the area hire out horses, or run trekking trips, especially around Pommeréval and Ventes. On the western side of the forest in Saint-Saëns, ancestral home of the composer, there's a particularly luxuriant golf course, with a genuine château for a clubhouse. Northwest of the forest is the main cider region of the Seine-Maritime, marked on the tourist office's *Route de la Pomme et du Cidre*. This is the base for France's major commercial cider producers, such as Duché de Longueville at **Anneville-sur-Scie**, which offers tours and tastings.

Dieppe's Pacific Rim

Dieppe, like Boulogne, is a Channel port that's well worth exploring rather than just passing through. It's a small city, with a compact old centre of narrow streets and little alleys, but still a busy, living port. Its name comes from the Old Norse for 'deep', and the deep-water harbour, the mouth of the River Arques, comes right into the middle of the town, lined with cafés, restaurants and shops, some neat, some a bit tatty, so that, uniquely among the Normandy ports, it has something of the bustle and sharp-edged air of a Mediterranean seaport town. Dieppe also has some of the most irresistibly eye-catching food shops and one of the best markets in Normandy.

The town has always lived, in different ways, from the sea: as a port and later, in the 1820s, as the first town in France to follow Brighton and become a seaside resort.

Its history has also been bound up perhaps more closely than that of anywhere else along the Normandy coast with England.

le Colombier. Offranville

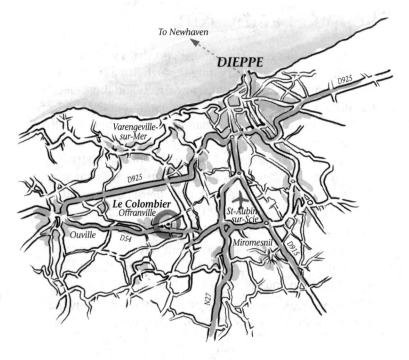

As far as food is concerned, Dieppe is most famous, as you would expect, for fish and seafood, especially served with the classic *dieppoise* sauce combining Norman cream with white wine and mushrooms, but its cosmopolitan traditions mean it also has more varied cuisine to offer. Xavier Poupel is a French chef who worked for many years abroad, in the USA and, especially, Australia. Since 1993 he and his Australian wife Janette have been established in a very pretty 16th-century house in the village of Offranville, just outside Dieppe, and their restaurant, Le Colombier, has won a fast-growing word-of-mouth reputation. Considered exotic by conservative Normans, his cooking combines Pacific-rim (and other) influences still within a recognisably French style. Light, subtle and enjoyable, it's a very original departure from the strict limits of French tradition.

If you are coming from central Dieppe, follow the signs for the Rouen and Paris road (N27/D915), which within the town is called avenue Gambetta, a long, straight hill (from the new ferry terminal, on the east side of the port, you must follow signs to '*Centre Ville*', cross the harbour on quai du Carénage and then turn right into a one-way system around the seafront to get on to avenue Gambetta). Stay on the N27, which separates from the D915 outside Dieppe, as far as St-Aubin-sur-Scie, where there is a right turn to Offranville. Follow the blue signs marked '*Parc du Colombier*', and the restaurant is almost impossible to miss.

Le Colombier

Le Colombier, Parc du Colombier, 76550 Offranville, ℗ 35.85.48.50. Open Tues–Thurs noon–2.30pm, 7–9.30pm; Fri noon–2.30pm, 7–10pm; Sat 7–10pm; Sun noon–2.30pm. Open for reservations only Sat midday, and Tues–Thurs evenings from Oct to Mar. Booking advisable. Menus at 95F (not Sat, Sun or public holidays), 148F, 195F; carte *average 270F.*

Offranville is a quiet, attractive village with a striking 16th-century church and a huge, much older yew tree at its centre, and a low-key leisure park, the Parc du Colombier, with a mini-golf course, a riding centre, an old manor house and a fine rose garden. Le Colombier is by the entrance to the park, an archetypally Norman half-timbered house dating from 1505. Inside, it has been beautifully restored, in a smart, rather country-house style reworking of a French *cadre rustique*. Great bunches of dried flowers hang in the grandly impressive original stone fireplace, and gold and beige linen and fresh flowers on each table add to the feeling of comfort. Through the windows you can see ducks in a small pond in the garden, where you can eat or have coffee outside when weather allows (note, though, that the restaurant is not normally open for Saturday lunch, so on Saturdays you should plan on dinner, or check whether you can reserve for midday).

As you read the menu while sampling the *mises en bouche*—maybe cherry tomatoes stuffed with a fish pâté, or deliciously crumbly cheese pastries—the range of ingredients and influences picked up by Xavier

Poupel on his travels becomes apparent. One of his most popular specialities, from the 148F menu, combines crab and sushi with a saffron sauce, and other sauces feature unusual spicing and citrus fruits. The most out-of-the-way offerings on the *carte*, meanwhile, are ostrich steaks with Australian peppers, and a sophisticated prawn curry (with couscous). There are plenty of other dishes that are more obviously French, however—such as market-choice fish with *foie gras*, or *suprême de volaille*—and the more exotic elements are never allowed to overpower the other, fine-quality Norman ingredients. To the well-dressed local families who settle in around the tables for Sunday lunch some of the fare probably seems pretty daring, but it's interesting to see French food approached with the kind of global eclecticism now common in the English-speaking world.

From the main, 148F menu, if the crab and sushi are not for you, try the *ravioles d'escargot à la crème de shitaki* to start. The ravioli are perfectly cooked, firm to bite into, and the flavour comes less from the snails than the earthy-but-subtle taste of the shiitake mushrooms. Another alternative first course is an excellent *soufflé de chèvre*, with a great range of textures from creamy to powdery. To follow, *filet de canard aux épices et cacao* introduces you to another ingredient which Xavier Poupel handles with notable skill—chocolate. The duck is superb quality meat; the savoury chocolate sauce is no rarefied delicacy, but thick, complex and finger-licking rich. *Noisette de veau aux coquilles St-Jacques*, on the other hand, from the same menu, comes with a lighter sauce of orange and ginger.

The wine list is already substantial for a relatively new restaurant, with some excellent Graves and Rhône wines for around 100F. The final courses are a bit more conventional: the cheeseboard, naturally, features a good selection of Norman cheeses, and desserts might include a satisfyingly fruity traditional *tarte aux pommes* as well as more complex things such as a fragrant *sorbet aux cinq parfums*. There is still, though, a noticeably high proportion of sweets made with spices and/or chocolate to choose from, before you finish your meal with coffee and some very chocolatey *petits-fours*.

Magrets de Canard à l'Aigre-doux

(Serves 4)

4 duck breasts
125g/4½oz butter
1 tablespoon chopped shallots
3 dessert apples, peeled, cored and sliced (reserve the trimmings)
100ml/4fl oz cider vinegar
250ml/9fl oz cider
2 tablespoons honey
250ml/9fl oz duck stock
1 tablespoon Calvados
salt and pepper

Trim the duck breasts and season with salt and pepper. Heat 25g/1oz of the butter in a heavy frying pan, add the duck breasts and brown well on both sides over a high heat. Reduce the heat and cook for about 2–3 minutes. The duck should be very pink, almost bloody, inside. Transfer to a serving platter and keep warm.

Add the shallots and apple trimmings to the pan and sweat until tender, then add the vinegar. Raise the heat and bring to the boil, stirring to scrape up the sediment from the base of the pan. Cook until the liquid is reduced by about three-quarters, then stir in the cider and 1 tablespoon of the honey and boil until reduced by half. Add the Calvados, flambé, then pour the sauce through a fine sieve into a clean pan. Dice 75g/3oz of the remaining butter and whisk it into the sauce a little at a time. Season to taste and keep warm.

Melt the remaining butter and honey in a frying pan, add the apple slices and cook over a medium-high heat until lightly caramelized. Slice the duck breast and serve with the sauce, garnished with the apples.

---

touring around

If you come into Dieppe on a Tuesday, Wednesday, Thursday or (best of all) Saturday morning, make straight for the centre of town and the ample place Nationale and adjacent place St-Jacques around the church of the same name, which are then taken over by the wonderful **market**. On Saturdays, the stalls also spread along the Grande-Rue, the now-pedestrianised main street running from the quays of the harbour along the north side of place Nationale. There's a seemingly endless choice of fruit, meats, vegetables, fresh flowers, herbs, terrines and, especially, cheese and butter, as well as clothes, bargain-basement shoes and other miscellanea. Most food products are brought in directly by farm producers, and this is one of the best places in the area to find regional specialities.

The market packs up about 1pm, except on Saturdays, but Dieppe's permanent shops are equally impressive, especially, and unusually for a town of this size, for luxury foods (there's also a Mammouth hypermarket, on the N27 south just outside town). As well as fish, Dieppe is known for chocolate and sweets, and the **Grande-Rue** contains a string of spectacular *chocolatiers*. At No.18 in rue St-Jacques, which converges on the Grande-Rue from place St-Jacques, is L'Epicier Olivier, domain of the father of Philippe Olivier of Boulogne. While his son specialises entirely in cheese, Claude Olivier offers a smaller choice of excellent cheeses but also fine wines, coffees and many other delicacies. Almost opposite is the Traiteur-Charcuterie M. Duhoux, where the windows proudly proclaim its status as the '*Champion de France du Boudin Blanc*' (White Pudding), as well as displaying a fascinating range of other sausage and terrine variations.

From the market squares, several short, narrow streets connect with the **port**, just to the east. This area did become fairly run-down, but in the last few years substantial restoration work has been set in motion. The smarter cafés and fish restaurants are mostly along the quai Henri IV, the continuation of the Grande-Rue along the north side of the harbour; to the right along quai Duquesne, despite creeping gentrification, some of the arcades still contain slightly shabbier bars and shops selling things like discount electrical goods, confirming the impression that Dieppe is a real seaport.

From the 1850s until 1994, the Newhaven ferry sailed right into the harbour to dock, giving Dieppe the most impressive approach of any of the Channel ports (the new ferry terminal is just outside the main harbour, on the eastern side). Part of the outer harbour alongside quai

Henri IV, the *Avant-Port*, has now become a yacht marina, but even so the business of the port, the movement of ships, cargoes and little boats, is still an integral feature of the centre of the town. If you carry on inland down quai Duquesne you will walk alongside the fishing port, where most mornings you can see a dazzling array of superbly fresh fish and shellfish being unloaded, and equally dazzling stalls offering the day's catch, especially scallops, for direct sale, if you have any way of taking them away with you.

Dieppe first became an important port to the Normans after their conquest of England, and grew to a substantial size during the Middle Ages, both as a port on the Road to Santiago and as a stronghold that was fought over several times during the Hundred Years' War. Its greatest expansion, though, came in the 16th and 17th centuries, when Dieppe seamen were among the first in northern Europe to join in the vogue for exploration and to sail to other continents. In the 1520s, when they sought to join the trade with Africa and the East Indies, they found their way blocked by the Portuguese, who had arrived first. King François Ier of France authorised a Dieppe shipbuilder, Jean (or Jehan) Ango, to raise a fleet of privateers, which battered the Portuguese into submission. Ango died Dieppe's richest man, and has been a local hero ever since, so much so that his name still crops up all over the town.

Returning into town from the port, you will almost inevitably wander back to the market squares and Dieppe's largest church, **St-Jacques**, the pinnacles and buttresses of which loom up at the end of many of the streets and alleys in this area. It's in a much poorer state than most Norman Gothic churches, in obvious need of restoration, but impressive nonetheless. The oldest part is the nave, from the 13th century, but its greatest feature is the 14th-century rose window on the west front, especially beautiful in the evening light. The line of chapels around the church were mostly built as donations by Dieppe shipowners after 1500, including one, the Sacré-Cœur, with very fine late-Gothic vaulting, and another with the tomb of Jean Ango.

From the church, rue St-Jacques leads off to meet up with the Grande-Rue in the intimate **place du Puits-Salé**, the centre of Dieppe outside market hours. It is presided over by the **Café des Tribunaux**, one of the truly grand traditional French cafés. First built as a cabaret hall in the 18th century, it looks like something much more official, and in fact did serve as Dieppe's town hall at one time. As a café, it was an important place to be during the years when Dieppe acquired a large artistic community. One of the first painters to come here was the English artist, long resident in France, Richard Bonington, who encouraged his friends Turner and Delacroix both to visit Dieppe and paint its sea and sky in the 1820s. Later, Monet painted the church of St-Jacques, and Pissarro street scenes. Other artists seen in Dieppe were Whistler, Renoir, Gauguin, William Nicholson, Degas and especially the latter's friend Walter Sickert, a near-fixture in the town over forty years, who did much to introduce the ideas of the Impressionists into English art. In this century, Braque, Miró and Barbara Hepworth have also been drawn to Dieppe. Virtually all of them passed at some time or other through the Tribunaux, which seems the ideal setting for an artists' café. One figure most often associated with the place was Oscar Wilde. He first visited Dieppe in happier circumstances in 1878, invited by Sickert, and came back here, broken and depressed, immediately after his release from prison in 1897, staying for several months while writing *The Ballad of Reading Gaol*, and spending long hours at the café.

After an aperitif at the Tribunaux, unless it's Saturday, it should be time to go out to Le Colombier for lunch, after which you could perhaps explore Offranville and visit the Château of Miromesnil before returning to Dieppe. Otherwise, or if you are coming back to the town, continue west from place du Puits-Salé to the end of rue de la Barre or any of the old streets parallel to it, where all roads immediately begin to climb a steep hill, crowned by the dramatic castle, now the **Château-Musée** (*open June–Sept, Mon, Wed–Sun, 10am–noon, 2–6pm; Oct–May, Mon, Wed–Sat 10am–noon, 2–5pm, Sun 10am–noon, 2–6pm; closed Tues; adm 20F*), which glowers down at you from many places in Dieppe. Built mainly in the 14th and 15th centuries, it's a rambling complex of ramparts, rooms and separate buildings, with some great views over the town and the sea.

The museum collection inside is an attractive mixture which, apart from a few nautical exhibits and an entertaining display on the history of sea bathing in Dieppe, mostly divides into two halves. One is made up of paintings, especially by artists associated with Dieppe. Its greatest treasure, however, is its extraordinary collection of Dieppe ivories. When Dieppe was at its commercial height in the 17th century, its sailors wandered the coast of Africa trading for great quantities of ivory tusks, all of which were brought back and worked on here by local carvers who became renowned for their skill. They produced combs, fans, crucifixes, thimbles, pens, decorative scenes and all kinds of other articles in fine ivory; all are represented here, and, whatever you feel about the fate of the elephants, reveal a quite staggering level of painstaking, sensitive workmanship.

From the castle, take the steps down the seaward side of the hill to reach the seafront. At the foot of the hill is the **square du Canada**, which commemorates both the 'Canadian Martyrs', Jesuit missionaries killed by Indians in Quebec in the 17th century, and more recently a terrible military mess, the Dieppe Raid of 19th August 1942, when a predominantly Canadian force of 6000 men paid an appalling price—three-quarters of them killed, wounded or captured—to demonstrate to the Allied commanders that a frontal assault on a Channel port was not a viable prospect.

In Dieppe, as in Deauville, the line of hotels and houses looking seawards along the main promenade, boulevard de Verdun, is a considerable distance from the actual seafront, and the space between them is occupied by a mini-golf course, a *jardin d'enfants*, a swimming pool, tennis courts and the inevitable thalassotherapy centre (*see* p.131). The beach is shingle, but is actually the closest one to Paris, which may have been an important factor in prompting the Duchesse de Berry to introduce the English fad of sea-bathing into France here in 1824. Despite the rise of the more ostentatious *Côte Fleurie*, Dieppe remained fashionable for the next century. Nowadays, the seafront's grandeur seems a little faded, but like all old seaside resorts it still has plenty going on in summer. It also has a more modern attraction in the **Cité de la Mer** (*open April–Sept, daily 10am–12.30pm, 2–7pm; Oct–Mar, Mon, 2–6pm, Tues–Sun, 10am–noon, 2–6pm; adm 25F; 15F 4–16s; free under-4s*), at the very eastern end of the front, an aquarium and exhibition on all things to do with the sea that can work well with kids, but is not as sophisticated as Nausicaá in Boulogne.

For the end of the day on Saturdays, or after lunch on others, there are also places to be explored closer to Le Colombier. In Offranville itself there is the **Musée Jacques-Emile Blanche** (*open April–Oct daily 10am–6pm; adm 20F*), with paintings in a pretty setting in case those in the Dieppe museum are not enough, and well-signposted just across the main N27 road near St-Aubin there is the **Château de Miromesnil** (*open May–15 Oct, Mon, Wed–Sun, 2–6pm; closed Tues; adm 30F*). Begun in 1589, it's a very elegant example of a Henri IV-style, brick and stone château. The house has had two famous residents: the Marquis de Miromesnil, one of the enlightened ministers of Louis XVI who attempted ineffectually to reform the *ancien régime* in the years leading up to the French Revolution, and Guy de Maupassant, who was born here in 1850. This happened rather by accident, since his father was given to living above his means and rented several châteaux and other residences around the region; the family moved on from Miromesnil four years later. Particularly impressive, though, are the lush grounds and gardens outside, and especially the approach, an immensely long beech-lined avenue. In the woods of the park there is also a lovely 12th-century chapel, with some fine 16th-century wood panelling inside. In the interior of the house, the most interesting rooms are the study and bedroom of the Marquis.

The house does have certain quirks. As in most privately-owned French mansions, little thought has gone into the display, and, more especially, the interior can only be visited with a guided tour, usually given by a woman with a very old-schoolteacherish air and an umbrella, who confirms everything you've ever heard about the authoritarian nature of traditional French education. It's the Basil Fawlty school of tour guiding, and would drive you mad if it weren't also funny. She does promise to speak English, but it might be better not to have such individual attention.

Benedictine Luxuries

Some towns are conventionally pretty, all scenery and fine architecture, or have distinctive museums or cultural monuments; some may be no beauties but are strong on life and atmosphere. Others manage to combine a little of all of these qualities in different measures. One such is Fécamp. Like Dieppe and the other ports of northern Normandy, it sits in a gash in the long chalk cliff that lines this coast, dubbed the Côte d'Albâtre (Alabaster). At Fécamp the break in the cliffs is especially narrow, so

Palais Bénédictine, Fécamp

that they stand huge, white and impressive above the town, squeezing most of it into a snug valley running inland. Its harbour is similarly an inlet much longer than it is wide, still very much a working port with a fishing fleet, but now shared with an increasing number of yachts.

In the year 1001 Duke Richard II of Normandy established one of the largest Benedictine abbeys in France in Fécamp, and during the Middle Ages it was among the most important pilgrimage centres in Europe, thanks to its shrine of the Precious Blood of Christ, believed deposited there by Joseph of Arimathea. Fécamp was also one of the favoured capitals of the Norman Dukes, and William the Conqueror threw lavish revels here at Easter 1067 to celebrate his conquest of England.

Much later, it became a gritty deep-sea fishing port. From the 1830s on it also followed Brighton and Dieppe to become one of the first seaside resorts.

When the Fécampois wish to celebrate or tackle Sunday lunch in style, they commonly head for Claude Guyot's Auberge de la Rouge, just outside town. It's an impressive, half-timbered Norman inn, a hundred years old and supposedly named after the first owner and her red hair. M. Guyot is an ebullient, wiry man in his fifties, a great football and sports fan who runs marathons when he's not in his kitchen or giving courses to younger chefs; he has also marked out a very high standard over many years with his fine, sophisticated variations on classic Norman and French cuisine, made with an exquisitely delicate touch. When you're feeling a desire to be pleasantly pampered, La Rouge is ideal.

getting there

The Auberge de la Rouge is in St-Léonard, a small village about two kilometres south of Fécamp town. From the centre of Fécamp, by the place Charles de Gaulle and the church of St-Etienne, follow the signs for the road to Le Havre (D925), which begins as the rue Charles-le-Borgne. After a steep climb up a hill and a few bends this will bring you straight through St-Léonard, where the Auberge is unmissable on the left, shrouded by a few trees, and with its own car park alongside. If on the other hand you are approaching from Le Havre via Goderville, you will pass the Auberge on your right on the same road before reaching Fécamp.

Not very widely publicised is the fact that there is now a direct link between Fécamp and Britain, a passengers-only fast catamaran service from Brighton, with two sailings daily in each direction between 1st April and 30th September. The trip takes about two hours, and the boat arrives in Fécamp on the Grand Quai, in the centre of the port. From there, it's best to take a cab to get to St-Léonard.

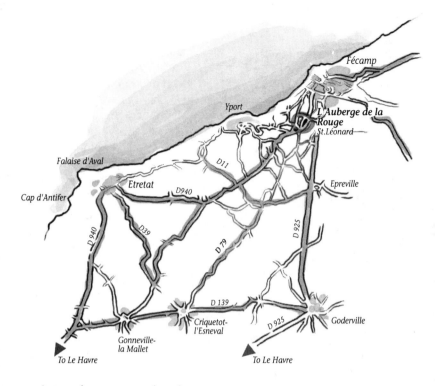

L'Auberge de la Rouge

Auberge de la Rouge, Route du Havre, St-Léonard, 76400 Fécamp,
© 35.28.07.59. Open Tues–Sat, noon–2.30pm, 7–9.30pm; Sun
noon–2.30pm. Book a day in advance, more for Sun. Menus at 105F, 195F,
280F; children's menu 50F; carte average 250F.

You enter the Auberge via a large gateway and an especially pretty
leafy garden, with a pond, a fountain, and loungers, chairs and tables
where you can sit outside to eat or drink in summer, or just take the
air. The same comfortable degree of luxury is continued inside, in both
surroundings and service. The old inn has been elegantly renovated
throughout, with a few well-appointed guest rooms. The dining room
is decorated with some model boats and nautical prints to recall
Fécamp's maritime traditions, and has snug armchair seating, fine
silver and enough carpeting to create a satisfying hush. The red-jack-
eted waiters exude traditional professionalism, but M. and Mme Guyot

Auberge de la Rouge

and their staff are friendly and charming rather than stuffy, and few other restaurants at this level would have such a well-equipped baby-changing room as the Auberge provides, with enough toys, wipes and other accessories to supply a small crèche.

The menu changes regularly. The main *carte* is divided between *cuisine créative* and *cuisine traditionelle*, although M. Guyot's versions even of local standards such as Fécamp salt cod in a cream sauce are never just plain home cooking. There is no lack of original, complex dishes in the different set menus either, but perhaps most impressive are the specials of the day, often fish chosen '*au hasard du marché*'—according to market availability.

Already to be appreciated in the preliminary *amuse-gueules*, such as some little quails'-egg tarts, is one particular aspect of M. Guyot's cooking, his delicious pastry— he has won several awards for his *pâtisserie* and desserts, of which more later. A superbly refreshing summer starter, from the 195F menu, is the *assiette sauvage aux deux saumonées*, wonderful quality smoked and unsmoked salmon intertwined on a bed of lettuce with a fine lime vinaigrette. There are also such delicacies as warm oysters with a cress and cider mousse.

The first courses concluded, there comes a modern variation on the *trou Normand* or 'Norman Hole'. In Maupassant's time it was the custom at Norman country dinners for the men at least to take a slug of Calvados between each course, supposedly to clear a 'hole' for the next round, and some traditional folk are still stout enough to keep this up today. At La Rouge you are given a little cup of Calvados sorbet, which is much more refined. Also true to the area are the various duck dishes, especially, among the main courses, the variations on *canard* or *caneton Rouennais à la presse*, a bird that's un-bled and then squeezed in a special press to create supremely tender meat, while the juices extracted are used to create a sauce that in this case is truly spectacular, rich, dark and yet not at all heavy. It often comes with tagliatelle, and a fine *ragoût* of forest mushrooms. If it's among the day's specials, though, don't miss the fabulous *bar grillé au beurre d'échalote*, one of Claude Guyot's regular specialities. The fish is of the best and perfectly cooked, with a woody, smoky tinge in the flavour from the grilling. The whole ensemble is, in the tradition of Norman cooking, decadently buttery, but so well-executed that you never notice, unless you really want to worry about it. If you are mixing meat and fish around the table, there is on the ample wine list a fragrant Sancerre rosé, at 160F not a cheap bottle, but delicious.

After such rich delights something drier is required. The cheeseboard at La Rouge is a picture, a shop window for Normandy cheeses; the choice is difficult, but to stay local there's a fine dry Neufchâtel, and a tangy *fromage au Calvados* that makes for a vigorous pick-me-up. Space has to be reserved, though, for the last course: hot desserts (which, as you will be advised, need to be ordered with the other courses) are, rather unusually, among M. Guyot's specialities. A gratin of fresh fruit (apple, melon, pears) in pastry with a "*sabayonade*" sauce is a fruit pie of a different order; *crêpe soufflée aux effluves de Bénédictine* is eggy but with a subtle alcoholic tang. As a final touch, the *petits-fours* with the coffee might be little tarts of woodland fruits, with more fine, crumbly pastry.

Feuilleté Cauchois 'du Père Mathieu'

(Serves 8)

8 large Conference pears
250g/1lb granulated sugar
12 good-quality dessert apples such as Reine des Reinettes or Cox's
100g/4oz unsalted butter
3 tablespoons honey
150ml/¼ pint B & B*
4 egg-yolks
375ml/½ pint sweet cider
8 puff-pastry cases, 10cm/4" diameter
mint leaves to decorate

For the crème pâtissière:

4 egg-yolks
100g/4oz caster sugar
500ml/1 pint milk
25g/1oz plain flour
25g/1oz cornflour
4 tablespoons ground almonds
4 tablespoons double cream
4 tablespoons B & B*

For the caramel sauce:

200g/8oz granulated sugar
250ml/1 pint whipping cream

First make the crème pâtissière. Beat the egg yolks with the sugar, adding a little of the milk if necessary. When pale, mix in the flour and cornflour. Bring the milk just to boiling point and stir it into the egg mixture. Return to the pan and bring to the boil, stirring constantly until smooth. Pour into a bowl and cool slightly, then mix in the ground almonds, cream and B & B. Set aside.

Peel the pears, leaving the stalks on, and core them from the bottom. Put the sugar in a large pan with 1 litre of water and heat gntly until dissolved. Add the pears and poach until tender.

For the caramel sauce, put the sugar in a small heavy-based pan with 2 tablespoons of water and heat very gently until all the sugar has melted. Bring to the boil and cook until it becomes a rich brown caramel. remove from the heat and immediately pour in the cream (stand well back as it will splutter dangerously). Stir over a gentle heat until smooth and set aside.

Peel, core and finely dice 8 of the apples. Heat half the butter in a frying pan with honey, add the apples and fry until golden and tender. Sprinkle with a little B & B and set aside. Peel and core the remaining apples and cut each one into 8 slices. Sauté them in the remaining butter, sprinkle with a little B & B and set aside.

Put the egg yolks, cider and remaining B & B in a bowl set over a pan of simmering water and whisk with an electric mixer to make a sabayon: it should be thick and mousse-like.

To assemble the dessert, remove the tops of the pastry cases and spread a layer of crème pâtissière in each one. Stand a pear in each case and surround with the diced apples, then decorate with the apple slices. Spread the sabayon over everything except the pears and glaze (a small domestic blow torch is useful for this). Finally, pour a little caramel sauce over each pear and decorate with mint. Serve the remaining caramel sauce separately.

*B & B is the Brandy-and-Bénédictine mix produced by Bénédictine. This is sold mainly in the USA, and is available in the UK only from Harrods and a few other outlets. Straight Bénédictine can also be used, although the flavour will be slightly different.

---

touring around

In the town of Fécamp, visitors' eyes tend to be drawn towards its most spectacular attraction. The **Palais Bénédictine** (*guided tours Nov–mid-Mar, daily 10.30am, 3.30pm; mid-Mar–end-May, Sept–Oct daily, 10am–noon, 2–5.30pm; end-May–Aug, daily, 9.30am– 6pm; adm 25F, 12.50F 10–17s*) has pinnacle towers, baronial staircases and fine stained glass, and must be the world's grandest distillery. It was built for the founder of the company, Alexandre Le Grand, and stands comparison with William Randolph Hearst's San Simeon as one of the most extravagant creations of the pirate-prince era of capitalism.

The recipe for Bénédictine liqueur was invented by an Italian monk at Fécamp Abbey in about 1510, and for centuries it was made only by the monks for medicinal purposes. The Le Grands were a local family of beer and wine merchants, and when the abbey was dissolved during the French Revolution an erudite Le Grand forebear had bought up many relics and monastic documents, preventing them from being destroyed. In 1863 Alexandre, then aged 33, was browsing through these papers when he came across the recipe, and a new life opened up before him. He was not content just to tinker with the liqueur a little and put it on sale in the family shop. With a remarkably modern vision, he chose to advertise his product aggressively, using some of the best poster artists of the great age of French graphic art, and to go for exports. The French had only a certain capacity for a sweet liqueur, and, from the first, Bénédictine's market was the world.

The results were immediate. Le Grand also sought very deliberately to create a prestigious image for his brand, to root it in history; providing a palace for his distillery naturally added to the mystique, and suggested a continuity with the ancient abbey. Then, in January 1892, the recently finished Palais burnt down. Undismayed, Le Grand promptly rebuilt it on an even bigger scale. He did not live to see it completed, dying in 1898, two years before its inauguration. The grandest parts of the Palais were built as a museum to house the collection of artefacts, mostly medieval and Renaissance, amassed by Le Grand—religious statuary, paintings, carved wooden chests, English alabaster altarpieces, Limoges enamels, and furniture, with highlights that include some magnificent 15th-century illuminated manuscripts. The collection is also engagingly quirky and personal; there is a whole room, for example, full of 16th- to 18th-century doorknobs, keys and door-knockers. Tours of the Palais last about an hour and a half.

Opposite the main entrance to the Palais Bénédictine is the **Fécamp** tourist office, for maps of the town. Take the street downhill beside the Palais, rue du Domaine, to reach rue de Mer, and turn right for the centre of the town. Early Fécamp, and the abbey that once exercised control over a large part of the surrounding area, grew up on higher ground some way inland; the fishing community by the port was almost a separate village until the last century. Rue de Mer emerges into place Charles-de-Gaulle, where, if it's Saturday morning, the market will be in progress. The main shopping streets are also close by, around rues Jacques-Huet and Alexandre-Legros.

From the landward end of rue A-Legros, rue Leroux leads into the oldest part of Fécamp, and to the abbey. The main surviving monastic buildings, rebuilt in the 17th and 18th centuries and Classical-Baroque in style, now form the *Hôtel de Ville*. Alongside them is the abbey church, the **Eglise de la Trinité**, actually larger than many cathedrals. Like the rest of the abbey it was given an 18th-century neoclassical façade, but inside it's a fine example of early Gothic in light-coloured stone, airy, plain and an interesting contrast to the Bénédictine's decorative overkill.

Its visual impact stems especially from the fact that it's unusually long (127m) for its width. This is the fourth church on this site. The legend that some of the Precious Blood had made its way to Fécamp was known in the 7th century, and a small women's convent grew up at the shrine. At the end of the 10th century, in fulfilment of a vow to his father, Richard I of Normandy, and to mark the first millennium, Duke Richard II built a far grander church and attracted the Bene-dictines to found a men's abbey. The tombs of both Richards are now in the south transept. So many pilgrims came to Fécamp, though, that this church too became inadequate, and it was entirely rebuilt in Romanesque style in 1106, only to be destroyed by fire in 1168, and replaced by the present, Gothic church, mostly completed by 1220.

The Precious Blood is still there, in a reliquary on the marble altar from 1510, by the Italian Renaissance sculptor Viscardo. More striking, and in front of the altar, is a rare Romanesque reliquary chest In the south transept there is an exquisite, vivid carving of the *Entombment of the Virgin* in polychrome stone, from 1495, but most unique may be the giant, ornate 1667 clock in the north transept, which indicates the time, month, season and even the tides. Opposite the main entrance to the church some ruins remain of the palace of the Dukes of Normandy; in the streets off to the left, such as rue Arquaise, there are still quite a few medieval houses.

From the abbey a walk seawards veering to the right, through rue Jacques Huet and the shopping streets around the market, will bring you eventually to quai Bérigny, alongside the port. Commercial and fishing traffic is now largely confined to the inner basin; the outer harbour is mainly a *port de plaisance* for yachts. A feature of Fécamp harbour is that the breakwaters of the outer harbour are lined with wooden walkways, and a stroll along them is a very pleasant way to see the port. Just up the street from here, at 6 rue de la Mer, there is a great junk-and-antique shop, the Brocante de la Rue de la Mer.

At the end of the harbour, just around the corner on the sea front (called boulevard Albert Ier), there's an imaginatively presented modern museum, the **Musée des Terre-Neuvas et de la Pêche** (*open Sept–June, Mon, Wed–Sun, 10am–noon, 2–5.30pm; closed Tues; July–Aug, daily, 10am–noon, 2–6.30pm; adm 20F, free under-18s; same ticket also admits to Musée-Centre des Arts*) dedicated to Fécamp's maritime traditions. Of great interest to anyone with nautical leanings, it also covers a good deal of social history, including the development of Fécamp as a seaside resort. The front was the other major 19th-century addition to the town, running along the beach to end at the **Casino** and a footpath up to the cliffs. The beach is all pebbles and not much good for swimming, but fine for windsurfing or a paddle and a frolic.

If you have time and transport, continue 20km west along the coast from Fécamp to **Etretat**, site of the most celebrated cliffs of the Côte d'Albâtre, battered by the sea into giant arches that look eerily like human creations. The northern Normandy coast was particularly important to the Impressionists, especially Monet, and nowhere more so than these cliffs; they also feature in two stories by Maupassant, for whom Etretat was another of his child-hood homes. It's more of a pure tourist town than Fécamp, a bit twee and with plenty of souvenir shops, but undeniably pretty all the same. And the sometimes precarious cliff walks, north (*amont*) and south (*aval*), with their superb dramatic views along the coast, are the kind of attraction that no amount of over-attention can spoil.

arch near Etretat

Monet's Paradise

Giverny

Light. Water. Colour. Fields with swathes of poppies and irises. Bright dresses and dappled sunlight through trees above tranquil, dusty paths. The Impressionists have left images of France that still have the power to seduce despite all their arch-familiarity. In the history of Impressionism, especially during its early years, Normandy played a major part: Boudin, one of the precursors of the movement, rarely strayed far from Honfleur, Monet was raised in Le Havre, and places along the Norman coast such as Trouville and Etretat inspired many artists. The Seine Valley, too, was the subject of innumerable river scenes. Nowhere, though, was better associated with a particular painter than Giverny, beside the Seine just inside the borders of Normandy, where Claude Monet lived from 1883 until his death in 1926.

Monet discovered Giverny by accident from the window of a train, but it isn't difficult to see why the Seine between Paris and Rouen was such an attraction to artists seeking light and nature. The river wanders quietly through bends and long meanders. In midstream there is a line of small islands, the odd boathouse and thickets of trees matched by the woods scattered along the banks, often climbing up steep hills and cliffs that at times make the valley almost like a gorge.

History has been marching along the Seine Valley since Roman times. Along the river are towns such as Vernon with Romanesque and Gothic churches, and Renaissance and neo-classical châteaux. In this idyllic valley, the best place to eat is naturally on a leafy terrace overlooking the river. This can be done in traditional style at the Hôtel de Normandie, a classic country hotel in Les Andelys, beneath the looming remains of a castle built by Richard the Lionheart, Château-Gaillard.

getting there

Les Andelys is easily accessible from Le Havre or Caen via the A13 autoroute: exit at junction 18 (Louviers) and take the D135 east, signposted to Les Andelys, an attractive road through forest. This will bring you into the town on the bridge across the Seine. After the bridge, turn left, go past the tourist office, and the entrance to rue Grande is on the left; however, a one-way system will oblige you to make a circuit to the right and come into the street from the opposite end, in which case the hotel is easy to find on the right. From Paris, leave the A13 at junction 17 and take the D316/D313 through Gaillon, which will bring you into Les Andelys to meet the road across the bridge. From Dieppe or further north, avoid Rouen with the road through Buchy and Fleury-sur-Andelle, and turn right at the main street of Les Andelys to reach the river.

L'Hôtel de Normandie

Hôtel de Normandie, 1 rue Grande, Le Petit-Andely, 27700 Les Andelys,
℡ 32.54.10.52. Open Mon–Tues, Fri–Sun noon–2.30pm, 7.30–9.30pm;
Wed noon–2.30pm only; closed Thurs and all Dec. Book weekends. Menus
at 100F, 170F, 270F; carte average 200F.

As you come into the Hôtel de Normandie through the entrance hall, formerly an arched gateway into the courtyard of the old inn, the

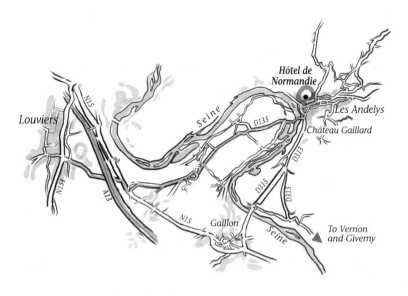

owner, Mme. Bourguignon, welcomes you from behind an impressive mahogany desk. Beyond is the courtyard, the terrace with outside tables, a mass of geraniums and busy lizzies in pots and hanging baskets, and the Seine. From the side of the terrace next to the riverside footpath there is a good view of the *Ile du Château* in mid-river. All you need do is take out your notepad and start sketching over the aperitifs. To secure a table outside, be sure to ask when booking; if none is available, or the weather is unfriendly there is a comfortable and also very pretty dining room inside, several tables having a view of the river.

One of a number of old inns that have been providing for travellers along the Seine-side road for the past two centuries or so, the Normandie is traditional inside and out, typical of the French *restaurant bourgeois*. The dining room is large but intimate, fitted out with solid wooden furniture and crisp linen. M. and Mme Bourguignon have been here for 35 years, and their son-in-law now presides in the kitchen; this is a restaurant that does what it has done for a long time—classic French and Norman cuisine—but does it well. The standards of presentation and seamless service, provided by the kind of waiters who look as if they've been practising since the age of five, equally bring to mind a certain timeless notion of comfort.

The 100F menu offers a good range of fine-flavoured Norman dishes: the home-made *terrine de volaille* is rich, strong and meaty, and comes as an education to anyone used to oily, production-line pâtés. To follow, try the *andouillettes à la Dijonnaise*. Mme Bourguignon will probably warn you that, as all traditional French restaurateurs know, Anglo-Saxons are supposed not to like such things, but really kidney is the most unusual flavour in this fine traditional sausage, and it's beautifully offset by the Dijonnaise mustard sauce. On the 170F menu, meanwhile, are such dishes as a salad with excellent fresh prawns to start, a *pavé* of fresh salmon with a sorrel sauce and some perfectly grilled lamb chops in Provençal herbs.

The comfort of the surroundings, and the relentless cosseting by the ever-present staff, build up an inescapable feeling of leisurely well-being. As might be expected, the wine list is extensive, but the Côtes du Castillon Bordeaux (95F) is a light, full-flavoured red that goes excellently with this kind of food. Following on from the cheese course—with good *chèvre*, Livarot and especially Camembert—desserts include a delightful lime sorbet that, served on beautiful little dishes, is a picture in itself. On the other hand you could complete the old-fashioned touch with gâteaux of the kind that were always seen on old-style English sweet trolleys and so often disappointed. Here, while still very sweet, they're wonderfully light, with rich flavours of mocha and cream. Drinking aromatic coffee while admiring the gentle progress of the river seems the only fitting conclusion to such a feast.

Ris de Veau Vallée d'Auge

The Vallée d'Auge sauce is a classic Norman recipe, used with chicken, pork and many other meats as well as sweetbreads.

(Serves 4)

400g/14oz calf's sweetbreads
dash of vinegar
1 onion, roughly chopped

2 sprigs of thyme
1 bay leaf
6 tablespoons oil
4 dessert apples, peeled, cored and sliced
200g/7oz mushrooms, thinly sliced
2 tablespoons Calvados
125ml/4fl oz crème fraîche
salt and pepper

Soak the sweetbreads overnight in water to cover with a dash of vinegar, changing the water 2 or 3 times. There should be no blood in the water at the end of the soaking time. Drain and rinse the sweetbreads, then put them in a pan of cold water with the onion, thyme, bay leaf, salt and pepper. Bring slowly to the boil and poach for 5 minutes. Drain and rinse under cold water, then remove all the skin and membrane and cut into slices.

Heat the oil in a frying pan, add the apples and mushrooms and sauté until softened. Add the sweetbreads and cook for 2–3 minutes, until golden, then remove from the pan along with the apples and mushrooms. Cover and keep warm. Pour the Calvados into the pan and boil until reduced by half, then add the crème fraîche, reduce the heat and simmer for a few minutes until slightly thickned. Return the sweetbread mixture to the pan, season to taste and serve.

touring around

Les Andelys are plural because there are two of them, Le Petit-Andely, built next to the river to provide supplies for Richard the Lionheart's castle, and the much older Le Grand-Andely, founded by the Romans, and set a little way from the Seine up a narrow valley. Since the last century they have been joined into one town by a long, straight main street. For an overview of the town and, more to the point, magnificent views over the Seine valley and miles of surrounding countryside, climb immediately up to **Château-Gaillard**. From Le Petit-Andely there's an invigoratingly steep walk up to the castle, beginning by the tourist office; by car, you must follow a well-signposted one-way system all the way through Le Grand-Andely and round via a fairly precipitous track, coming upon it from behind.

When Richard Cœur-de-Lion returned from his famous imprisonment in Austria after the Third Crusade, he found that his former childhood friend, fellow Crusader and, it has always been rumoured, lover Philippe Auguste of France was planning to end the effective independence of the Duchy of Normandy. To stop him, Richard resolved to build the most advanced fortification yet seen in Europe, incorporating all the lessons he had taken from Crusader and Arab castles. In a prodigious effort it was built in only one year, in 1196–97. Philippe was deterred for a few years, but after the Lionheart's death his hapless brother John seemed an easier adversary, and in 1203 a French army besieged Château-Gaillard. The castle fell in March 1204, and with that the dual Anglo-Norman monarchy came to an end. Château-Gaillard, though, continued to be an important stronghold through the wars of the later Middle Ages and into the French Wars of Religion after the 1560s, so much so that in the 17th century King Henri IV and later Richelieu ordered that it be demolished. Their demolition work and centuries of pilfering by local builders have taken their toll on the castle, but the sections that remain are still massive and awe-inspiring. The giant, bullish, 16ft-thick walls of the keep seem to grow out of the rock, and, visible for miles, look as if they could still at least partly fulfil their original purpose. The opening times apply only to the keep (*open 15 Mar–15 Nov, Mon, Thurs–Sun, 9am–noon, 2–6pm, Tues, Wed 2–6pm only; adm 18F*), around which there are hourly guided tours; you are free to wander round the other parts of the ruins at all times, and enjoy the views over the river, its islands and the plains beyond. They are especially spectacular at sunset.

Le Petit-Andely is an attractive quarter of little narrow streets with some half-timbered old buildings, and an open-air swimming pool by the river (*open May–15 Sept*). Le Grand-Andely, naturally larger, has an ample central square where the **market** is held on Saturdays. Not far away is the Collegiate Church of **Notre-Dame**, standing on the site of a monastery founded in the 6th century by Ste Clothilde, wife of Clovis, first of France's Frankish Kings. Inside, there is some beautiful 16th-century stained glass, and, in the chapels, two fine altar paintings by a local painter of some renown, Quentin Varin. Varin was the first teacher of Les Andelys' most famous son, Nicolas Poussin, the greatest of all French Baroque painters, born just outside the two towns in

1594. Unusually, though, Poussin seems to have felt very little devotion to his *terroir*; he scarcely ever came back here after leaving to study in Paris in his twenties, and did most of his major work in Rome. However, his home town does have a small **Musée Nicolas Poussin** (*open Mon, Wed–Sun, 2–6pm; closed Tues; adm 20F*), not far from the market square (actually place Nicolas Poussin). It has one of his major paintings (*Coriolanus Answering the Tears of his Mother*) together with a few articles associated with him and an eccentric collection of unrelated artefacts and pictures by a variety of local artists.

In **Giverny**, all eyes naturally turn to the **Fondation Claude Monet** (*open April–Oct, Tues–Sun, 10am–6pm; adm 35F; 25F students; 20F 7–12s; free under-7s*). Here you are only about 70km from Paris, and Monet's house and gardens are fixtures on all the city coach tour programmes. They are therefore very often full of people, especially in midsummer, and it's worthwhile trying to visit towards the beginning or the end of the season, and on a weekday.

Monet moved here in 1883 with Alice Hoschedé, a friend of his first wife who had been abandoned by her husband, and their several children by their respective first marriages. They later married. When he first arrived, Monet, then 43, only rented the house and its main garden, called the *Clos Normand*; as he became more successful, though, he was able to buy them and remodel the garden exactly to his liking, and in 1895 he added an additional plot in which to create, from nothing, his Japanese Water Garden and lily pond. The Water Garden was separated from the main plot by a railway line and a dusty track. This is now a main road, but access from one side to the other is made easy by a pedestrian underpass paid for by the Texan millionaire and some-time diplomat Walter Annenberg. The current immaculate condition of the house and gardens, in fact, is due in great part to American benefactors. When Monet's last surviving son left the property to the French Académie des Beaux-Arts in 1966, it was in a sorry state, and long and expensive restoration work was necessary.

Each of the gardens has a different character. *The Clos Normand* was originally a traditional French garden with neat, formal paths, but Monet's love for colour soon overcame these limitations. These are not gardens for those obsessed with precisely defined flower beds and straight lines: they are all about abundance, exuberance, explosions of colour. The Water Garden meanwhile is leafy and centred on the pond, often surrounded by white wisteria. This naturally attracts the biggest crowds, especially the Japanese bridge, but one of the best features of Giverny is that you are free to wander as you like.

The house is almost as pretty as the gardens, beautifully light and, remarkably, still possessed of a cosy and almost lived-in feel. Most striking and surprising in a house of that time are the colours: summery yellows in the dining room, blue tiles and duck-egg woodwork in the kitchen and a day room. Decorating virtually every wall is one of the world's finest collections of Japanese prints. They are the original examples actually acquired by Monet, arranged exactly as he hung them; in his spacious, comfortable studio, though, there are only reproductions of the paintings he owned and some of his own works, for the originals of which you will mainly have to go to the Musée Marmottan and other Paris museums. The last stage in the visit to the house is the warehouse-like studio Monet had built in order to work on his giant near-abstract water-lily paintings, the *Nymphéas*, in the years before his death in 1926. Today, it contains more reproductions, and, naturally, a powerfully equipped souvenir shop.

Outside, along Giverny's main street, today rue Claude Monet, several pretty old houses are now occupied by painters offering Monet-ish flower paintings, a veritable neo-Impressionist industry. On the other side of the road is the lavishly appointed **Musée Américain** (*open April–Oct, Tues–Sun, 10am–6pm; adm 30F*). In the 1890s, several young painters, mostly Americans, arrived in Giverny to follow the master's example, and this museum, founded by a former US Ambassador to France and his wife, is intended to showcase their work and that of other American artists living in France around that time. Monet's reactions to his fan club were mixed: some became his friends and one, Theodore Butler, married his stepdaughter and is buried in the Monet family grave in Giverny: others he just found irritating. Their work as seen in the museum prompts a similar response. With some the uncharitable thought occurs that they might have done better to stay at home and try and be more original, but there are also some fine pictures by artists such as Mary Cassatt.

Moules, Movers and Shakers

Fleeting glimpses of French actresses and Euro-celebrities, sharply preserved matrons promenading with little dogs, Belle Epoque roués staggering ruined from the casino, men and women with flawless skin lolling in unbelievably comfortable chairs on beachfront café terraces, a precise sense of chic and luxury: these are the images and ideas conjured up by Deauville, legendary capital of the Côte Fleurie. This stretch of coast at the mouth of the Seine has been the seaside of Paris since the last century, when Deauville, above all, became the self-styled 21st *arrondissement* of the capital, and in the 1900s anyone who was anyone could be found at some time every summer on parade along its neatly clipped seafront. More recently its position has been challenged by the more reliable weather of other resorts further south, but Deauville has fought to maintain its status, promoting its overall ritziness and its role as a venue for prestige events.

All this *ultra-chic* and *très distinguée* opulence might seem a bit intimidating, or a bore, and of course Deauville isn't cheap, but take it with a pinch of salt and it's fun. It's quintessentially French: nothing to do with quaint rural practices, but a place based on very Gallic traditions of well-being, style, and a proper observation of social customs; being here is not about getting away from it all, but about getting into it. The Parisian *hauts-bourgeois* who are the greatest sustainers of the town like to do things in a certain way, and Deauville is one resort that still has a definite Season.

And alongside it is Trouville, separated only by the river Touques but remarkably different. The beach at Trouville was a favourite weekend escape for Parisians when Deauville was still a stretch of sand dunes. However, while Deauville has remained a pure resort, Trouville is a real town as well, with a life of its own that carries on through and outside the holiday season, seen in its harbour, its fishing fleet, and in one of France's very finest town markets. Trouville has quirky little streets where Deauville has long, well-trimmed drives; it's just as much of an immersion in *la vie française*, but laid-back, amiable and hip in a way its neighbour rarely can be. It's more enjoyable to eat on the Trouville side of the river, and not only because it's usually cheaper. Along the quay overlooking the Touques in Trouville there are some of France's best, most bustling brasseries. Most famous of all is Les Vapeurs, renowned for both its style and the products of its kitchen, especially seafood. It has unquestionable cachet, better known than many much swankier places across the river, and this is one case of a reputation that's very richly deserved.

getting there

Approach Deauville/Trouville on the main N177 road from Caen, Rouen and the *autoroute* A13 and you will enter the towns on the Deauville side, and shortly come to the pont des Belges, the only bridge between them. Cross the bridge, and the quai Fernand Moureaux runs off towards the sea on the left, parallel with the river. About halfway up there is a bank of bars and brasseries, and Les Vapeurs is right in the middle. If you are coming from the east and Honfleur on the D513, you will arrive at the Trouville end of the bridge, in which case you should turn right along the quay.

Note, also, that during the summer season there is also a direct flight between Deauville's small airport and London Gatwick.

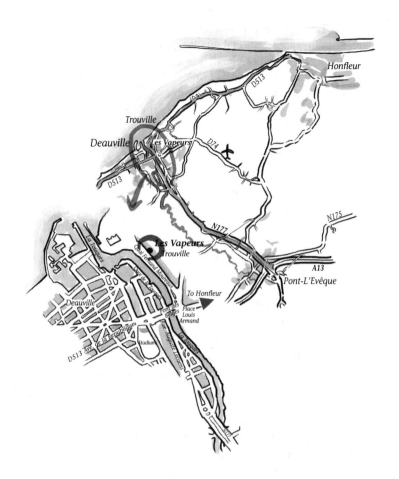

Les Vapeurs

Brasserie Les Vapeurs, 160 quai Fernand Moureaux, 14360 Trouville,
℡ 31.88.15.24. Open daily 8am–1am , closing time may vary in winter
according to trade. Booking always advisable. Carte average 150F.

When restaurant owners in other countries call their place a brasserie,
this is what they are hoping to achieve—this same mixture of buzz,
bustle, light unfussy décor, fine but accessible food and easygoing,

open-all-hours atmosphere. The added element here is the special care, seen in the exceptional quality of ingredients and touches such as the plentiful fresh flowers, that is needed to sustain a place like this over many years. It was opened in 1927 by the grandfather of present owner Gérard Bazire as a plain fisherman's bar, and despite its growth in reputation has retained more or less the same Art Deco fittings, with plenty of mirrors now adorned with an accumulation of souvenirs and signed photographs. It seems quite small from the entrance, but is labyrinthine inside, with several upstairs rooms.

Gérard Depardieu and Antoine de Caunes are regulars, and over the years virtually every French entertainment star anyone has ever heard of and many Hollywood and international names as well have signed the *Livre d'Or*, among them the director of *Diner* and much else besides, Barry Levinson, who wrote that you can eat here better than in any diner. There are also obscure fashion types, and people who work somewhere in French TV, in high season vying for the best tables alongside the zinc bar or on the pavement outside. Even with all this celebrity hubbub, though, the place still manages to generate a comfortable warmth, with locals coming in just to eat a quick lunch alone, and plenty of ordinary punters among the poseurs.

Mutterings have been made about the service at Les Vapeurs, with suggestions that, Deauville and Trouville being offshoots of Paris, this is also a den of the kind of French waiters who can flatten an ego with one flick of an eyebrow. My own experience is that once they've got over showing you their smattering of English the waiters here can be genuinely friendly in a rapid-fire way, and are certainly not to be compared with the hostile Parisian waiter of yore. Les Vapeurs does get busy, and they don't hang about, but requests for changes or extras are met with professional aplomb, and they don't harass you off a table once you're on to the coffees.

Since this is a brasserie, there is only a *carte*, and eating a full meal can become expensive, particularly if you have some of the fish specialities, but it's perfectly acceptable to have just one or two plainer dishes (note, also, that M. Bazire now has a restaurant next door, Les Voiles, with more restricted hours and a set menu at 119F and children's menu at 59F). Starters are straightforward, with a sizeable selection of simple, fresh salads. There's also plenty of food for people who like to use their fingers, such as one of Les Vapeurs' noted specialities, *crevettes grises*—shrimps, swiftly boiled in salt and pepper. You pop them in in their shells, minus only heads and tails, although real aficionados eat the tails too.

Main courses include steaks, and above all many varieties of superbly fresh fish, all landed right in Trouville, some of which are fixtures on the menu, like the (expensive) sole; others are seasonal market specials such as red mullet, generally plainly grilled or served in a classic sauce. What many people around you will be dealing with, however, are the mussels. There are signs offering *moules-frites* all along the French coast, but Les Vapeurs is home to what is probably the definitive *moules marinières*, a superlative, addictive concatenation of subtle flavours that contrives to explode and melt in the mouth simultaneously. Once you've finished the ample bowl you can only start planning to come back for more. If you want your mussels with more traditional Norman richness, try them *à la crème normande*, an equally delicious combination of seafood, cider and cream. The chips are excellent too, and the brasserie's steady supply of perfectly chilled Muscadet is an ideal accompaniment.

Don't pass on the classic desserts. A *crêpe suzette* with Grand Marnier is wonderfully fruity and boozy, and the charlotte with raspberries and the *tarte Tatin* are beautifully made and packed with best-quality fresh fruit. Moreover, with them there appears on the table a whole earthenware tub of *crème fraîche*. The mere sight of it must cause fainting fits in any self-respecting Californian movie executive.

Matelote Trouvillaise

The Norman matelote is the only one of these classic fish stews made with sea- rather than freshwater fish, and is one of M. Bazire's occasional speciality dishes. It can vary greatly, and can be made with any white fish instead of sole and red mullet.

(Serves 4)

675g/1½lb cleaned baby squid
1 bunch parsley, chopped
4 large potatoes, cut into chunks
1 carrot, cut into chunks
2 large onions, 1 carrot, cut into chunks
1 sprig thyme
1 bay leaf
150g/5oz unsalted butter, diced
250ml/8fl oz dry cider
2 red mullet, each approx 300g/11oz
1 sole, approx 600g/1¼lb
8 scallops
100ml/4fl oz crème fraîche
salt and pepper

Poach the baby squid in 1 litre of barely simmering water for 5–8 minutes, until the flesh turns opaque. Remove the squid with a slotted spoon, cut into pieces and set aside.

Scatter the parsley over the base of a large heavy pan and arrange the potatoes, carrot and onions on top together with the thyme, bay leaf and butter. Add the cider and the liquid from cooking the squid. Season to taste, then bring to the boil and simmer for 30 minutes, until the vegetables are tender. Add the red mullet and sole to the pan and poach very gently for 3–4 minutes; the liquid should barely be moving. Add the scallops and squid and cook for 1–2 minutes .

To serve, remove all the seafood and vegetables with a slotted spoon and place in warmed shallow soup plates. Strain the liquid into a small soup tureen, season if necessary, then swirl in the crème frâiche and serve immediately with the fish.

touring around

It may have been beaten by Dieppe as France's first seaside resort, but thanks to a better beach and its good connections with Paris **Trouville** quickly became more popular. The first beach huts appeared in the 1840s, and when Napoleon III began to bring his court here in the following decade its popularity was assured. The great forerunner of Impressionism Eugène Boudin, and later Monet and Renoir, all painted here, and the view along the wooden boardwalk or *planches*, with flags fluttering in the wind, must be one of the most familiar images in mid-19th-century French painting. After the élite had transferred their allegiance to Deauville, Trouville continued to draw the crowds. Maupassant, in his 1888 novel *Pierre et Jean*, described the beach as looking like 'a long garden full of brilliantly coloured flowers', covered in 'sunshades of all colours, hats of all shapes, dresses of all shades'.

Trouville's beach has been its fortune, a sweep of soft sand running away to the cliffs in the far distance to the east, fine for frolicking in the waves even though it can be a hike to reach the water at low tide, and backed by the *planches* for all of its length. It's a relaxing, old-style seafront, with bars, ice-cream stands and some grand old 19th-century beach villas along the *planches*, and still fills up on summer weekends.

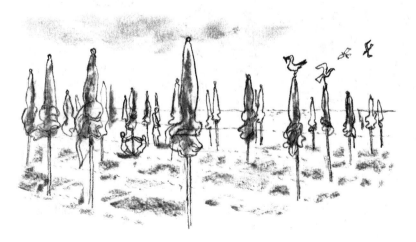

Part-way along there is an **aquarium** (*open Easter–mid-Nov, daily, 10am–noon, 2–6.30pm; mid-Nov–Easter, daily, 2–6.30pm; adm 30F; 20F under-16s*) for a rainy day, with displays of all kinds of marine life. Even Trouville's casino, at the point where the seafront meets the river Touques, and home to the 'Louisiana Follies', has more of an end-of-the-pier than a jet-set look to it.

Away from the beach Trouville is an engaging, idiosyncratic town, with little narrow streets intersecting and winding up suddenly steep hillsides, and a good deal of bizarre Norman holiday-town architecture combining half-timbering and pebbledash, and housing some interesting antique, fashion and curio shops. On rue Général Leclerc, the main street that runs parallel to the beach, there is the **Musée Montebello** (*open Easter–end Sept, Mon, Wed–Sun 2–6pm; July–Aug 2–6.30pm; closed Tues; adm 10F*), a small museum with some charming works by Boudin and other Trouville painters, and also some exhibits on other aspects of the history of the town.

Trouville has another other major focus of activity as well as the beach: the long quay along the Touques, where fishing boats are moored in line to unload their catch, and also the location of Les Vapeurs and other good bars and restaurants. The best time to come here is on Wednesday and Sunday mornings, when the tree-shaded space along the quays is also the site of Trouville's wonderful **market** (*between July to September some stalls are also there virtually every day*). It's a fascinating combination of luxury food display and jumble sale. Because Trouville and Deauville together offer a large, generally free-spending number of customers, many of Normandy's finest producers of traditional foods bring their wares here: farmhouse cheeses, terrines, pâtés and confits of duck, *andouilles* and other gutsy products, ciders and Calvados, honey, cakes and traditional breads. The only permanent building is the fish market, where the day's catch is put on sale just a few feet from where it is landed. The displays of *tourteaux*, sea bass, mussels, prawns, *bigorneaux* and other less familiar sea creatures are spectacular; the lack of fishy odour is testament to their freshness. This is also, though, a market whose eclecticism demonstrates Trouville's quirky small-town identity, and as you wander around you'll find stalls offering anything from scarves featuring Johnny Halliday or Nirvana, unidentified stretches of elastic, a big old clothes stall with three items for 60F and extremely tacky cardigans, to American quilts, fire extinguishers, rare books and some vaguely Baroque furniture. It's wonderfully vibrant and rough-and-ready, and nothing to do with the supposed stuffiness of the Côte Fleurie.

The market ends at the bridge across the river, called the Pont des Belges because of the curious fact that Deauville and Trouville were liberated in August 1944 by a Belgian Brigade operating with the Canadian Army. On the other side, you can walk down the neat, shaded path along the Touques, or stroll into the broad avenues of **Deauville**. The town is another product of the decadent Second Empire. In 1860 Napoleon III's half-brother the Duc de Morny strayed across from Trouville and decided to develop the empty dunes on the left bank of the river as a much more exclusive, and so more profitable, resort. Another major contributor to its development was a speculator called Eugène Cornuché, who at the turn of the century rebuilt the seafront, and the casino. Deauville's two great heydays were either side of the First World War, and in the Jazz Age flappers danced the night away at parties in the town's extravagant villas, and entertainment stars such as Mistinguett and Maurice Chevalier were obligatorily snapped in photo opportunities on the seafront every year.

Since Deauville is an artificial town, its promoters were able to control building and impose particular styles, above all the one known locally as '*Anglo-Normand*', with much use of mock-traditional half-timbering in giant mansions several storeys high, giving the impression of a Pays d'Auge manor house after a severe dose of steroids. Walk around the quiet, neatly kept streets of the town and you can find a fascinating variety of such creations, with pepperpot towers, turrets, Swiss-chalet roofs, gingerbread-house windows, elaborate pagoda-ish cornices and all kinds of other fanciful details, all within smart gardens surrounded by tightly clipped hedges. It's the presence of so much mock architecture in Deauville that gives the place its distinctly Beverly Hills, slightly dotty look. There are not many shops, and probably more *esthéticiennes* than food stores.

Right next to the Pont des Belges is one of the most engagingly silly of the *Anglo-Normand* edifices, the half-timbered railway station. Carry on past it and veer to the right, and you will come to the heart of the town. Away to your right again are Deauville's two large yachting marinas. At the centre of town is the shiny white **casino**, overlooking the beach, looking a bit like a lower floor of the White House without the top. On either side of it are two of the three Empress-Dowagers of Deauville hotels, the Normandy and the Royal. The third, the Hôtel du Golf, perhaps the largest half-timbered cottage ever built, is on Mont Canisy at the back of the town, next to its golf holes, one of the finest courses in France.

Unusually, the casino and the grand hotels are separated from the seafront by a flat, open area, lined with flowerbeds, that now contains such services as tennis courts, an indoor swimming pool and the esplanade of the Centre International de Deauville or CID, the venue for exhibitions, festivals and conferences. Beyond that, finally, is the beach, lined with more wooden *planches* that form Deauville's historic promenade. The bars along the front—Le Ciro's, the Bar du Soleil, the Bar de la Mer—are perhaps the original beach cafés; they still draw in the visiting glamour today, busily air-kissing across the tables. You also see Deauville's more regular clientèle along the promenade, participating in their rituals as many have for years. The French middle classes have a persistent fondness for little dogs, and parts of Deauville could be considered a preserve where all the poodles and Pekinese that have disappeared from the rest of the world have been taken for safety. Every so often pretty young people may appear and push a piece of paper towards you, promoting something. After the bars come to an end there are lines of rather elaborate, well-kept beach cabins, the little fences between them painted in imitation Hollywood Boulevard style with the names of all sorts of international film figures who presumably have passed through.

Next to the esplanade by the casino there is a large centre for thalassotherapy: basically bombardment with sea water through a high-pressure hose. *La Thalasso* fits all the requirements of a French middle-class health fad: you don't have to do anything, it's all done to you, and it's as much about looking good as it is about health. It's also supposed to be very good for *le stress*, and a basic two-session treatment can be had in Deauville from 1250F. There are now *thalasso* centres all round the French coast, and the Deauville establishment is naturally one of the most luxuriously equipped.

Deauville's Season runs essentially through July and August. In the last twenty years, though, since the town now has to work much harder to keep up its prestige, this has been extended on either side. Programmes listing all the events organized each year are available from the tourist office, by the Mairie.

One major thing to do in Deauville is to go to the **races**, for this is one of the most important centres of the French horse world. There are two tracks, La Touques for flat racing and the more casual Clairefontaine, which hosts some flat races but is mainly used for steeplechases and trotting. Both have lavishly equipped, beautifully maintained buildings, naturally enough in giant *Anglo-Normand* manor house style, and hold regular meetings through the summer season, with additional races and thoroughbred sales at La Touques in mid-October. Clairefontaine also offers free guided tours, every day in season at 10.30am.

Some events in Deauville, such as, at the race track, the polo tournament held at La Touques in August, and the Grand Prix de Deauville, the traditional end to the season held at the same track at the end of the month, are definitely the kind of occasions you would not want to turn up at without the right hat. Others are much less so. Deauville most lets its hair down during the film festival, the **Festival du Cinéma Américain** in early September, which generally previews American movies some time before their European release dates, and always ensures that some major Hollywood figures such as Clint

Eastwood, Tom Hanks or Robert de Niro put in an appearance, amid much flashing of lights and rippling crowds. Oddly enough, it's also much easier to get into than other trade-orientated festivals such as Cannes, and so more of a hit with the public than the critics.

From November to mid-spring, while Trouville stays alive, Deauville largely closes down. A few people still come up for weekends to catch the sea air, but many of the grand houses are tightly shuttered up, the lines of beach umbrellas are tied up like so many coloured pillars, and the streets are oddly but atmospherically quiet. Note, though, that this is also the town from which Jean-Louis Trintignant drove Anouk Aimée back to Paris in *Un Homme et une Femme*, so if you are here on a rainy day you could always drive round looking moonily at the windscreen wipers and going *Yaba-daba-da, Yaba-daba-da* ad infinitum.

If you've had enough of Deauville, then follow the D513 west from Deauville, through the neat, orderly little seaside towns that make up the rest of the **Côte Fleurie**. Part-way along, the road stands back from the coast to avoid the cliffs of the Vaches Noires, beneath which there's a great walk at low tide. Almost hidden in amongst these precise resorts is the ancient town of **Dives-sur-Mer**, from where William the Conqueror's main fleet set sail for Hastings. Its port has since largely silted up, but it still has a fine Romanesque and Gothic church and a superb 15th-century covered market hall, which hosts another wonderful market on Saturdays.

Deauville may have reinvented itself, but the Belle Epoque still lives in **Cabourg**, just across the Dives river from Dives-sur-Mer, where Marcel Proust came for his adolescent holidays, and which he immortalized as 'Balbek' in *Within a Budding Grove*. All roads in Cabourg lead to the Grand Hôtel, around which the town was created. It looks exactly like the kind of hotel that would have been patronized by the Margaret Dumont character in the Marx Brothers movies, but now trades shamelessly on its Proustian associations by offering wildly expensive teas in its *salon de thé*, with no refund if the madeleines fail to unlock the floodgates of memory in publishable form. In the casino alongside the hotel there's a bar called *Le Temps Perdu*, which could be seen as an invitation to a very expensive lost weekend.

Cider and Flowers

Three of the four classic
Norman cheeses—Camembert,
Livarot and Pont-l'Evêque—and the
best of all Normandy ciders all come
from the Pays d'Auge, an area of rambling,
intertwined valleys that spreads roughly from east of Caen
across towards the River Risle, and from near the coast at
Honfleur down to beyond Vimoutiers in the south. Known as
a region of agricultural abundance since the early Middle Ages,
it has also provided the classic image of the Normandy countryside: half-timbered, thatched-roofed farms, manor houses
and villages, with roses climbing the walls, scattered between
apple orchards, woods and open fields across green valleys.
Meander along the narrow lanes, some of them almost tunnel-
like between ranks of giant, wildly beautiful beeches, and there
are any number of farms that offer their own cider, Calvados,
preserves and sometimes rarer delicacies for sale, while fine
cheeses and dairy produce can be found at the spectacular
local town markets. Follow your nose—sometimes literally, for
the air often carries a fragrant but noticeable scent of apples. If
the fragrance brings on hunger pangs, an ideal place in which

to get further immersed in the atmosphere of rural calm is the wonderful Deux Tonneaux (Two Barrels) in Pierrefitte-en-Auge. With a barrel for a sign, creaking timbered walls and a garden alongside with tables beneath apple trees and a fabulous view, it's a traditional Norman village inn and *bar-tabac* that even locals are surprised to find still exists, offering cider from the barrel and equally traditional country dishes made with the best of local produce.

getting there

Pierrefitte is a few kilometres south of Pont-l'Evêque, in the north of the Pays d'Auge. From the A13 Caen-Rouen *autoroute*, take the exit for Pont-l'Evêque to join the other main east-west road, the N175, at the crossroads in the middle of the town, where you should turn left towards Caen. If you approach Pont-l'Evêque from

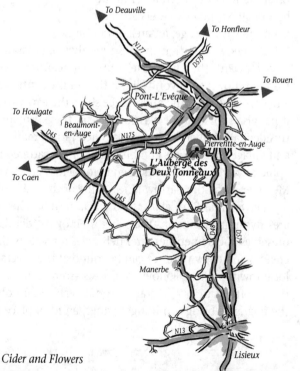

the north, from Deauville, Honfleur or the Pont de Normandie on the N177/D579, turn right at the same crossroads. On the western side of Pont-l'Evêque there is a turn to the south off the N175 on to the D48, signposted to Lisieux, and a short way down this road, past the *autoroute*, there is a right turn for the D280A to Pierrefitte-en-Auge. The Auberge is unmistakable in the centre of the village.

L'Auberge des Deux Tonneaux

L'Auberge des Deux Tonneaux, Pierrefitte-en-Auge, 14130 Pont-l'Evêque,
℗ 31.64.09.31. Open Sept–Nov, Feb–June, Tues–Sat noon–9pm, Sun
noon–4pm; also open July–Aug, Mon, noon–9pm; closed 12 Nov–1 Feb.
Booking advisable. Carte *average 100F.*

Auberge des Deux Tonneaux

The tranquil village of Pierrefitte-en-Auge is not that far from the *autoroute* and the busy N175, and yet it seems entirely oblivious of them. A scattering of farms and barns up and down a steep hillside overlooking the broad valley of the River Touques, the whole village is *protegé*, and just about every building is half-timbered except the church. The Auberge des Deux Tonneaux stands by the roadside opposite the latter. Built in the 17th century, it looks very much the kind of place a musketeer might once have chased a serving wench around in. Outside, its brown-timbered walls lean and bulge at odd angles beneath the dense eaves of thatch, and out of each window spill great clumps of potted geraniums. The garden is on a raised terrace at one side; anyone from the area will tell you it's best in May, when the apple blossom enhances the great vista over the green valley spread out beneath you. At the back of the garden there's an additional dining room with long tables and pews for seating, where red-faced farmers take lunch in big noisy groups.

Inside, the snug main dining room has oak beams, a massive oak bar, oak tables neatly covered in check oilcloth, and an impressively ornate gold-plated grandfather clock in one corner. The windows sport little embroideries and a collection of coffee pots, and through the glass beyond them the view over the Touques framed by those red geraniums. However, Mme. Jacqueline Rayer and her charming young staff run it very definitely as a local restaurant, not a heritage site (*note that, despite the 'official' opening times, they may sometimes close mid-afternoon on quiet days*).

The Deux Tonneaux offers '*plats typiques*', and straightforward Norman cooking is what you get: omelettes, salads, hams, sausages of various kinds, award-winning tripe, rabbit *Grand-mère*, chicken and so on, with apples, cider and mushrooms turning up in several dishes. If you want a first course, there's a green salad in a very pleasant mustard vinaigrette as well as the larger, mixed salads. Dishes may be simple, but what makes them spectacular is the quality of the entirely local ingredients: the gutsy terrines, *rillettes* (shredded, potted goose) and other meat products are all made at the Auberge itself, and the sheer goodness of such things as tomatoes and the deep-yellow eggs used in the omelettes hits you as soon as you taste them. An *omelette campagnarde* comes filled with potatoes and their own home-dried ham, while the meaty *andouillette* bursts open when you cut it and is full of strong, varied, earthy flavours. For a larger meal, you can also order ahead for a succulent whole roast farm chicken (for a minimum of three people).

To drink, there are wines, beers and the usual alternatives, but it's only natural in this setting to have one or two of the earthenware jugs of farm cider, dry or sweet—the dry cider from the barrel is fruity, but still very refreshing. For something a bit more smooth and refined, there's also local corked cider (*cidre bouché*).

After the main course, you can naturally have cheese (a creamy Pont-l'Evêque only), and there are some delicious fruit-filled classic Norman apple desserts. The eye, though, is irresistibly drawn towards another speciality of the house, crêpes. They come in a range of fruity and alcoholic combinations, but even one innocently named '*crêpe au chocolat*' arrives powerfully doused in Calvados as well as a thick, aromatic chocolate sauce. It's all a sensuous experience, especially if you take time at the end to sit in the garden and watch the trees waving in the breeze down below. When you leave, you won't miss (because they're stacked all around the bar) the pots of the Auberge's terrines, preserves and wild mushrooms, and bottles of cider and Calvados, to buy and take away.

Lapin Façon Grand-mère au Cidre et au Pommeau

1 rabbit, jointed
1 heaped tablespoon seasoned flour
75g/3oz butter
2 onions, sliced
2 carrots, sliced
250g/9oz mushrooms, cut into quarters
4 tablespoons Pommeau
1 tablespoon chopped thyme
1 bay leaf
500ml/1 pint cider
chopped parsley to garnish
salt and pepper

Dust the rabbit pieces in the seasoned flour, shaking off any excess. Heat the butter in a large pan, add the rabbit and brown well on all sides. Remove from the pan. Add the onions, carrots and mushroom to the pan and cook gently until lightly coloured, then add the Pommeau and bring to the boil, stirring to scrape up the sediment from the bottom of the pan. Return the rabbit to the pan, then stir in the thyme, bay leaf, cider and salt and pepper. Simmer for about 1 hour or until the rabbit is tender. If the sauce is too thin, you can remove the rabbit from the pan and boil the liquid until reduced and thickened. Return the rabbit to the pan, adjust the seasoning if necessary, and serve sprinkled with chopped parsley.

touring around

The northern Pays d'Auge, roughly above the N13 Caen-Lisieux road on the map, is the prettiest part of all, where the valleys are most leafy and sheltered and virtually every small town and village is made up predominantly of *maisons à colombage* or half-timbered houses. Norman half-timbering uses more, thinner uprights than its English equivalent, giving buildings a more stripier look, but the three basic elements of the technique—the *poteaux* (structural timbers), *écharpes* (diagonals) and *colombages* (the thinner pieces between the main timbers)—provide an apparently infinite variety of design possibilities, with complex zigzags, buttresses and counterposed panels creating a fascinating diversity. They tend to sprawl into several equally impressive buildings, for it has been the practice for the original house to become a barn or cowshed once a larger one could be built.

This is also the most important area for ciders, the location of the official *Route du Cidre*, which is well signposted along the roads. Farms that meet the exacting demands of the *appellation contrôlée* for Auge ciders and sell direct to the public are indicated by small signs with an apple and the words '*Cru de Cambremer*' by their gates. The local cider authorities also set a recommended price for direct-sale ciders. All local tourist offices have leaflets on the *route* and cider producers in the area, and on the special farm open days that are often held between spring and early autumn.

If you come into the Auge on the N13, from Caen, turn north at Carrefour-St-Jean on to the D16, following the *Route du Cidre* sign, and then on to the D49 for Beuvron. Very shortly the countryside begins to resemble a small-scale Kentucky. As well as apple country, this is also prime horse-breeding territory, generally for *le Trot*, trotting races, rather than flat racing; between the orchards there are plenty of lushly carpeted meadows containing some very sleek, elegant horseflesh behind white-painted fences. The Manoir de Sens at **Victot-Pontfol** is an opulent manor house with neatly trimmed lawns that's both a cider and a stud farm, and also offers very smart *chambres-d'hôtes*.

Beuvron-en-Auge describes itself as one of the '*plus beaux villages de France*', and few people would argue. It's a remarkable ensemble of traditional Norman houses, mostly first built between the 16th and 18th centuries, and the delightful main square, where they are lined up alongside each other, their timbers forming crosses, arrowheads and other intricate patterns between clay washed in a range of surprisingly different, gentle shades, is a demonstration of the ingenuity and imagination of the region's anonymous builders. One of the highlights is the large 16th-century **Vieux Manoir** on the south side of the *place*, with some fine, gargoyle-like carvings, but really the whole village is the attraction. As one of the most beautiful of all the Auge's many beauty spots, Beuvron inevitably gets congested on summer Sundays, but it's very hard to take away its charm. The little timber market hall, in the middle of the square, now contains a restaurant and several shops, and the village also has plenty of craft and souvenir shops. Most are a little expensive, but one that is not is the Ferme de Beuvron, a farm cooperative in one of the few brick buildings to be seen, on the north road out of the village, which has particularly good preserves and the unusual *confiture de lait* made by Mme Odile Gasson of Méry-Corbon, a kind of very liquidy toffee.

Leaving Beuvron to the north, turn right on to the tiny D146 for Clermont, one of the leafiest of country lanes. Don't miss the sign to the left for the **Chapelle de Clermont**. A footpath leads through a canopy of dense beeches to the chapel, on a precipitous crag where you suddenly emerge to find sweeping views over the Dives valley to the west. Believed to have been founded in the 12th century or earlier, and then rebuilt in the 15th, the chapel is wonderfully simple, whitewashed inside and with some fine locally carved statues of saints around the walls, including an oddly cute Virgin and Child.

This is a good place to begin cider-hunting. Auge ciders are often slightly fruitier than other Normandy ciders, but also with more subtle flavours. The apple harvest runs from late September to November, and the dryness of the cider depends on how long it is left to ferment in the barrel, although cider apples more than six months old must by law be made into Calvados. Once bottled, cider, unlike Calvados, does not change significantly with age. Most farms produce some very sweet *cidre nouveau* for Christmas, but more normal *demi* and dry (*brut*) ciders do not become available until March or April, and so the best time for tasting and buying is from mid-spring to summer. By autumn the large producers will still have ciders on sale, but smaller farms will often have sold their production for the year. In general there are two kinds of cider producers in the Pays d'Auge. Some are unmistakably farms where, having been attracted in by the apple sign and '*Cidre–Calvados-Vente Directe-OUVERTE*' outside, you may find yourself wondering whether you're being had on, as not even the dog takes much notice of you until someone finally appears and with very few words unbolts the large half-timbered sheds where the cider is kept. Others are much more sophisticated operations, often around large manor houses, and with separate farm shops. Whether producers are one or the other has no relevance to the drink's quality, and excellent ciders can come from either kind. Some farmers will also show you round their cider sheds, but in large and small farms it's advisable not to call during the sacred hours of lunch, 12.30 to 2pm, or too late in the evening.

A fine example of a farmhouse producer is Gérard Desvoyé of St-Aubin-Lebizay, east of Clermont. He won't make any fuss of potential customers, but the many cups and other awards on shelves in his cider shed attest to the quality of his ciders, especially the superbly smooth and subtle *brut*. He also has good Calvados, Pommeau, apple vinegars and jams. An excellent larger producer is Pierre Huet, in a magnificent Norman manor, La Brière des Fontaines, on the D101 road just south of Cambremer. The Huet family have produced cider here for five generations, and the friendly staff offer guided tours (*in English, on request*) of their large cider sheds and distillery. As well as fine ciders, Huet is also renowned for its Calvados, of which there is a great range of varieties reaching up to a superb 30-year-old Cordon d'Or for over 400F, and even reserve 50-year bottles for 700F.

A little way south of Cambremer in St-Laurent-du-Mont, on the road towards Crèvecoeur, there's another very good small-scale cider maker, Robert Turmel, with one of the most ravishing of all Pays d'Auge farmhouses; and just outside St-Laurent on the D50 road towards Lisieux there is the farm of J-A Motte, who makes first-quality *chèvre*, both plain and with tarragon and other herbs. From there it's not far to the château of **Crèvecœur-en-Auge** (*open April–June, Sept, Mon, Wed–Sun, 11am–6pm; July–Aug, 11am–7pm; closed Tues; adm 20F*).

This immediately suggests a book illustration of a Norman motte-and-bailey castle; its oldest ramparts were built before its lord joined Duke William in invading England, while the other half-timbered buildings around the grassed-over courtyard were built and rebuilt over the following centuries. Most impressive is the giant dovecote, an imposing indication of the status of the castle's 15th-century owners, since only the aristocracy were allowed such buildings in medieval Normandy. Curiously, Crèvecœur has since the 1970s been owned by a foundation created by the Alsatian Schlumberger engineering family, who have lovingly restored it to house a museum on oil exploration, as well as temporary exhibitions of more direct Norman interest.

You could potentially cover all or part of this area in a morning, before heading north to Pierrefitte for a long lunch. If, though, you happen to be in the area on a Monday, make all allowances to get to the Pays d'Auge's largest market, to the south in **St-Pierre-sur-Dives**. It has been held here virtually every Monday morning since the early Middle Ages, and the town largely developed around it. The *halles*, the giant covered market hall at its centre, was first built in the 11th century, and has been altered and faithfully rebuilt several times since after fires and other disasters, the last in 1944. It's a powerful reminder that, for all its prettiness and the adoption of tourism, the Pays d'Auge remains very much a rural area, and it can be a culture-shock: all around there are geese, ducks, chickens, rabbits and any other small farmyard animal you can think of, and all of them alive. To buy food that isn't still animate, look outside, where the market also sprawls over two very large, open squares. Close to the *halles*, there are stalls with superb local meat and *charcuterie*, wonderful fruit and vegetables, and some of the very best Camembert, Livarot and other local cheeses. At others, farm people in for the day can buy all-weather jackets, toys, machinery, leather bags and virtually anything else they might need, before the market, very traditionally, begins to pack up around half-past noon.

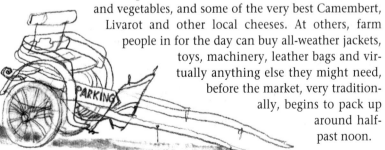

The southern Pays d'Auge, east of St-Pierre-sur-Dives, is not quite as scenic as the north, but is the best area for cheese, whether Camembert of different strengths, the milder, slightly more crumbly Pont l'Evêque, powerful, tangy Livarot or the pungent Pavé d'Auge. Unfortunately, owing largely to modern regulations and to the fact that much cheese is produced by local cooperatives, opportunities to visit farm producers are scarce, and the best places actually to buy cheese are the area's markets, apart from St-Pierre especially Orbec (*Wed and Sat*), Livarot (*Thurs*) and Vimoutiers (*Mon and Fri*). Interested cheeseophiles also have a choice of **cheese museums**. The one in St-Pierre, above the tourist office (*open Easter–Oct, Mon, Wed–Sun, 10am–12.30pm, 2–6.30pm; adm 22F*) is hugely informative on cheese-making, to an extent that even French-speakers find overwhelming, and more engaging (and accessible to English-speakers) are the older little museums in **Livarot** (*open April–Oct, Mon–Fri 9am–noon, 2–6pm, Sat 10am–noon; closed Nov–Mar, Mon, Tues; adm 15F*) and **Vimoutiers** (*open Mar–Oct, Mon, 2–6pm, Tues–Sun, 9am– noon, 2–6pm; Nov–Dec, Mon 2.30–6pm, Tues–Fri 10am–noon, 2.30–6pm, Sat 10am–noon; closed Jan, Feb; adm 15F*). All of them naturally also have cheese for sale.

As a complete alternative to food-tasting, just south of St-Pierre-sur-Dives there is the **Château de Vendeuvre** (*open 10am–6pm daily, May–Sept; Sat, Sun and holidays only, Mar–April, Oct–Nov; Closed Dec–Feb; adm 40F; 20F under-18s*), a Louis XVI bonbon of a stately home that could be a revelation to anyone who thought the French aristocracy had been on hard times since 1789. Gutted in 1944, it has been lavishly and beautifully restored by the Comtes de Vendeuvre with all of its original, pastel-shaded décor, a fascinating example of the sugary style of the Marie-Antoinette era, plus a remarkable collection of furniture and bric-à-brac and life-size automata in each room. Especially entertaining is the kitchen, where the automaton actually appears to talk manically as it shows off the different pots and pans. Moreover, in the Orangerie the Comtesse has the world's largest collection of miniature furniture. The attention of the Comte, meanwhile, seems more centred on his Jardins d'Eau-Surprises, a fanciful water garden with elaborate concealed fountains. It's all very twee, but very entertaining, and for once in a private French château gives you plenty to look at for the (rather high) admission fee.

The Beaches and the Tapestry

The wide arc of the Lower Normandy coast, stretching west from the Bay of the Seine and the River Orne to the Cotentin, is a fine, open coastline, gentle in parts and more rocky and abrupt in others, and at one time it must have been possible just to appreciate it as such. Today it's hard to dissociate this coast from the events of summer 1944, or its familiar place names—Ranville, Arromanches—from their emotional resonances. Even on French maps this area is marked as the Plages du Débarquement, and since the 1994 anniversary every point of historical significance has been smartly signposted.

Surprising, perhaps, to first-time visitors is the sheer length of the stretch of coast covered by the D-Day invasion beaches, close to 60 miles from end to end. The eastern section from Ouistreham to Arromanches, corresponding to the British and Canadian beaches of Gold, Juno and Sword, is otherwise known as the Côte de Nacre or 'Mother-of-Pearl Coast', a near-continuous, quite narrow beach fronted by a line of old-fashioned, inexpensive French seaside towns. Obviously nowhere chooses to be a battlefield, but for

the machine-guns to have sliced up the sand and the flail tanks crashed ashore here seems particularly bizarre; it's as if they'd invaded Bournemouth.

The D-Day sites and museums may be an obvious centre of attention in this area, but its more conventional attractions shouldn't be ignored. The Bessin is actually one of the best farming areas in Normandy, the tranquil home of crème fraîche. Its old stone villages are truly rural and especially pretty, with massive Norman church towers, and the region's large farms are often extraordinary, huge and castle-like, having been fortified against earlier English invaders in the Hundred Years' War. And, a short distance inland, there is the capital of the Bessin, Bayeux, a charming town, miraculously undamaged by the war, and which of course houses one of the greatest of all medieval artefacts, the Bayeux Tapestry.

Midway between the beaches and Bayeux, its streets normally patrolled only by tractors, is Crépon, population 203. It has some of the finest stone farms and manor houses of any of the Bessin villages, and in one of them, La Rançonnière, belying the hamlet's rustic appearance, there is now a hotel-restaurant offering some of the most sophisticated food in the area.

getting there

Crépon is a crossroads of several country lanes. From Arromanches, take the main Ouistreham road, and then halfway up the steep hill at the back of the town take a sharp right turn on to the D65, signposted for Creully, which will eventually bring you into Crépon. Go straight through the village, and on the south exit, round a sharp left bend, is La Rançonnière. The gateway through its turreted walls is quite narrow, and it's advisable to take a wide turn at it to breach them and get through into the well-kept courtyard. From Bayeux, take the D12 road for Douvres, and in Sommervieu carry on on to the D112 for Crépon (actually straight on), instead of following the main road to the right. From Caen, take the D22 road, signposted to Creully and Arromanches.

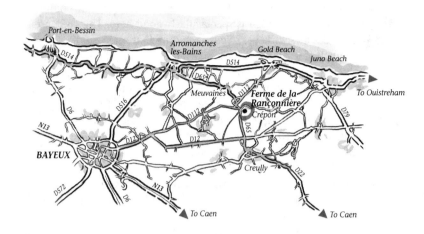

Ferme de la Rançonnière

Ferme de la Rançonnière, Route d'Arromanches, 14480 Crépon (Creully),
℡ 31.22.21.73. Open daily noon–2pm, 7–9pm (June–Sept until 9.30pm);
Closed 9–26 Jan. Book a day in advance. Menus at 60F (Mon–Fri lunch
only), 88F, 128F, 185F, 255F; children's menu 55F; carte average 200F.

The oldest part of La Rançonnière, a tower on one side of the courtyard, dates from the 15th century, and the farm buildings shelter
within a massive sandstone outer wall, the watchtowers, crenellations
and other fortifications of which were still being added to until the
18th, such was the fear in these parts of the English and other
marauders. Today, though, the grassy courtyard contains flower-beds
and some café-style tables. The father of Mme Agnès Vereecke, the present owner, bought the place as a farm shortly after the war, and the
family opened it as a hotel twenty years ago. It's now mainly run by
Mme Vereecke's daughter, Isabelle Sileghem, and her husband.

The restaurant is large and attractively barn-like, with thick stone walls
and fireplace, oak beams and long tables clad in white linen with bou-
quets of pinks on each one. It fills up at weekends but will probably be
much quieter at other times, unless you happen to coincide with one
of those big groups of work colleagues, 98% male, who always seem to
find the time to go out to lunch *en masse*, even midweek.

They will very possibly be tucking into some form of poultry or similar game, which is spectacularly good here. The 185F menu includes a remarkable *salade champêtre* that offers smoked *magret* of duck, *foie gras* and roast quail in the same platter; the duck is rich, almost ham-like and wonderfully subtle, the quail, fresh, savoury and bursting with flavour. The 88F menu features a daily special that might be chicken or duck with a *sucré* of pears, or a sauce of *Pommeau*, the Calvados and cider liqueur. The freshness of the fowl is quite tangible on the tongue, and all have so much taste they make the standard supermarket chicken a different creature altogether. Sauces are rich, often fruity, but made with a fine light touch, and complement the meat perfectly: pine kernels and hazelnuts with the quail, a *fondue* of leeks with guinea fowl.

At this point it's probably time to come clean about just why the poultry here is so good. Although no longer a working farm, La Rançonnière still takes in quality domestic poultry and other fowl from around the district for slaughtering and dressing (on another side of the building), to supply this and other restaurants, and for making terrines and other related products. For French people this closeness to source is a major selling point—while here you'll probably see a regular stream of people drive up to the little farm shop by the gate, having come here from Bayeux or further away just to buy farmhouse terrines and cheeses.

There are of course alternatives to poultry: fine dishes involving other meats or fish—again local—such as brill with *pleurotte* mushrooms, or a salad of smoked lamb with an apple *confit*. There's also an ample wine list, including a 1990 Marc Brédif Grand Vouvray that's a revelation if you've always thought of Vouvray as far too sickly a wine. Cheese is another speciality of the house, and of those on the board several are their own, and all are local; there is a particularly excellent, strong but subtle Livarot and Pavé d'Auge.

The desserts bring you back from country tradition to more urbane delights—the *pâtisserie* pleasures on offer may include a vanilla custard so exploding with fresh vanilla that its perfume wafts gently around your nose for the rest of the day, or a great, gooey coffee and chocolate mousse. After that, and maybe a Calvados with the coffee and *petits fours*, a wander into the field of clover at the back of the farm will round out the contentment.

Suprême de Pintadeau à la Fondue de Poireaux

(Serves 4)

2 leeks, finely chopped

125g/4½oz chilled unsalted butter

4 boned guinea-fowl breasts

3 tablespoons port

5 shallots, chopped

500ml/1 pint crème fraîche

salt and pepper

Sweat the leeks in 25g of the butter until very soft, and set on one side. Then, brown the guinea fowl breasts briefly on both sides in a pan. Pour in the port and flambé. When the flames have died down, remove the breasts, put in an ovenproof dish, season and cook in an oven at 200°C/400°F (gas mark 6) for about 15 minutes.

To make the sauce, add the shallots and crème fraîche to the pan and allow the mixture to reduce by half or until it reaches the desired consistency. Add the leeks to this sauce, dice the remaining butter and whisk in, a few pieces at a time, until the sauce is glossy. Season to taste, and serve with the guinea-fowl.

---

touring around

Crépon itself is an attractive, peaceful place, with a very traditional *bar-tabac*. At the centre of the village is the 12th-century Romanesque church, with a huge, typically solid Norman tower, and inside some impressive 17th- and 18th-century Baroque woodwork. South from Crépon is the dramatic romantic pile that is the château of **Creully**. A remarkable mix of medieval base, looming towers and Louis XIII additions, the château is briefly open to the public each summer (*guided tours only, July, Aug only, Tues, Wed, Fri, 10am–noon, 3–6pm; adm 10F*). Visitors wishing to see more of this area, though, tend to choose between the beaches and **Bayeux**—perhaps on different days—for both of which Crépon is ideally situated.

The **Bayeux Tapestry** is the kind of historical artefact that can seem very familiar, but actually becomes far more impressive close up. It was commissioned by Odo, William the Conqueror's half-brother and Bishop of Bayeux, to hang in his new cathedral here, completed in 1077, as a monumental piece of propaganda presenting the Normans' justification for their invasion of England. Functioning like an early comic strip, it tells its story with great narrative drive, but most fascinating are the incidental details of 11th-century life that appear along the way—scenes of shipbuilding and farming, mythological scenes, sailors hitching up their tunics as they jump on to a beach, the English shown with long red moustaches, just as they still are in Astérix books. The tapestry is nowadays excellently presented in the **Centre Guillaume le Conquérant** (*open mid-May–mid-Sept, daily, 9am–7pm; mid-Mar–mid-May, mid-Sept–mid-Oct, 9am–12.30pm, 2–6.30pm; mid-Oct–mid-Mar, 9.30am–12.30pm, 2–6pm; adm 30F*), a former seminary, easy to find in the centre of Bayeux. A visit will take two and a half hours, if not more. It includes an audiovisual display, a film, shown alternately in French and English, and an extensive exhibition on the historical background. It might seem a lot, but it is imaginatively and attractively done, and leaves you fully informed by the time you actually reach the tapestry, where an earphone commentary will take you through it scene-by-scene.

As you leave the Tapestry Centre, a turn right or left in front of you will take you into the narrow streets of old Bayeux, remarkably unscathed in 1944 due to the town being liberated one day after the invasion. Veer right, and you will come to the long main street that's the spine of the old town, called rue St-Jean at this point and by different names at others. Along it there are several fine old houses, and at the far end, in place St-Patrice, there is a good market on Saturdays. Back in the centre, a turn down rue Cousinier will take you to Bishop

work on the land, from the Bayeux tapestry

Odo's **cathedral**, home of the tapestry for centuries. It has been added to many times since the 1070s, but the massive mainly original nave is still a beautiful work of classic Norman architecture. Just as fine is the crypt, with some wonderful frescoes of angels from the same time, and the delicate tomb of a 15th-century canon. And, outside the cathedral, look out too for the 16th-century half-timbered house opposite on rue du Bienvenu, which has some great carvings on the upper storeys, including a very coy-looking Adam and a more provocative Eve on either side of the Serpent entwined around a tree.

Bayeux is also the site of the largest British war cemetery in Normandy, and, just opposite, is the **Musée-Mémorial de la Bataille de Normandie** (*open mid-Mar–May, Sept–mid-Oct, daily, 9.30am–12.30pm, 2–6.30pm; June–Aug, daily, 9am–7pm; mid-Oct–mid-Mar, daily, 10am–12.30pm, 2–6pm; adm 30F, 12F 10–18s; free under-10s*) There are war museums of all sizes and for different tastes in Normandy—a full list can be found on leaflets provided at tourist offices, and a special discount pass is available, a good investment if you're considering visiting several. Either of the two largest can provide an overview. Conventional militaria enthusiasts and those with a more immediate interest in the Normandy campaign itself may find most interesting the Bayeux museum, which has tanks, trucks, artillery, aeroplanes, all kinds of other equipment and any number of uniforms, arranged on sometimes slightly wobbly shop dummies, plus a hugely comprehensive display of newspaper cuttings and other material that, if you take time to read it all, enables you to follow the campaign almost day-by-day. As in many of the similarly traditional smaller museums, all these military accessories can fade into a blur for the uninitiated, although in amongst it all there are still personal details and items that cut through to the quick, such as the various pieces of paper which infromed the family of Canadian airman James Lanfranchi that he wouldn't be coming home. Again, a visit to the museum can easily take two hours.

In contrast, the Caen **Mémorial-Musée pour la Paix** (*open Sept–May, daily, 9am–7pm; June–Aug, daily, 9am–9pm; closed 25 Dec, 1–15 Jan; adm 63F, 55F 10–18s, over-60s; free under-10s*) is a state-of-the-art facility opened only in 1988, a sculptural slab of a building with a gash for an entrance to recall the violence of war, in a beautifully landscaped park on the north side of the Caen *périphérique* ring road (so that it's not necessary to go into the city to visit it). Its different sections are often highly imaginative, strongly visual mixed-media displays as much as traditional museum exhibits, with a strong sense of drama, and the visit culminates with an hour-long, three-screen film centred on the Normandy battles. The Mémorial also seeks to present a global picture of the causes of the war from 1918, the political and social background, and life at the time. A full visit to the Mémorial, including the film will require over two hours.

To see the D-Day coast itself, maybe after visiting one of the main museums, it's best to start at one end. Just off the Caen-Ouistreham road at **Bénouville** is the **Pegasus Bridge** over the Caen Canal, taken by the British 6th Airborne Division at midnight on 5th June 1944. Like many Normandy sites it all seems very peaceful, especially with a gentle breeze across the water and the canal dredger quietly chugging away. In a scrubby, brambly field at the Ranville end of the bridge the places where the paratroops' gliders landed, remarkably close to the target, are precisely marked; across the bridge is the Café Gondrée, the 'First House Liberated in France', where the Gondrée family have been dispensing hospitality to British veterans ever since, and which is now itself almost as much a museum as a bar. There's also the small official **Musée des Troupes Aéroportées** (*open mid-Mar–May, Sept–mid-Oct, daily, 9.30am–12.30pm, 2–6pm; June, daily, 9.30am–12.30pm, 2–7pm; July–Aug, daily, 9am–7pm; closed mid-Oct–mid-Mar; adm 17F, 12F 10–18s*). A son-et-lumière is presented nightly at the bridge between April and October.

At **Ouistreham** the road turns west along the beaches of the Côte de Nacre, now popular with windsurfers and lined with holiday homes, some quite grand, others much more modest, between the centres of the small seaside towns. Sand spreads inland along the sides of many of the streets, kids pad around barefoot, and there are plenty of bars and snack stands with *moules-frites* and shops offering freshly-caught *tourteaux* and *homards*. Every so often the seafront is interrupted by a tank set in concrete, with a plaque. **Luc-sur-Mer** is a little more substantial than most of the other towns, with a large, glossy modernised casino dominating the front, and a thalassotherapy centre that's a lot cheaper than Deauville's; at **St-Aubin-sur-Mer** the casino is more modest, but has a striking Art Deco-style mosaic façade, perhaps a sign of former glory. **Courseulles**, meanwhile, is a more modern resort, with a pretty yacht marina. From here, if by this point it's lunchtime, it's a quick drive inland to Crépon.

Beyond Courseulles the holiday cottages thin out, and lush meadows grazed by brown and white Normandy cows come right down to meet the beaches. A few kilometres further on, though, is one of the most visited points along the coast, **Arromanches**, still ringed, like so many giant, peculiarly angular beached whales, by several of the huge concrete and iron blocks of the Mulberry harbour, the entirely artificial port created here to supply the landing forces. For a few weeks the busiest port in the world, Arromanches is otherwise an attractive small beach town, with two main war-related exhibits, the **Musée du Débarquement** (*open Sept–mid-May, daily, 9–11.30am, 2–5.30pm; mid-May–Aug, daily, 9am–6.30pm; closed first three weeks Jan; adm 30F, 25F over-60s, 15F under-14s*); and **Arromanches 360**, a high-impact film show using a 360° wrap-around screen (*shows Oct–Easter, daily, 10.10am–4.40pm; Easter–Sept, daily, 9.10am–6.40pm; adm 20F, 17F under-12s*).

West of here the cliffs rise rapidly, while the main coast road cuts inland through hedgerows and small, quiet villages that don't feel as if they're near the sea, although for walkers the GR261 footpath keeps mainly to the cliff edge. Atop the cliffs at **Longues-sur-Mer** are the bunkers of the last of the German batteries along this coast that still has its guns in place, battered and rusting and pointing impotently into the sky. It's also a very beautiful place, with paths surrounded by heather and blackberries, and superb views out to sea and along the shoreline.

Port-en-Bessin is, unlike most towns in this area, a working fishing port, with a real harbour and a good market on Sundays; it's also the location of one of the oddest of the Normandy museums, the private **Musée des Epaves Sous-marines du Débarquement** (*open May, daily, 9am–noon, 2–7pm; June–Sept, daily, 9am–7pm; closed Oct–April; adm 30F, 10F under-18s*). Since 1968 owner Jacques Lemonchois has had the sole concession from the French government to salvage all the various kinds of scrap metal sunk off the Normandy coast, and the 'Museum of Wrecks from the Landings' is in effect his yard. There are whole tanks, ships' turbines, guns, plates and all kinds of smaller items such as coat hooks, razors and old pennies from sunken ships, all rusted a uniform brown. It has a strangely ghoulish feel, more so than the other museums. Beyond Port-en-Bessin the road reaches Colleville, St-Laurent and Vierville (all 'sur-Mer'), now signposted to the world as **Omaha Beach**. The US invasion force lost over 1000 men here, more than on any of the other beaches. It's actually a very fine, open stretch of sand lined with just a few bars and beach houses, although not many people seem to use it as such. The **Musée Omaha** (*open Mar–June, Sept–Oct, daily, 9.30am–12.30pm, 2.30–6.30pm; July–Aug, daily, 9.30am–7pm; closed Nov–Feb; adm 20F, 10F under-18s*), is privately run and a little tatty, but has some details such as toothbrushes, Army-issue condoms and the US soldiers' guide to France, with all of 40 pages.

On the cliffs above Omaha is the **American Cemetery** (*open 9am–6pm daily*), a transplanted piece of American monumental architecture, finely landscaped and with some of the most sharply trimmed lawns and flower beds you'll ever see. Nearly 10,000 of the US dead from France and Belgium were brought together in this one huge plot, an eloquent demonstration of the sheer scale of the loss. Just west again is **Pointe du Hoc**, where Colonel James Rudder and his US 2nd Ranger Battalion scaled the cliffs in a few minutes flat on the morning of D-Day in an attempt to silence a German battery on top, and now American territory, ceded as a memorial. Although the landscape remains pitted and cratered, it's now a beautiful, tranquil place, with yellow sandstone cliffs above a small rocky beach where gulls and waders pick for shellfish, and from where you can watch a fine sunset over the Cotentin peninsula.

Seafood on the Rocks

Oysters, mussels, prawns, clams and lobster, and fish such as sole, sea bass and monkfish, are the most renowned produce of the northeast Cotentin, the rugged coastline that winds round from Cherbourg to meet the flatlands and beaches of the central Normandy coast. The ports around the coast have traditionally had their special assets: lobsters at Barfleur, or oysters, renowned for their unique, vaguely nutty flavour, at St-Vaast-la-Hougue.

The old fishing harbours of the area are small and full of character, built of granite like the rest of the tip of the Cotentin, grey and severe when the weather sets in, brighter when the sun appears. Their airy tranquillity and relaxed pace belies their proximity to bustling Cherbourg only a few miles away.

Between the villages the shoreline is a succession of rocky headlands, cliffs and crags, interrupted by beautiful little coves and a few fine beaches, with excellent walks and views along the way. Inland, the countryside becomes surprisingly leafy and lush, with rich pastures and pockets of thick woodland, producing vegetables, beef and hams that, while less well-

known than the local fish and seafood, are also of very high quality. There are plenty of places to sample the area's specialities. For a truly memorable display of local produce, though, make your way to the Moderne in Barfleur, an easygoing, unassuming hotel where M. Evrard Le Roulier prepares food with a superb combination of quality of ingredients, attention to detail, skill and a notable inventiveness.

getting there

Barfleur is easy to reach on the straight D901 road direct from Cherbourg (27km), or from the south on the D902 via Quettehou. The town forms an arc around the surprisingly large harbour, with one broad main street, rue Thomas-Becket, which you will inevitably come on to whether you arrive from Cherbourg or the south. About halfway down on the right, looking towards the sea, there is a side street with a large *boulangerie-pâtisserie* on the corner: turn up this street and in about 200 metres you will come to the Hôtel Moderne.

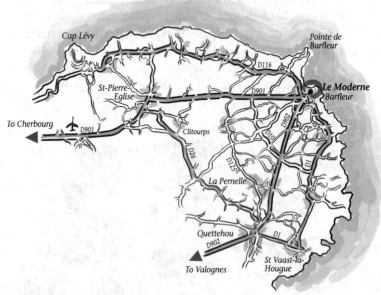

Le Moderne

Restaurant-Hôtel Moderne, 1 place Charles de Gaulle, 50760 Barfleur,
© 33.23.12.44. Open April–Sept, daily, noon–2pm, 7–9pm; Oct–Mar, Mon,
Thurs–Sun only, noon–2pm, 7–9pm; closed 15 Jan–15 Mar. Book weekends.
Menus at 85F (Mon–Fri only), 110F (Mon, Thur, Fri midday only), 134F,
183F; carte *average 200F.*

From the outside, the Moderne looks just as a well-established small French harbour-town hotel should look, with an outside terrace and a Mansard roof. Once inside, through a round hallway which has a touch of Art Deco and the odd fishtank, the dining room is light, bright and airy, with a few pictures of Norman coastal scenes around the walls. The atmosphere is comfortable, but not at all stuffy. While M. Le Roulier is at work in the kitchen, his wife is in charge front-of-house and chats away with the many locals and regulars, who at weekends slip behind the tables with complete familiarity and give the restaurant a distinctly homelike feel.

The menu promises *une cuisine traditionelle*, but M. Le Roulier makes many distinctive departures of his own. The care taken to create the wonderful, crunchy home-baked *pain de campagne* and the home-made terrines and desserts equally may once have been traditional, but is certainly not routine.

Once you'd been here a few times you would probably try some of this *charcuterie maison* for a first course, but on an initial visit it has to be the seafood: on the 134F menu, St-Vaast oysters, or *crevettes de la côte*, a superlative plate of plainly boiled local prawns with more of that great home-baked bread, as simple as they could be. Around you, fellow prawn-eaters set about their plates with an interesting variety of styles: some set their heads down to tear off shells with resolute determination; others take them one at a time, with several pauses for breath, in which case downing the whole plate can take a while—not that anyone will hurry you along. The 183F menu, meanwhile, offers a magnificent *cocktails de fruits de mer gratinés*, mussels, crayfish, clams, scallops, oysters and other delights in a light, spicy gratin that beautifully enhances the flavours of the seafood.

When the starters have finally been sent on their way, some diners don bibs to engage in the ritual of consuming the local lobster, in which case the beasts of the day are brought to your table still kicking, for you to have an informed discussion on their qualities and make your choice. More original, less hands-on but equally spectacular are dishes included in the menus, such as, from the 183F, M. Le Roulier's *brochette de lotte*, fine pieces of monkfish wrapped in English bacon and cooked in a cider vinegar sauce. Equally non-traditional in Normandy, from the 134F menu, are the excellent *cassoulet* and another house speciality, the magnificent *choucroute de poisson*. Alsatian *choucroute*, like its parent German *sauerkraut*, can sometimes be all acid, but it's not remotely so here. It's delicately buttery, and surrounded by an orgy of smoked salmon, fresh salmon, two kinds of white fish (perhaps sea bass and monkfish), mussels and an oyster, all in a superb *beurre blanc*.

To help it along there's plenty of refreshing cold Muscadet, for around 90F a bottle. Another leisurely pause precedes the usual Norman cheese course, and home-made desserts such as a light crème caramel, or *millefeuille* with a fresh *coulis de framboises*. M. Le Roulier emerges to make his customary tour of the tables a little after 2pm, to catch up on local conversation and receive the thanks of all present.

Brochette de Lotte

(Serves 8)

1.5kg/3 ¼lb monkfish fillets
8 bacon rashers, cut into 32 strips
2 onions, peeled and sliced into rounds
olive oil
200ml/7fl oz fish stock
4 tablespoons cider vinegar
250ml/8fl oz crème fraîche
salt and pepper

Slice the monkfish into 32 cubes of about
4cm/1½". Wrap each one in a strip of bacon,
and then thread on to 8 skewers, 4 to each
skewer, alternating the fish with the onion slices.
Brown the kebabs very quickly in some oil in a hot
frying pan until golden. Lay the kebabs side by side in an ovenproof dish.

Thoroughly mix together the fish stock, cider vinegar and crème fraîche,
and season to taste. Pour the sauce around the kebabs without covering
them. Place in a hot oven at 180° C/350°F (gas mark 4) for about 10 min-
utes or until the fish is just cooked, and serve immediately.

touring around

Largest of the northeast Cotentin ports is **St-Vaast-la-Hougue** (from
Cherbourg, take the D26 road south from the D901, through the rich,
green countryside of the Val de Saire). It's a broad, attractive harbour,
with plenty of bars and restaurants around the waterfront, and in the
centre of the view an eccentric 19th-century Mariners' Chapel and
imposing granite lighthouse. There's still a sizeable fishing trade, and
a good general market on Saturdays. The famous **oyster beds** are just
south of the town, and offer visits and tastings on some days in July
and August (*by reservation only; for information contact tourist office*). St-
Vaast also has a marina that's well patronised by both the French and
British yachting communities, and there are generally several sails
running up and down outside the harbour. South of the port a narrow
spit of land runs down to La Hougue point and the dramatic pile of
Fort de la Hougue, a military installation closed to the public,
looking as if it rises straight out of the sea. On either side of the spit
there are coves and beaches which, weather and tides permitting, are
good for paddling around or even swimming.

The seas offshore were the scene of a famous naval encounter, the
battle of La Hougue, a clash that gave rise to France's own nautical
Charge of the Light Brigade. In 1692 Louis XIV hatched a plan for his
greatest Admiral, Tourville, to sail with his squadron from Brest, rendezvous with reinforcements from the Mediterranean, pick up 30,000
mostly Irish soldiers encamped at St-Vaast and carry them across the

Channel before the English and Dutch fleets could join together to oppose him. Once there, in association with English Jacobite plotters, they would restore James II to the British throne. However, bad weather prevented the French Mediterranean fleet from making its way up the coast; Tourville calculated that the same winds would make it much easier for the Anglo-Dutch fleet to join forces, and pointed this out to his superiors, but was told not to question the King's orders. Once the Admiral had set sail, Louis received news that, as predicted, the Allied fleet had made their rendezvous, and that the Jacobite conspiracy in England was no more than a damp squib. A fast boat was sent to call Tourville back, but failed to find him in the bad weather. On 29 May 1692, Tourville with his 44 ships rounded Barfleur point, to find an Anglo-Dutch fleet of 100 ships in front of him. In a scene that seems pure romantic literature, the French commanders all agreed that the only sensible course was to turn back to Brest; however, Tourville read them the King's orders to engage the enemy, they accepted they had no choice, and then continued to sail onwards, to the amazement of their opponents. To everyone's still greater astonishment, in the fighting that lasted the rest of the day the French actually came off slightly the better. During that night and the following day, though, part of the French fleet was scattered by the winds, while the rest took refuge in the harbours of the Cotentin, where there was no protected naval port, a shortage often lamented by French admirals. The English fleet were able to sail into St-Vaast and set fire to many of Tourville's best ships, ending any possibility of a French invasion in support of James II.

Following the battle, somewhat after the horse had bolted, Marshal Vauban was sent to St-Vaast to build defences at Fort de la Hougue and on the low green island of **Tatihou**, which looms in the background of the harbour of St-Vaast and adds much to the interest of the view. Since 1992, the island has been open to the public, and is now one of the most attractive places to visit around the coast. You get there by amphibious vehicle, tickets for which are bought at *Accueil Tatihou* on the quay in St-Vaast (*crossings May–Sept, daily, 10am–12.30pm, 2–5pm; Oct–April Sat, Sun only; tickets 50F return; 25F under-10s*). If you're going on to Barfleur for lunch, arrive early, and note that it's advisable to book in midsummer.

As well as a chance to wander around one of the largest and most complete of Vauban's many fortresses, Tatihou offers an engaging range of other things to do. There's a maritime museum, centred around artefacts, from weapons to plates, recovered from ships sunk in the 1692 battle, and a workshop that builds and restores traditional Norman fishing craft; also, each summer the island hosts an imaginative series of temporary exhibitions, theatrical shows, festivals and concerts. One of its primary permanent attractions is that, since the island was kept isolated by the military for centuries, most of it is a pristine expanse of grassy moorland, rocks and dunes, great for walking and a conservation area especially rich in sea birds such as cormorants, terns and gulls.

North of St-Vaast there is a pretty road that runs right along the shore to Jonville and the Pointe de Saire, past some more good beaches. Inland from here, just across the D902 road about halfway between St-Vaast and Barfleur, is one of the Cotentin's most renowned beauty spots, the remarkable village of **La Pernelle**. Its main street improbably runs almost straight up a near sheer-sided ridge to a little granite church at the top; from alongside there are limitless views, eulogised by a whole host of local literati, over the Cotentin, down the coast and out to sea. They also naturally attracted the attention of the Germans, who installed an observation post, which is still there, and a long-dismantled gun battery that in June 1944 caused considerable trouble to the US troops landing at Utah Beach, 30 kilometres to the south. Nowadays there's also a very pleasant bar-restaurant, should you wish to study the view at a leisured pace.

Barfleur itself is a charming, uncommercial little granite fishing port that's noticeably less busy than St-Vaast, even though there's usually a fair number of yachts and dinghies sharing space with the fishing boats in the harbour. There's rarely much traffic to disturb the people chatting in the middle of the street, but part-way round the apparently unnecessarily wide arc of the waterfront there's an attractive quayside café, the Café de France, where you can take in the activity after lunch. A squat 17th-century church dominates the vista at the end of the harbour, next to the tiny beach amid the rocks where some brave souls occasionally take to the waters.

Owing to its treacherous rocks. Barfleur does have the distinction of possessing France's oldest lifeboat station, opened in 1865, and one of its tallest lighthouses, on **Pointe de Barfleur**. You reach the point through the interesting old village of **Gatteville-le-Phare**, with a huge open square and a fine, monumental church with a twelfth-century tower, which as so often with Norman churches looks more like a fortress than anything else. Gatteville is also the jumping-off point for the GR223 footpath, which can take you via perhaps a bus-ride through Cherbourg all the way round the Cap de la Hague on the other side of the Cotentin and down to Avranches. Barfleur lighthouse is, like all the Cotentin lights, an impressively stark monument in an isolated, wind-blasted spot, where the air can clear most headaches, and which is also popular with adventurous fishermen. Extraordinarily tall and thin, the lighthouse is usually open to visitors, but may be closed for security reasons. There is one step up for every day of the year, and those who reach the top are rewarded with wonderful seascapes and views, on a good day, round the peninsula from La Hague and down to Grandcamp at the mouth of the Vire.

From Barfleur point, if you're in a hurry to get to Cherbourg, you can cut back on to the D901 and be there in not much over twenty minutes. More entertaining, though, is the winding D116 west from Gatteville. The road runs a little inland, through tiny, close-clustered villages between hedges and still-narrower side lanes, with every so often some more beautiful views of rocky inlets between cliffs. Just past halfway there's a turn off to the right to **Cap Lévy**, another point that's a great place for a windswept walk.

West of Cap Lévy you enter the Bay of Cherbourg, first seen to full advantage at **Pointe du Brulay**. Just below it is **Anse du Brick**, a little seaside resort in its own right, where the coast opens up to leave a well-sized beach that's popular with surfers and can be packed in summer. Perched on the cliffs above there's a selection of bars and restaurants, all with the same great view. West again, and the road runs straight into Cherbourg through a string of little towns each with their own *plage*, where the city's residents and a good number of visitors take to the sands on hot July weekends.

The Restaurant at the End of the World

La Hague peninsula is a 15-mile arm of granite reaching out into the sea west of Cherbourg. From the edge of the city's harbour, you enter a world of increasingly narrow lanes sometimes virtually enclosed by towering hedgerows, and then opening up into bog and moorland running right to the rim of the massive cliffs that fall away into the surf. Intermittently, you come across little stone villages, huddled against the weather, that look as if they might house communities of Celtic Methodists were it not for the stout old Norman Catholic churches in the middle of each of them. In the centre of the peninsula, meanwhile, in valleys and corners sheltered from the wind, there are microclimates that are surprisingly lush and leafy. La Hague is exceptionally beautiful when the sun shines, when the wild flowers are in bloom along the cliffs and you can watch the changing colours of the sea below; it's also a romantic and wild place to visit even if the weather is less favourable, when giant waves crash against the rocks and the Atlantic blasters are enough to clear anyone's head.

At the very end of the peninsula, where the landscape is at its most rugged, there is a little rocky inlet, long a refuge for

Auberge de Goury

endangered mariners, with a lighthouse that looks exactly how a lighthouse ought to look. This is Goury. There is a lifeboat station, a shingle beach, a few boats, six or seven houses and, sometimes, a van selling sandwiches. There's also a seemingly unnecessarily large tourist office, for the cape can attract its share of visitors in summer. Still, it is the sense of isolation that predominates, and this seems an unlikely location for a fine-quality restaurant. However, at the centre of the clutch of grey granite cottages is the Auberge de Goury, chiefly offering, as the sign says, 'Spécialités de Mer'. Here, owner M. Retout has presided since the end of the 70s with amiable hyperactivity, throwing out rapid snatches of conversation to regulars in between attending to some of the cooking and much else. The style is casual and straightforward, but devotees often make their way here all the way from Cherbourg and beyond just for midweek lunch. When the weather's fine, you can sit outside and eat while watching the waves; at other times, when the wind is up, stout stone walls and the smell of the log fire, on which the Auberge's superlative grilled fish is prepared, make you feel snug and sheltered, so you can revel in the sensation of eating so well in a place once considered one of the ends of the known world.

getting there

There is a relatively quick route from Cherbourg to the end of La Hague, along the D901, which runs along the south side of the peninsula and will take you there in about half an hour to 45 minutes. To make a trip of it, though, take the much smaller D45 road, a right turn off the D910 on the way out of Cherbourg in Hameau-de-la-Mer (signposted to Querqueville), and then return by the south route. For most of its length the D45 winds along the north side of La Hague, with a few hairpin bends along the way. Most people will want to stop at least at a few points along the road, but if you drive down it directly you should reach the Cape in a little under an hour. Both roads meet in Auderville, where on one side

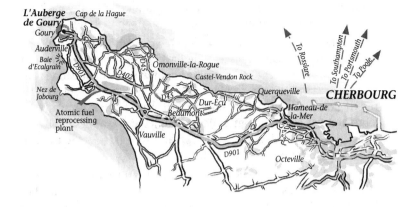

of the widening of the roads that could be called the village square there is a narrow lane signposted to Goury.

Alternatively, the energetic should know that the long-distance footpath GR223 also runs all the way round La Hague peninsula, keeping to the edge. It's clearly marked, and those who take it all the way should certainly be hungry by the time they get to Goury.

L'Auberge de Goury

L'Auberge de Goury, Port de Goury, 50440 Auderville, ☎ 33.52.77.01. Open 5 Mar–1 Nov, daily, noon–2pm, 7–9.30pm; 2 Nov–4 Mar, noon–2pm only. Book a day in advance, more for weekends. Menus at 85F, 110F, 135F, 180F, 260F, 280F, 305F; carte average 180F.

The menu at Goury carries a little note which, as well as informing you about luminaries such as Bertrand Tavernier, Jean-Claude Brialy and others who have passed through here, extols the virtues of patience and a willingness to wait in order to get the best out of your food. This could be seen by suspicious souls as a pre-emptive strike, but it seems only fair to view it more generously as a reflection of the attention to detail shown in the individual preparation of each dish— plus one other consideration: some of this food takes a fair while to eat. If there is any delay, it's as well to accept the offer of, maybe, a glass of champagne and a plate of *crevettes grises*, and stand at the little wooden bar for a few minutes while examining the décor, your fellow diners, and the lobsters and crabs manoeuvring in their tank.

The restaurant is comfortably characterful and traditional, but without any forced attempts at a 'heritage' image—parts that are genuinely old, such as the main dining room with its plain stone walls and open fireplace, are recognisably so, while others, such as the recent extension, are simple and modern. The clientele, similarly, are a broad mix—a few foreigners, local couples and families of all ages, and during the week groups of workmates who have obviously converged upon it from miles around.

If you eat just one course here, it has to be the grilled fish (perhaps red mullet, sea bass, sole, turbot or monkfish, according to what's best locally that day), cooked by M. Retout himself on the wood fire in the main dining room. Tinged with subtle flavours from the woodsmoke, it's a revelation of how good simply but perfectly cooked fresh food can be. He uses mainly chestnut and hazel for the fire, and complains that it's increasingly difficult to find wood of sufficient quality, but fortunately seems to be assured of a supply for some time to come. There's some grilled fish (often tuna) and a selection of smoked fish among the choices in the 85F four-course menu, while the 110F *menu du terroir* offers grilled lamb, as well as crab mayonnaise; if you can, though, make a day of it and go for the 135F *menu gourmand*. For one thing, even with fluctuations in exchange rates it's still an incredibly good deal; for another, there are few more relaxed places in which to come to terms with the concept of a five-course meal.

There are several choices for first course, but the star must be the *assiette de fruits de mer*, a giant pile made up of oysters, mussels, prawns, langoustines, half a large crab, *bulots* (large whelks), *bigorneaux* (sea snails) and other things you may never have seen before. This edges you into the meal gradually by forcing you to take your time and get to grips with your food, literally. Once you've finished, it's time to sample the grilled fish, or try the *feuilleté* of monkfish or a fishy *surprise du jour*, which might be a superb bowl of *moules à la crème*, the sauce alone delicious enough to be offered separately as a soup.

mussels

After that the meat course might be expected to come as a bit of a let-down, but the grilled lamb that's a fixture on the menu, cooked on the other side of the fire from the fish, is a first-quality slice of meat, and as an alternative there's a meat dish of the day that might be an excellent version of a Norman classic such as *jambon au cidre*, with strong, salty ham and a rich sauce. This is also the stage where those feeling the absence of greenery get some vegetables, and some *frites*.

The final stages are just as much high points of the Auberge. In a region where competition is not exactly lacking, M. Retout also has an especially excellent cheese selection, with good, powerful Rincette and a great rich *chèvre* as well as fine examples of all the more usual Norman standards such as Camembert and Pont-l'Evêque. The palate thus dried a little, there's still one more house favourite to come, one of the range of sometimes fairly alcoholic Norman apple or pear desserts, or maybe just a sorbet or the rather eggy *crème brûlée*, before you finish up well into the afternoon with a good strong coffee.

The more expensive menus mainly feature lobster, hence the price. To drink, there's a reasonably priced wine list, with a good Saumur at 75F and Muscadet at 65F that both go excellently with the fish. All this might seem a very *grande bouffe* indeed, but each course is so well executed, and presented at such a comfortable pace, that you never feel weighed down. And, as you contemplate what you've enjoyed, you're unlikely to feel any need to eat again that day.

Douillon aux Pommes

The Douillon Normand is one of the simplest of the region's many classic fruit desserts, which can equally be made with pears (a douillon aux poires). For each person, take a large green apple, core it, and wrap it entirely in puff pastry; brush with beaten egg, place on a baking sheet and put in a hot oven, 200°C/400°F (gas mark 6), and cook for 30 minutes or until the pastry is golden and the apples are tender (test with a skewer). Once cooked, serve them quickly on top of crème fraîche sprinkled with sugar, and, just before serving, add some apple compôte mixed with a dash of Calvados to the top of each douillon.

touring around

The greatest glory of La Hague is the scenery. As you travel west along its northern flank you begin to get dramatic views over the sea from the fern- and heather-covered cliffs, while in between the road snakes back inland around abrupt narrow bends encased by dense hedgerows. Those who don't want to take on the whole of the coastal footpath can still walk along it for a kilometre or so, as access to it is well indicated at several points along the D45 with the sign 'Sentier littoral'. A favourite walk, reachable via Gréville-Hague and Gruchy, is the one out to the viewpoint opposite **Castel-Vendon**, a giant rock standing just offshore.

La Hague was also one of the areas of strongest Viking settlement in Normandy, and most of the place-names ending in -ville indicate villages founded by Norse chieftains (Querqueville, 'Koki's ville', Auderville, 'Odern's ville', and so on). In **Querqueville**, almost before you have properly left Cherbourg and with a great view back across the harbour, there is the tiny, 10th-century, pre-Romanesque **Chapelle de St-Germain**, possibly the oldest church or chapel anywhere in western France and almost certainly the oldest still in use. It's a beautifully plain, simple little building with bare rough-stone walls, almost hidden in the shadow of the larger later village church. A little to the west there is a turning for the mainly 16th-century château of **Nacqueville**, a fine combination of French Renaissance château style and local granite that once belonged to the de Tocqueville family (*guided tours only, Easter–30 Sept, Mon, Wed, Thur, Sat, Sun, every hour 2–5pm*). It stands in one of the peninsula's sheltered valleys, and has a luxuriant, partly English-style landscaped garden that explodes into flower in May. Further west again, but not open to the public, there looms beside the road the much older manor of **Dur-Ecu**, a massive, turreted granite pile that looks as if it could easily have been designed for a movie of an Edgar Allan Poe story starring Vincent Price.

The peninsula may feel remote today, but nevertheless it has played its part in *la vie française*. **Gréville-Hague**, in a loop in the D45 away from the coast, was the birthplace of Jean-François Millet, and he painted its squat, typically Norman stone church several times before moving on to his more familiar themes of peasant life in the Seine valley. **Omonville-la-Petite**, almost lost in another protected valley and so exceptionally lush and pretty, was the last home of one of the great figures of modern French culture, the poet Jacques Prévert, author of *Paroles*, fixture on French A-level syllabuses, and of the scripts for many of the classics of the golden age of French cinema such as *Le Crime de Monsieur Lange, Le Jour se lève* and *Les Enfants du paradis*. He died here in 1977, and his widow stayed on in their house, a pretty cottage with an exuberant garden, until her own death in 1993, since when it has been opened up as the **Maison de Jacques Prévert** (*open Easter–end Oct, daily, 2–6pm; adm 10–20F*). Visitors must park next to the village churchyard, where both Préverts and their daughter Michelle are buried, and then walk up a quiet lane. Rather than a display of Prévert effects, much of the house has been made into an exhibition space that each year hosts a single exhibition devoted to a related theme or one or another of his activities or acquaintances. The subject for 1996 will be his close friend Miró, who visited here several times, and the museum's director says that, given the range of Prévert's contacts and interests, they have material for several years yet. There is also a video and many photographs of Prévert, which allow us the conclusion that he shared with Jean Gabin the distinction of having perfected the well-known French technique of talking, eating and generally living with a cigarette clamped permanently in one side of the mouth at a 45-degree angle. Sometimes a tape plays, of Yves Montand singing another Prévert creation, *Les Feuilles d'Automne,* for which he wrote the lyrics, and the evocation of a certain period of French life couldn't be more complete.

Omonville-la-Rogue, actually some way from la-Petite, is an attractive little fishing port. Here the road rejoins the coast, and from here west the terrain loses much of its leafiness and becomes much more wind-blasted and moor-like. Before reaching Saint-Germain-les-Vaux and Auderville near the Cape the road comes upon tiny **Port Racine**, an inlet of grey shingle with a few boats usually tied up that a sign proclaims to be '*le plus petit port de France*'. This claim doesn't seem to have been arrived at in any scientific manner, but since there are only two reasonably substantial buildings in the place, one of them a hotel, nobody's likely to argue.

The coastline on the south side of La Hague is less inhabited and more open than the north, with sweeping bays of giant cliffs above empty, sandy beaches. From Goury, take a sharp turn off the D901 road in Auderville, signposted to Ecalgrain and Jobourg. This will take you to the viewpoint overlooking the **Baie d'Ecalgrain**, a magnificent arc of sand and surf, and then to the **Nez de Jobourg**, at 128 metres often described as the tallest cliffs in Europe. From both points you can easily see Alderney on a clear day. Again, there are plenty of opportunities for walking along the GR223 footpath.

After you rejoin the main road at Jobourg village it soon becomes surprisingly wider and newer. This indicates that you are about to pass the truly vast bulk of the **Beaumont-La Hague atomic fuel reprocessing plant**, one of the symbols of official France's notorious modern love affair with all things nuclear. As in all such installations, they're falling over themselves to invite the public in to have a look around, and anyone interested will find leaflets at all local tourist offices. From Beaumont, the only town on the peninsula, you can continue on the D901 straight back to Cherbourg, or turn south on to the D318 for another wonderful open bay, the **Anse de Vauville**, where there are miles of cliffs and sand dunes, a bird sanctuary (*guided tours only, contact local tourist offices for details*), an unusual, semi-tropical botanical garden in Vauville village (**Château de Vauville**, *open May–Oct, Tues, Sun only, 2–8pm, July–Aug Sat also; adm 30F*), and, at the south end, beaches where it's actually suggested you should swim or windsurf as well as just watch the breakers.

In the Normandy *Bocage*

The *bocage* country of Normandy stretches across the Cotentin peninsula and much of western Calvados and the Orne, a countryside of innumerable villages, solid stone houses, small, scattered farms and fields separated by giant stone-bottomed hedgerows, all spread over rolling hills between patches of thick woodland. The fields are rarely more than a hundred yards wide, and at times so small that their grass becomes almost invisible between the hedges.

Abbey of Hambye

The word '*bocage*' is probably best known in English to those with an interest in the Second World War, for this is also the countryside that caused such utter misery to the US Army following the D-Day landings, when the region's trademark hedgerows gave the Germans ready-made defences that had to be taken one by one. For just one example, if you drive down the Cotentin from Cherbourg and take the main D900 road between La Haye-du-Puits and Lessay, which will require about fifteen minutes, it's a sharp thought to consider that it took the American 8th Corps eight days to get down this same stretch of road in July 1944, at a loss of 5000 casualties. It takes a real leap of the imagination to conceive of these horrors here today, when the hedges are picturesque instead of threatening and an absolute calm pervades the countryside.

The southern Cotentin, inland from Coutances and Avranches, is one of the most beautiful parts of the *bocage*. The beech woods are denser and more extensive, and the broader hills further north give way to steep inclines along lush, neat little valleys, with a web of tiny lanes that wind along and across them, sometimes meeting each other, sometimes not, begging you to lose your way and then catching you by surprise with an idyllic view as you come round a hill. In the early Middle Ages, when most of the region was still covered by forest, several monasteries were founded here.

Today, also, this is one of the best areas in Normandy to sample farm ciders and other traditional foods and crafts. Cheese, for once, is not foremost among the region's products, but there are plenty of small cider producers that welcome visitors, and the Cotentin's ham, duck, lamb, beef and their derivatives are renowned.

And, when it comes to exploring the very French concept that food is always better at source, where better than an *auberge du terroir*, officially recognised as serving only local produce. The welcoming Auberge du Mesnil-Rogues occupies a straightforward granite building, with a small bar by the door and the restaurant just beyond, and had the distinction of being the only French village *auberge* 'officially twinned' with an English village pub, an arrangement that only lapsed because of a change of landlord at the English end. Presided over by the aptly named Joseph Cotentin, who, it's fair to say, looks as if he well enjoys his food himself, the Auberge is dedicated to presenting country produce at its best.

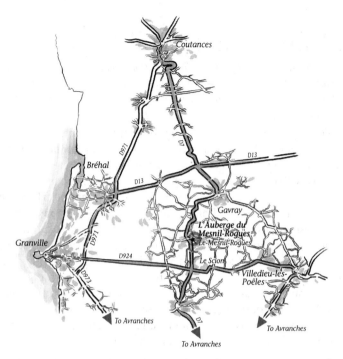

getting there

The main roads from Cherbourg southwards meet at Coutances, to divide again just south of the town; take the turning off to the left, the D7 inland, signposted to Gavray and Villedieu. At Gavray, in the Valley of the Sienne, the D7 veers to the southwest, and runs through a pretty stretch of rolling bends. After about five kilometres, look out for the turn for Le Mesnil-Rogues off to the left—it's quite well signposted, with both the village name and a sign for the *auberge du terroir*, but it's a sharp, narrow turn and easy to pass by. In the village, a short way from the main road, it is on the other hand impossible to miss the Auberge, right by the roadside.

If you're approaching from the south, the turn off from the D7 is less abrupt, to the right about two kilometres north of the cross-roads at Le Scion.

L'Auberge du Mesnil-Rogues

Auberge du Mesnil-Rogues, 50450 Le Mesnil-Rogues, © 33.61.37.12. Open Easter–15 Sept, daily, noon–3pm, 7–9pm; 16 Sept–Easter closed Tues, Wed. Book a day in advance, more for weekends. Menus at 50F, 65F, 80F, 100F, 135F, 140F, 160F; children's menu 40F; carte average 150F.

The centrepiece of the main dining room at the Auberge is the massive old, distinctly manorial stone fireplace, which Mme Cotentin passes every so often to check on the meat grilling there over beech logs—every Friday a whole ham is slowly spit-roasted there, ready for the night's specials of *jambon façon York cuit à la broche*. There's no deliberate rusticity here, though, for this is something to which few French restaurants aspire; the rest of the room is perhaps surprisingly neat and smart, with striped and flowery wallpaper, pretty tablecloths and flowers on the tables, and there's a large additional dining room that's positively ornate, but which regularly fills up with big, noisy family groups for Sunday lunch. This is a family restaurant in more ways than one—outside, across a small garden, there's a very well-equipped play area, with slides and climbing frames, and requests for high chairs and other infant accessories are happily answered.

An *auberge du terroir* this may be, but this doesn't mean the food here is unsophisticated. M. Cotentin worked for several years around the Paris region before returning to his particular *terroir*, and as well as Norman tradition there are very well-developed skills evident in his cooking. His range of menus, provide an opportunity to sample them for an exceptionally reasonable outlay. There's also a shortish but satisfying wine list, with a Gros Point Bordeaux red for around 80F that's an excellent match for the meats.

Among the starters, as well as salads and local river fish there are plenty of home-made terrines and *foie gras*—try the *foie gras de canard chaud* from the 160F menu, with a texture both creamy and truffle-ish, and served in a rich raspberry vinegar. *Plats* for main courses include several variations on duck, lamb and pork, often with Norman cider, cream or cheese sauces, and fish dishes such as an admired *fumé de poisson*, but serious carnivores will rarely wish to let by the chance to try the grilled meats. The *pavé de daguet* (young venison, from the Orne near

Argentan) is a truly succulent slab of meat, with a subtle, smoky flavour and none of the coarseness of some game, served with a *sauce poivrade* that demands to be called lip-smacking. And then there's the *pavé de filet de bœuf grillé*. There's *steack-frites* and *steack-frites*, and this is of the definitive kind. The English are well-known in French restaurants for liking their meat well- (meaning over-) done, to the extent that at times the French just assume this is what you want. In this case, though, overcome prejudices and request it *saignant* or even *bleu*. Meat of this quality scarcely needs any cooking at all, and to have it burnt dry really is an awful waste. Between mouthfuls, roll your tongue around a *frite*, and wonder how a humble chip can be so delicate.

After some Livarot from the excellent cheeseboard, desserts present a difficult choice. If you're looking for comfort food there's an excellent *teurgoule*, the Norman rice pudding, with fine cinnamon flavours and a thick, crispy crust on top. It's hard, though, to miss out on the *coupe normande*, a fabulously fresh and fragrant apple sorbet soaked in Calvados—one of the great ice-cream experiences. At the end of the meal M. Cotentin emerges from his kitchen to tour the tables with a very genuine beaming smile, and the congratulations are certainly deserved.

Magret de Canard, Sauce Camembert

(Serves 4)

150g/5oz Camembert
4 duck breasts
200ml/7fl oz sweet white wine
150g/5oz crème fraîche
salt and pepper

Remove the rind from the Camembert and cut the cheese into 1cm/½" cubes.

With a small knife, lightly score the skin of the duck breasts in a criss-cross pattern to allow them to open up while cooking. Just before cooking, season with salt and pepper.

Take a cast-iron casserole dish, or a very heavy frying pan; preheat it dry. Then, when the pan is very hot, lay the duck breasts in it, with the skin side downwards. The heat will immediately melt the fat; lift the breasts up gently so that it can penetrate underneath. Cook this side for 5–7 minutes, making sure that the skin doesn't get too brown (and do not prick the meat). Then turn the duck breasts over and cook on the other side for 4–5 minutes. Transfer the breasts to a plate, skin side downwards, to keep warm.

To make the sauce, pour off the fat from the pan, and then put it back on the heat. Pour in the white wine and bring to the boil, stirring to scrape up the sediment from the base of the pan, and then add the Camembert. Allow it to melt, and then add the crème fraîche. Reduce the mixture until it reaches the desired consistency. Taste, and add seasoning if required.

Serve the duck breasts whole or in slices, with the sauce poured around.

touring around

If you're coming from Cherbourg on the D2 road, via Lessay, turn off to the right just north of Coutances in the village of Peley for the semi-ruined château of **Gratot**. With its pepperpot turrets, massive granite walls and moat that in places is well wide enough to be called a small lake, it looks just like a picture-book, fairy-tale idea of a castle, and indeed it comes with its very own fairy story.

The main part of the château is 14th-century, although additions continued to be made until the 18th. Gratot was the stronghold of the Argouges clan, the most celebrated of whom was the maverick Chevalier Jean d'Argouges, who played a double game in the Hundred Years' War and won eternal opprobrium in France by handing over Granville to the English for hard cash. The story refers to a local fairy who supposedly agreed to become mortal and marry an Argouges, on condition that he never mentioned death in her presence. They lived together blissfully happy for ten years, until one night she was taking an inordinately long time getting ready for a banquet, whereupon the flatfooted Chevalier stumped upstairs and asked if she was waiting until they were all dead: his fairy wife then slipped out the window, and this Argouges was left to weep away his life alone. Sceptics may be unimpressed, but the castle's peculiar 'Fairy Tower' (*Tour à la Fée*), with one rectangular room atop an almost round tower, is undeniably an ideal site for such a tale.

The last scion of the Argouges, a humble artillery captain, sold his château in 1777. Gratot then passed through various owners, but was still occupied, as a farm, at the beginning of this century. A wedding was due to be held there in 1914, when part of the roof fell in on the banqueting tables, fortunately before the guests had arrived. This finally convinced the last owner to give it up as a bad job. By 1968 it was entirely derelict, when restoration was begun by local volunteers. Today Gratot is a self-service castle: you can wander round it even when unattended, and are asked to leave a contribution (*15F adults, 10F 10–18s*) in an honesty box. The restoration group also provide dossiers in different languages, which in true French didactic style go on at great and sometimes infuriating length about philosophy, our relationship to the past and so on and so forth, in between giving pieces of useful information. Gratot is now used fairly frequently as a venue for festivals and other cultural events in summer. On other days, though, when you may well have it to yourself except for stray cats and the ducks in the moat, it has a mistily romantic aura.

Continue south, skirting Coutances, and another 20km along the D7 will take you into the Valley of the Sienne. At Lengronne, on the north side of the main valley, a turn off to the left (D13) leads towards one of the region's best-known monuments, the ruined Benedictine **Abbaye de Hambye** (*open Mon, Wed–Sun, 10am–noon, 2–6pm; closed Tues and 15 Dec–31 Jan; guided tours 10–11.30am, 2–5.30pm; adm 20F, 15F 7–18s*), looming lichen-clad above the trees. Founded in 1145 by Guillaume de Paynel, Lord of Hambye, and much-favoured by Henry II of England and Normandy, it was still occupied until the Revolution, after which it was plundered by locals for stone and rapidly fell into dereliction. Nevertheless, though battered and roofless, the abbey church still stands as one of the finest examples of Norman Gothic in the soaring simplicity of its unusually tall, narrow arches and its massive tower, still improbably perched almost intact on top of the giant arches, a full 100 feet above the nave.

Other monastic buildings are even more intact. The Monks' Parlour has a remarkable 13th-century decorated ceiling, painted very simply with flowers, while the kitchen has a truly magnificent giant fireplace; the Chapter House, virtually undamaged, is similar in shape and vaulting to that in Norwich, with which Hambye had close links during the Middle Ages. Guided tours of the abbey, in French only, last from an hour to an hour and a half; non-French speakers must tag along with an information sheet in English or other languages. You can wander around on your own, but note that if you do you will not have access to many interesting parts of the abbey, such as the Chapter House and the Parlour, viewable only with the tour (this is not made clear at the entrance, and the admission charge is the same).

From Hambye a string of lanes leads back westwards up hill and down dale towards Gavray and Le Mesnil-Rogues. Around you there are plenty of opportunities to taste cider and local produce. On a bend in the road in the tiny village of **La Baleine** is the Andouillerie de la Vallée de la Sienne, dedicated to producing high-quality examples of the Norman versions of those strong gut and offal sausages the English are supposed to shy away from, *andouilles* and *andouillettes*, by entirely traditional methods, smoking them over forest woods. This is one of the food and craft establishments on the Manche tourist board's *Route de la Table*; visit four or more of them and you qualify for a *cadeau surprise* of goodies (details from all tourist offices). For charcuterie enthusiasts, guided tours of the *andouillerie* are offered every day except Sunday in July and August (*adm 5F*); the shop is open daily except Monday throughout the year. In **Le Mesnil-Rogues** itself, meanwhile, look for the farm La Pinotière, which has good strong *chèvre*.

After lunch, perhaps, turn back from the Auberge in Le Mesnil-Rogues toward the main D7 road and go straight across it on to the little narrow road downhill to **La Meurdraquière**, site of two fine cider producers, their driveways on either side of a crossroads like bookends. The Cotentin ciders, though still nothing like rough cider, are in general a little drier and not quite so smooth as those from the Pays d'Auge; the best time to try them is from April to August, for the region's cider farmers are small producers, and may well have sold their stock by September, although most will have some sweet *cidre nouveau* on sale in the weeks before Christmas, and Calvados is available at all times. In La Meurdraquière, the Ferme de la Grenterie has an impressive cider shed dating from 1689, while if you wander into La Butte across the way M. Roland Venisse—who, unusually, generally does have some cider in stock all year round—will bluffly leave his apple-crusher to open up his shed and sit at a massive log table with you while you try out his especially fine *brut* cider and fairly ferocious Calvados. Both farms also offer *chambres d'hôtes*, for a 24-hour rural retreat. Also in La Meurdraquière there is another farm, La Percehaye, specialising in beekeeping and offering a range of farmhouse honeys.

A little south-west of La Meurdraquière, well signposted off the main D924 Granville road near St-Jean-des-Champs, is the **Ferme de la Hermitière** (another stop on the *Route de la Table*), one of the larger cider farms in the area, although still a place where no one except the odd goose may show much reaction when you drive into the yard. As well as its different products for sale—cider, unfermented apple juice, Calvados, Pommeau (an aperitif of cider and Calvados combined) and excellent, not overly-sweet *poiré* (pear cider)—owner Jean-Luc Coulombier offers guided tours of the centuries-old farm, its orchards, still and cider presses, with a video (shown in English on request) on cider-making and a year in the life of the farm. There's also a small cider museum and a play area, and the tours end, naturally enough, with a tasting of the product (*tours Easter–30 June, 2–6pm only; July–Aug, Mon–Sat, 10am–noon, 1.30–6pm, Sept, Mon–Fri only; adm 15F, free under-14s; open for sales all year*).

From La Hermitière, presuming you've had enough cider-tasting, look for the road, a little way east towards Villedieu on the south side of the main road, signed for St-Jean-des-Champs and the Abbaye de la Lucerne. This seems almost deliberately deceptive, for having got you on to this leaf-shrouded lane the authorities then omit to place any more signs to the abbey. It's best to accept the occasional false turning, appreciate the scenery, and try to follow the signs for St-Léger. Then, just when you think you're totally lost, you roll around a hill and there, nestling in a wood-clad valley like a medieval monastic vision, is the **Abbaye de la Lucerne d'Outremer** (*open Mon, Wed–Sun, 9am–noon, 2–6.30pm; closed Tues and 1 Jan–15 Feb; adm 20F, 10F 7–14s*).

La Lucerne is less well-known than Hambye (very possibly because it's harder to find), but, if you want to visit only one of the Cotentin's ruined abbeys, this should be it. It's more atmospheric, and you're left to wander around it on your own; it's also slightly less of a ruin, having survived better the post-Revolutionary destruction, and a good deal of restoration work having been undertaken in the last thirty years. The Choir especially has been restored, as has its superb 1780 organ, and is regularly used for services and organ concerts. A Gregorian Mass is performed there every Sunday at 11am, by a local choir.

The abbey's subtitle '*d'Outremer*' stems from its persistent loyalty during the Middle Ages 'across the sea', to England. In 1204, when King Philip Augustus of France seized control of the Duchy of Normandy, the monks of La Lucerne remained stubbornly loyal to their former duke, King John, in opposition to the French ecclesiastical stronghold of Mont St-Michel. Later, moreover, when the English reappeared in the area during the Hundred Years' War, the abbey again offered them its allegiance, providing a chaplain for Edward III. However, this did not prevent it later becoming one of the largest religious houses in France, and remaining so right up until dissolution in 1791.

The main church was built between 1164 and 1178. Given that by this time Notre-Dame in Paris and the other great works of early French Gothic were under construction to the east the style is remarkably simple and conservative, an unadorned Norman Romanesque little changed since the Conqueror's time; the thought occurs whether in the 12th century there was already in the Anglo-Norman establishment some tendency dead set against new-fangled architectural modernism. Even so, the building's very plainness gives it strength, and alongside the church, and only recently opened to visitors, there is a fine, slightly later and more Gothic Chapter House, above an impressive 12th-century vaulted cellar. And, in its valley the abbey seems always close to water: at the back of the church there is a small aqueduct, built in the 1800s when La Lucerne was briefly used as a textile mill, and alongside there is a near lake-sized pond, separating the main buildings from the 18th-century Bishops' Palace. This is now a private house, and visitors are asked not to go too close, but there doesn't seem to be any problem in sampling the religious experience of sitting by the pond side for a while on a sunny afternoon, allowing any recent food and drink intake to settle down peaceably while contemplating the ducks.

East of La Lucerne is the capital of the southern *bocage*, **Villedieu-les-Poêles**. The 'City-of-God-of-the-Cooking-Pots' is so-called because since the 12th century the town has been singlemindedly dedicated to the working of copper, pewter and other metals. It became so because in the 1100s Henry I of England gave the town to the Knights of St John, with trading privileges that encouraged industry; at the same time, the surrounding *bocage* was for centuries poor and overpopulated, and unemployed farm boys flocked into Villedieu to work in the metal trades and other crafts that developed there.

The stone and slate medieval town is charming and classically pretty, with an architectural style of its own. It is centred on one long main street along a ridge, called place de la République at the lower end and then narrowing into rue Général Huard, with narrow alleyways running away on either side into the courtyards of the old copper-workers' homes and workshops. It's also much visited, with shops selling copper, kitchenware and other local craft products almost end-to-end along the main street.

The town has several museums and open workshops to showcase its trades, notably the **Fonderie des Cloches**, rue du Pont-Chignon, one of the last completely traditional bell-foundries in Europe (*tours Tues–Sat, 8am–noon, 2–5.30pm; 15 Jun–31 Aug Mon also; adm 12F, 10F under-14s*), the **Atelier du Cuivre**, 54, rue Général Huard (*open mid-Sept–mid-June, Tues–Sat, 9am–noon, 2–6.30pm; mid-June–mid-Sept daily; adm 15F, 10F 10–16s*) and the **Musée de la Poêlerie et de la Dentelle** (Museum of Copperworking and Lacemaking, the latter formerly carried on by the town's women while the men worked the metal), in a fine 18th-century copper-workers' courtyard at 25 rue Général Huard (*open Easter–31 Oct only, daily, 10am–noon, 2–6.30pm; closed mornings Tues; adm 15F, 5F under-14s*). Between them they combine displays on the history of their crafts (and videos, today apparently obligatory in exhibits of this kind in France) with opportunities to see work in progress in an industry that's still kept very much alive using entirely hand-crafted techniques. And, if you know anyone who likes copper pots, this is of course the perfect place for gift buying. What's more, to help you the town, mindful of the possibilities for tat in such a souvenir magnet, has actually introduced an *appellation contrôlée* for genuine Villedieu copperware.

On the Bay of Mont St-Michel

In southwestern Normandy, all routes and eyes seem to converge on the extraordinary giant pinnacle of Mont St-Michel. Like a natural extension of the tiny rock on which it stands, the abbey can be seen towering above the surrounding empty wastes of sand and water from all angles, whether first seen sharply outlined from miles away on a clear day, or dimly glimpsed in silhouette through mists and the not-infrequent rain. First built to embody a particularly intense ideal of Christianity, it can still suggest a celestial vision against the sky. Even the giant arc of the bay itself seems to have been created as a great amphitheatre for the glory of the Abbey.

The *Merveille de l'Occident*, the 'Wonder of the Western World', as it has been known for centuries, is also France's greatest tourist attraction outside Paris. Pilgrims have been flocking here for well over a thousand years, and when people began to travel for pure pleasure in the last century it immediately became an obligatory stop for the first modern tourists.

mont saint michel

Consequently, as with the Vatican, St Mark's in Venice or any other site that's beyond mere fame, to see Mont St-Michel is usually to see it together with hundreds of other people. This can be disheartening, and to avoid the maximum crowds it's advisable to visit in spring, autumn or even atmospheric winter rather than high summer. However, one aspect of the holy mountain is that, for all its arch-familiarity, the more you know about it, the more extraordinary it becomes. The abbey looks astonishing from a distance but is truly staggering from close up.

And all around it is the bay, a mysterious expanse of constantly shifting sands, channels and salt marshes, known for its unpredictable weather, where the horizon sometimes seems infinitely far away to the west. It has the longest, deepest tides in Europe, with the sea a full fifteen kilometres away at low tide. This immense flatness contains an abundance of birds and shellfish, while the marshes around the bay's edge are used to graze the much-prized *pré-salé* or salt-marsh lamb.

A century ago Henry James and other luminaries who made their way to Mont St-Michel slept and ate at the hotel of Mère Poulard, sampling her famous omelettes (with *crème fraîche* whipped into the eggs). You can still eat there today, but meals on the mount rarely justify the restaurants' inflated charges. For a meal that doesn't disappoint (and that's also vastly better value), it's much better to make for the Auberge de la Selune at Ducey, only 15km from the rock, a very comfortable small hotel with exceptional, sophisticated cuisine.

getting there

All roads from Cherbourg and the Caen area converge at Avranches to form the N175, a motorway-standard road that sweeps around the Bay of Mont St-Michel into Brittany. South of Avranches, just past the Second World War museum, turn off on to the D103, signposted to St-Quentin-sur-le-Homme, for a more

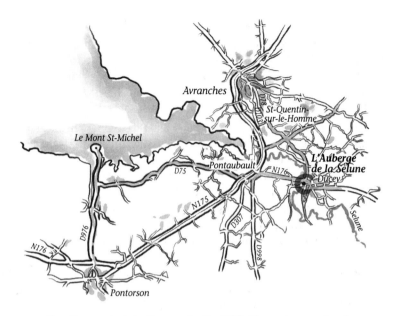

attractive route into Ducey via the D78. If you are coming from Avranches town, follow the signs to Mont St-Michel as far as the monument to General Patton, where the D78 to Ducey and St-Hilaire-du-Harcouët turns off to the left. In Ducey, the Auberge is just on the right immediately after the main crossroads. If you are coming from St-Malo or Mont St-Michel itself, turn off the N175 at Pontaubault on to the N176 for Ducey. Turn right immediately after crossing the river bridge into the town, and, again, the hotel is easy to see on the right.

L'Auberge de la Selune

Auberge de la Selune, 2 rue St-Germain, 50220 Ducey, ✆ 33.48.53.62.
Open Mar–Sept, daily, noon–3.30pm, 7–8.30pm; Oct–Feb, Tues–Sun only.
Booking advisable. Menus at 75, 115, 150, 190F; carte average 160F.

The Auberge stands on the banks of the River Selune, which before it gets lost in the Bay of Mont St-Michel is a fast-flowing river known for its salmon and trout. It looks entirely like a traditional four-square French country hotel from a distance, but under owners Josette and

Jean-Pierre Girres it has been renovated from top to bottom in the smartly modern/traditional style preferred in French hotels, with a light pastel dining room adorned with plenty of fresh flowers. Through the reception area you can also see the very pretty garden alongside the river, winner of an award for the best kept, *plus fleuri* hotel garden in Normandy. In summer, there are tables outside.

You might expect a small-town hotel like this to offer reliable, enjoyable regional food, with no great culinary departures. But, Jean-Pierre Girres will surprise you: his menus do include local standards such as salmon *béarnaise*, but he also introduces original, refined dishes of his own. Meals here are also exceptionally well-priced, above all the 115F menu, offering a range of dishes every bit as sophisticated as the more expensive lists. A star dish among the first courses on this menu is distinctly English in inspiration, the *pie au crabe* or crab pie, a great combination of fresh crab, shallots and other vegetables in pastry with a delicate *beurre blanc*. Alternatively, for something light and refreshing, try the salad of langoustines, the shellfish small and superbly flavoured, served with a salad of lettuce, avocado and raw mushrooms. There is also a *gâteau d'aubergine* with a red pepper coulis, an interesting dish that's remarkable for a French restaurant, as you realise halfway through, in that it's entirely vegetarian.

The generous list of main courses makes choice difficult. One of Jean-Pierre Girres' specialities, stuffed saddle of rabbit in cider vinegar, is a superbly rich, fruity yet subtle creation that shows off local ingredients to perfection. The rabbit is stuffed with a mixture of veal, pork, mushrooms and shallots, which, with the cider vinegar glaze, creates an entirely new flavour distinct from any of its constituent parts. Just as fine is the *truite soufflée à la Ducéenne*, a fascinating, complex dish in which delicate aromas of chives and tarragon appear under the classic Norman flavours of cider, butter and superbly fresh fish. Some of the salmon and trout served in the restaurant have been not only cooked but also caught by M. Girres, a keen fisherman who will organise fishing trips for hotel guests.

The cheeseboard, also part of the menu, is well-stocked, with good St-Paulin as well as Norman cheeses. Then, just as you are pondering how the main courses might have been put together, there arrive desserts that show the same inventiveness, delicacy and attention to detail, above all the spectacular *mousse de rhubarbe glacée au coulis de framboises*. The idea of rhubarb mousse may never have occurred to you up to now, but in the face of this wonderfully refreshing mix of flavours all memories of sticky puddings with thick custard fade away into the dim distance.

Truite Soufflée à la Ducéenne

(Serves 8)

8 salmon trout, each approx 180g/6 ½oz
parsley for garnish

For the stuffing:

500g/1lb salmon fillets
120ml/4fl oz crème fraîche
120g/4oz softened unsalted butter
5 eggs
handful of mixed fresh herbs, such as chives, chervil, parsley, tarragon
2 dessert apples, peeled, cored and very finely diced
100ml/3 ½fl oz Calvados

For the sauce:

100g/3 ½oz carrots, finely diced
100g/3 ½oz onions, finely diced
100g/3 ½oz button mushrooms, finely diced
250ml/8fl oz crème fraîche
500ml/16fl oz cider
100g/3 ½oz chilled unsalted butter
4 tablespoons Calvados

Dress and clean the trout, making an incision into the left side to extract the bone.

To make the stuffing, chop the salmon in a food processor, pass through a very fine sieve, add the eggs, cream and butter and whisk it into a mousseline. Put the apples in a frying pan and flambé in the Calvados. Let cool, and fold these and the chopped herbs into the mousseline. Season to taste, and then spoon the mousseline inside each trout.

Sweat the carrots, onions and mushrooms in a pan in 25g/1oz butter until soft. Spread them over the bottom of an ovenproof dish, and then lay the trout on top. Add the cider, and place in an oven, 190°C/375°F (gas mark 5) for about 20 minutes or until the fish is cooked through. Remove the trout and keep warm. Strain off the juices from the dish into a saucepan, and boil hard to reduce by about two-thirds. Stir in the crème fraîche, allow it to reduce again to the desired consistency, and then whisk in the remaining butter in small pieces a few at a time until the sauce is glossy. Just before serving, add the last amount of Calvados.

To serve, garnish with the chopped parsley.

---

touring around

The city of **Avranches** sits atop a clutch of giant granite hills that on one side fall away almost precipitously down to the great flat plain of the Bay of Mont St-Michel. Its history is inextricably bound up with that of the Mount. According to medieval manuscripts, in the year 708 the Archangel Michael appeared to Saint Aubert, Bishop of Avranches, and commanded him to build a shrine on what was then just a rocky outcrop covered in trees in the middle of the bay. Aubert, evidently an early rationalist despite his saintly status, dismissed this as a dream, and what's more did so again when Michael came a second time. The third time the angry Archangel gave him a sharp prod in the side of the head, and so the Bishop, duly called to attention, built the first small oratory on the Mount. The 19th-century church of **St-Gervais** in Avranches contains as its greatest relic the skull of Saint Aubert, with a small hole supposedly left by the Archangel's finger. When the belligerent Normans adopted Christianity in the 10th century, the warrior saint Michael, who fought the Devil sword in hand leaping from rock to rock, held a particular attraction with his obvious similarity to the old Norse gods, and his shrine became an object of special veneration and pilgrimage.

Also in Avranches is the **Plate-forme**, the small square where in 1172, at the instigation of Robert de Torigni, Bishop of Avranches and Abbot of Mont St-Michel, Henry II of England and Normandy knelt for a whole day dressed only in his shirt in penance for the murder of Thomas à Becket. This is also a vantage point from where, coming from the north, you have the first spectacular views out across the Bay, and of Mont St-Michel itself at its centre.

The **Mairie** (*open 15 June–Sept, daily, 10am–noon, 2–6pm; closed Tues in June only; adm 12F*) of Avranches contains a matchless treasure, the library of Mont St-Michel, saved from the abbey during the Revolution. A selection of its superb illuminated manuscripts, some of the finest in the world, is put on display each summer.

It's well worth exploring the villages along the bay west of Avranches, **Le Gué de l'Epine** and, north of the River Sée, **St-Léonard**, **Le Grand-Port** and **Genêts**. Along the shore the paths between the villages are beautifully peaceful, with sheep grazing in the salt marshes and the shifting horizons of the bay away in the distance; and a contemplation of the extraordinary, misty silhouette of Mont St-Michel, ever-present, is as important an experience as a tour of the abbey buildings, especially at sunset, when you can well imagine medieval pilgrims thinking they had come within the presence of the divine. At Genêts is the **Maison de la Baie**, a mine of information on local wildlife and nature which from May to October also organises walks across to the Mount at low tide. This is a journey which on no account should be attempted without a guide: legends abound about the giant tides and quicksands of the bay.

From the bay's shore, if you are making this journey in a day, you are well placed to get to Ducey for lunch. Afterwards, follow the road back to Pontaubault and take the D43 for **Mont St-Michel**. As the road winds across the flat, marshy fields, the abbey appears like a lodestar, sometimes hidden from view, at others re-emerging suddenly around a bend in the hedgerows.

As you finally come up to the causeway to the Mount you are reminded with a thump that you are entering one of the world's great tourist sites, as the base of the causeway resembles an American small-town motel strip, with ranks of shiny new hotels, petrol stations, souvenir shops and fast-throughput restaurants. Apparently it was ever thus: in the *Roman du Mont St-Michel*, written some time around 1160–1180, the monk Guillaume de St-Pair describes the annual

October main pilgrimage for the Feast of St Michael, when huge crowds converged on the bay from all directions, in procession with musicians, and bringing their livestock. All along the routes to the Mount, there were tents with entertainments, and vendors selling wines, cakes and every other kind of food: '*De totes parz aveit a vendre / Assez en out qui ad que tendre.*' ('On every side there were things for sale/They had plenty enough, those who had the means to pay.').

After this you then come on to the causeway proper, undeniably one of the greatest approaches in the world, with the Mount towering ever larger at the far end. Drivers are obliged to stop short of the rock and turn into one of the causeway car parks; if you are staying overnight on the Mount, resist any suggestions to do otherwise and continue to car park 1, nearest the entrance. From there a very narrow walkway leads to the first gate in the 15th-century ramparts, and the tourist office. Carry on through the massive **Porte du Roi**, the very model of a medieval citadel, into Mont St-Michel's only real street, the **Grande Rue**, which winds anti-clockwise around the rock. Tourist office literature optimistically refers to the shopkeepers of the Grande Rue 'maintaining a tradition born in catering to pilgrims in the Middle Ages'. This means in effect that they have been peddling junk for centuries. Apart from tat by the ton it is possible to find some quite good, if expensive, craft jewellery and ceramics, mostly in the shops away from the main street along the ramparts.

Mont St-Michel is proud of still being officially a town, with a Mairie in the former Governors' residence above the Porte du Roi, even though its permanent population is less than a hundred. As well as the abbey it has some other museums and exhibits, none of them especially impressive. Most respectable are the **Logis Tiphaine** (*open mid-Mar–mid-Nov, daily, 9am–6pm; April–Sept 9am–6.30pm; adm 20F*), a 14th-century house that once belonged to the wife of Bertrand du Guesclin, French hero of the Hundred Years' War, with some period furniture, and the **Musée Maritime**, with exhibits on the development of the bay itself. The **Archéoscope** is a multimedia show on the history of the Mount, and silliest by far is the **Musée Grévin**, a branch of the Paris wax museum (*museums and Archéoscope open mid-Feb–mid-Nov, daily, 9am–7pm; adm 45F; joint ticket available for all three museums, and the Abbey*). More interesting is the town itself. Although the Grande Rue can seem Disneyfied, it is real, an extraordinary image of a medieval street that's only a few feet wide for much of its length, with remarkably tall half-timbered gables apparently impossibly narrow and close together. About halfway up on the right is the St-Pierre, one of the more pleasent hôtel-restaurants on the street, if you wish to eat on the rock. Away from the Grand Rue, the town is a fascinating labyrinth of passageways, stairways and ramparts.

The Grande Rue eventually winds up and round into the Grand Degré or great staircase up to the **abbey**. Maupassant wrote that from different angles Mont St-Michel can look like either a cathedral or a fortress. It has also been called France's Pyramid, and has distinct similarities to the Potala Palace in Tibet. Vast quantities of granite were brought across the water from the Chausey islands to build it; if nothing else it was an astonishing feat of structural engineering in an era when only very simple tools were available, and no one knows how many of its builders died at their work. Neglected after the 16th century, the Mount was rediscovered and venerated by Romantics such as Châteaubriand and Hugo, and from there entered the universal Gothic imagination. Particularly striking are the abbey's proportions—some walls and windows are enormous beyond expectation, while other rooms are quite intimate.

The abbey is a complex building in which rooms and wings from different periods and styles are all intertwined, making it impossible to look at in chronological order. St Aubert's oratory was succeeded by the first substantial church on the rock in the early 10th century, but building work really accelerated after the Benedictines took over the Mount and founded an abbey in 966. The main church was begun in 1017 by Abbot Hildebert, and the most important parts were completed in 1058, under William the Conqueror. One of the greatest periods for the abbey was the late 12th century, under Robert de Torigni, who made it a major centre for the production of manuscripts and altered and extended the buildings in a Gothic-Transition style.

Part of the legend of Mont St-Michel is that it has never been captured in war. This really only applies to strictly non-French armies, for in 1204, when Philip Augustus of France was struggling to wrest Normandy from King John, Breton soldiers allied to the French King took the Mount and severely damaged it in a fire. In atonement the

King commissioned an entire new wing on the north side of the Mount, the masterpiece of high Gothic known as the *Merveille* or Marvel. In return, Mont St-Michel became a bastion of French power in Normandy, and later resisted the English throughout the Hundred Years' War. Alterations were still being made to the buildings up until the 18th century, but the abbey was closed and badly damaged during the Revolution. It was made into a prison, remaining so until it became one of France's first national monuments in 1874.

It is theoretically possible to visit the **abbey** (*open May–Sept, daily, 9am–5.30pm; Oct–April, Mon–Sat, 10am–4pm, Sun, public holidays, 9.30am–4.30pm; adm 36F; 23F 18–25s; 10F 12–17s; free under-11s*) without a guide, but note that if you do so you will find many sections closed to you. Mont St-Michel is, in any case, very difficult for first-time visitors to find their way round alone, and so it's worthwhile following the official tours (*for no extra charge, and in different languages*). The basic tour lasts about an hour, but still does not visit all of the abbey; extended tours are also available by appointment (*56F*). Since 1966, Millennium of the Abbey, there has again been a token religious presence on the Mount, currently consisting of three monks and one nun. Mass is held in the church every day at 12.15pm, and they also organise retreats.

When you finally reach the top of the Grand Degré, you emerge via another gatehouse on to the Western Platform, with a fine view of the bay across to Cancale, and where the guides begin their tours. Immediately surprising is the fact that the **abbey church** has a plain neoclassical façade, dating only from the 1770s. It once had a massive Gothic-Transition frontage designed by Robert de Torigni, but like his cathedral in Avranches this was structurally not all it should have been. It began to crumble in the 1300s, and when it finally fell beyond repair in the 18th century it took with it three of the seven arches of Abbot Hildebert's original 11th-century nave. Inside the church, though, you are immediately made aware of the extraordinary, mystical ambition of the abbey's builders. It was not built *against* the Mount, but *on top* of it, with the peak of the original rock precisely beneath the centre of the church's cross, so that the whole thing is actually a cathedral suspended in the air. Around the centre, and still immovable, are Hildebert's original four massive columns, the basis of the whole structure. They, and the remaining arches of the nave, form a classic of severe, plain Norman Romanesque. The choir, on the other hand, is in a light, graceful *Flamboyant*-Gothic style, completed only in 1521, and built after the original choir had also given way, in the 15th century. The church thus contains both the first and final phases of medieval architecture.

The tour route runs in a rough spiral downwards, broadly following the way the abbey was conceived, with the church at its apex, the monastic and official apartments below and rooms for the reception of poor pilgrims at the bottom. On the same level as the church is one of the most beautiful and famous parts of the *Merveille*, the wonderful Cloister from 1218–28, another monument suspended in space with sheer walls beneath it on two sides. In the middle there is now a large sculpture of a book in a glass case, a typical Mitterrand-era combination of the revered and the contemporary. The Cloister leads to the **Refectory** from the same period, famed for the complex diffusion of light through its windows. Today, like the church, it can appear very austere and granite-grey, but colour is the one major feature of the abbey that is now entirely missing: the main halls of Mont St-Michel were large precisely because the abbots entertained exalted guests so frequently, and they and the church would have been decorated throughout with frescoes, tiles and tapestries in lavish hues.

As you descend, the intricacy with which rooms lead into one another is constantly surprising. Beneath the Cloister is the rib-vaulted **Promenoir** from 1115, one of the finest examples in existence of the Romanesque-Gothic transition. It was built as a place for Monks to take exercise, but was also used as a refectory before the building of the one above, and Robert de Torigni entertained Henry II, Eleanor of Aquitaine and their court here in 1158. Beyond that is the mysteriously atmospheric crypt of the **Gros Piliers** or 'Great Pillars', a thicket of giant granite columns. Look up through a little hole in the centre of the ceiling and you suddenly realise you are underneath the choir of the church, which the crypt was built to reinforce.

The most elegant room in the abbey is the **Guests' Hall**, part of the Gothic *Merveille*, with one row of delicate columns down the centre. Here, late-medieval French kings were received on their visits to the abbey. The contemporary **Knights' Hall**, on the other hand, is much larger and more massive. Despite its name it was most usually the main working room of the abbey, where the monks copied manuscripts, with two giant fireplaces to keep them warm. The last room visited on the main tour is the mixed 12th and 13th-century **Almonry** below, where charity was distributed to poor pilgrims, and which now contains a bookshop.

After leaving the abbey buildings, walk around the windblown gardens on the north side of the Mount, a great place from which to look at the bay and especially admire the truly giant outside walls of the abbey, supported on buttresses that seem to soar up hundreds of feet out of the rock. You can also see the most modern part of the whole complex, the spire, only completed in the 1890s as part of the French government's post-prison restoration work. Another thing to watch for from the gardens or the town ramparts, with which they connect, is the incoming tide. The speed of the tides in the bay, which so terrified medieval pilgrims, has been often compared to a galloping horse. It's more like a steady walk, but nevertheless the sight of the encroaching waters is spectacular, especially during the spring and autumn high tides. Tide tables are provided at the tourist office.

If at all possible (and you don't mind paying again) make every effort to return to the abbey at night for **Les Imaginaires** (*open June–late-Aug, daily, 10pm–1am, last admission midnight; late-Aug–Sept, 9pm–midnight, last admission 11pm; adm 60F; 35F 12-25s; free under-12s*), when its rooms are invidually lit in imaginative, subtle patterns, with different modern music in each one. It is of course much less crowded, and, best of all, you are free to wander at will, or stay for hours examining the shadows in one room if you wish. You can also see parts of the abbey not included in the main tour, notably **Notre-Dame-sous-Terre**, the wonderfully simple 10th-century first church of Mont St-Michel, which actually supports the nave of Hildebert's church. Some of the music used in *Les Imaginaires* is a bit of the Jean-Michel Jarre variety, but it's one of the best son-et-lumière presentations ever created, and an unforgettable way of experiencing the atmospheres of Mont St-Michel, despite all the exploitation down below, in all their mystic power.

Intra-Muros in St-Malo

St-Malo, with a walled city still at its centre, enjoys the most spectacular location of any of the ports along France's north coast. The old city looks almost as much a part of the sea as the land, its spires and giant ramparts filling completely a spit of earth jutting out into the Atlantic at the mouth of the River Rance. Around it, the eye follows surf breaking over a scattering of tiny rocky islands, across to the green banks on the other side of the estuary. Its life has inevitably been tied to the sea. Mariners from St-Malo, called *Malouins*, sailed to every corner of the earth: to Canada, the Indian Ocean and Polynesia—the French and Spanish names for the Falkland Islands, the *Malouines* or *Malvinas*, stem from the fact that they were first discovered by men from here. This was the home port of many of France's greatest explorers.

The *Malouins* were also known for their bellicose independence. When the Duchy of Brittany was still independent in the Middle Ages, St-Malo appealed to the authority of the Kings of France against their Duke; at other times, they did the same thing in reverse, and at one point in the 16th century announced that they were 'neither Frenchmen, nor Bretons' and declared an independent republic. The city was already notorious in the 13th century for its pirates, who demanded tribute from ships in the Channel, and for close on 200 years after the 1600s St-Malo carried on worldwide wars virtually all of its own against England, Holland, Portugal and any other challengers, through its legendary privateers, or Corsairs, whose names—Duguay-Trouin, Surcouf—crop up all over the city today as favourite sons. This privateering inevitably led to retaliation, and St-Malo was attacked several times by British and Dutch fleets. To resist them, small forts were built on many of the islands offshore.

Today, these forts and the ramparts still give the city something of the air of a bristling maritime stronghold. Inside, the atmosphere is now entirely peaceful, yet very individual. Within the walls of the old city, known as Intra-Muros, chasm-like narrow streets between tall granite houses open up into ample squares, lined with cafés. Outside, at the very foot of the ramparts, there are beaches that fill up with *Malouins* and visitors each summer. Miraculously restored after the Second World War, it's a city that has retained its old character but has a vigorous modern life, visible in its shops, markets, café life, theatres and festivals. Away from the walled city, there are the basins of the port and the broader streets of modern St-Malo, but also small wooded promontories and sheltered, rocky coves ideal for sailing.

In culinary matters, St-Malo, as might be expected, has always relied heavily on fish and seafood, and also shown an open-minded willingness to mix Breton tradition—*galettes*, mussels—with other elements from Normandy, the rest of France and further afield. Hence it's only fitting to eat here at the Marco Polo, a little restaurant tucked away in one of the cobbled streets Intra-Muros where a very able young chef offers light, imaginative variations on local cuisine incorporating an intriguing range of international influences.

getting there

Coming into St-Malo from anywhere inland, follow the signs for 'Centre-Ville', and more specifically Intra-Muros (the old city). From the ferry terminal for boats from Britain or the Channel Islands, turn left along Quai St-Louis, and the city walls are within easy walking distance. Either route will eventually bring you to Porte St-Vincent, the main entry for vehicles into the walled city. Just outside it is the tourist office and a large free parking area; drivers are well advised to use it, as parking inside the walls is heavily controlled, and expensive.

.alk through the gate, and you come directly into place Châteaubriand, the main square of the old city. Turn right to the end of the square and take the rue Châteaubriand, one of the most characteristic streets of the old town and the last turning out of the square on the left. The second turning off to the left is then rue de la Corne-de-Cerf, and the Marco Polo, identifiable by its bright green-painted frontage, is in front of you on the corner.

Marco Polo

Restaurant Marco Polo, 20 rue de la Corne-de-Cerf, 35400 St-Malo,
☎ 99.40.92.62. Open Sept–June, Tues–Sat, noon–2pm, 7.30–10.30pm;
July–Aug, daily, noon–2.30pm, 7.30–11.30pm; closed two weeks Jan. Book
dinner weekends. Menus at 65F (midday only), 95F; carte average 130F.

Inside, the Marco Polo is pretty and modern, painted in bright, fresh yellows and greens with starfish stencilled around the walls. The explorer theme is also reflected in photos of scenes from the Middle East, Africa, Latin America. The cushioned wicker chairs are extremely comfortable, and the quiet friendliness of Christine Barthe, who serves, adds equally to the charm of the place and its relaxed atmosphere.

Her husband Jean-Paul Barthe is local and largely self-taught as a chef, and so does things that might have been struck out as heretical by a graduate of a more traditional French kitchen education. His menus offer some international dishes—pasta, even a very fine apple crumble—and many of his own creation—the excellent salads and *assiettes*—as well as others from the recognisable Breton/Norman arsenal such as *moules à la crème* or *porc au cidre*. All, though, feature his own imaginative touches, often quite un-French combinations of fruit, fish, vegetables and meat. This is not a place to go to find pure local tradition, but an easygoing restaurant offering light, original food. It's also exceptional value, for not only do the menus offer a range of sophisticated dishes for under 100F, but exploration of the carte will, for once, be only a little more expensive.

He is particularly expert at marinades, seen to advantage in the range of delicately flavoured salads. From the *carte*, the *salade Marco Polo*—potatoes, tomatoes, peppers, cucumbers, shallots, haddock and *haricots de mer*—is beautifully done, and delightfully refreshing: every ingredient is perfectly fresh, but the stars have to be the salt haddock, wonderfully fishy but never acrid, the *haricots*, and the dressing, a complex, very original combination of fruit and herbs. The 95F menu offers fresh salmon subtly marinated in lime, a perfect modern dish. There are also a few vegetarian-friendly salads and first courses.

Main courses divide equally between meat and fish. The *émincé de porc, poivre et ail* features finely spiced cubes of meat, their flavour intermingling nicely with the garlic, served with melt-in-the-mouth homemade tagliatelle. Among the fish and seafood options is tagliatelle is served with mussels and basil, or there are also more conventional *assiettes* of local prawns or oysters. From the menu, try the *porc sauté au cidre*, with a more delicate variation on the traditional Norman cider sauce, and served with slices of apple and more of that excellent tagliatelle.

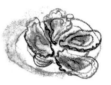

The wine list is shortish but to the point, with a good mix of Côtes du Rhône, Muscadet and Loire valley wines, again very reasonably priced. Save both time and space for the desserts, for they are another highlight of Jean-Paul Barthe's cooking. The list is substantial, making choice tantalising. A *croustillant de poires, miel et amande* is a crunchy purse of pastry filled with a perfectly blended mix of fruit and nuts, and served with a crème anglaise it seems unfair to translate simply as 'custard'. And then there's his apple crumble, included in the menu. You might expect a French cook to do things with extra lightness, and this, with a rich flavour of cinnamon, doesn't so much crumble as dissolve.

Carpaccio de Poissons

(Serves 6)

700g/1 ½lb salmon fillets
300g/11oz white fish fillets such as pollack, hake or halibut
juice of 5 limes
olive oil
4 tablespoons fresh coriander leaves, chopped
3 tablespoons pink peppercorns, crushed
salt and pepper

In this recipe, the lime juice 'cooks' the fish, but it is important to make sure that the fish is as fresh as possible.

For the marinade, measure the lime juice and whisk in an equal quantity of olive oil. Season to taste.

Rinse the fish fillets and dry them, and put into the freezer for about 45 minutes to firm up. Cut the white fish into wafer-thin slices and arrange them flat in the centre of six large serving plates. Do the same with the salmon, and arrange them around the white fish. Pour the marinade over the fish. Press the slices of fish very gently so that they soak up the marinade, then add the coriander, sprinkling it over each plate, and do the same with the crushed pink peppercorns.

Allow the fish to sit for 10 minutes before serving.

---

touring around

Although St-Malo has a substantial 19th- and 20th-century sprawl, its heart is still the walled city, and the best way to get an idea of it is to take a walk around the **ramparts**. They are regularly interrupted by giant gates and bastions. The **Porte St-Vincent**, with the arms of St-Malo and Brittany above the gates on the outer façade, has been the old city's main entrance since the 18th century. In the pedestrian passageway alongside the main gateways is a tiny barred chamber where anyone who tried to enter the city after the ten o'clock curfew, in force until 1770, was locked up for the night.

To the left of St-Vincent, looking towards the city, is the former principal entrance, the **Grande Porte**, with two massive 15th-century drum towers. The **Bastion de la Hollande** on the sea-side of the walls contains the kennels of the famously ferocious watchdogs, released on to the beach every night during the 18th century to deter any nocturnal interlopers. There are different views at every point around the walls: the main gates overlook the basins of the modern port, with a marina immediately below; further round the circuit, look across to the small harbour islands and the green shore of Dinard across the bay, which lend variety to the scene and make the Rance estuary one of the most beautiful in the world.

The beaches, where you can paddle, swim or windsurf, add an individual touch to the martial old city and extend around the western and northern sides of the ramparts, continuing into the long Grande Plage along the sea front of modern St-Malo. On one side, the Plage de Bon-Secours, there is a walled-off salt-water swimming pool for extra safety. Water buses across to Dinard leave from the Cale de Dinan, by the western corner of the ramparts. Another favourite excursion in St-Malo is to paddle across at low tide to the **Fort National** (*open to* *visitors*), one of the small bastions built on a rocky outcrop: slightly further out (so that it's more important to watch the tide), is the island of **Le Grand Bé**, burial place of the writer Châteaubriand, the arch-romantic, some-time French Foreign Minister and egomaniac who demanded to be buried here, and was accordingly given a virtual state funeral by his home town in 1848.

The present configuration of the ramparts is due to Marshal Vauban, the great military engineer whose ubiquitous presence in the innumerable fortifications put up around France under Louis XIV indicates a remarkable level of energy in an age when even great generals were dependent on horse- or sail-power to get around. St-Malo was then France's most important commercial port, and in 1689 Vauban was sent here to provide the city with a comprehensive system of defences. They are among his greatest work, and, interrupted several times by Anglo-Dutch attacks, were only completed after his death: the old city was considerably extended, especially towards the Porte St-Louis on the south side. The other great change in old St-Malo at this time stemmed from the city council, who after a disastrous fire in 1661 banned the use of wood and made stone—usually granite—obligatory for all buildings within the walls. It is thanks to this, and to the plain, rather severe lines favoured by Vauban's soldier-architects, that St-Malo sometimes has the look of a Gallic Aberdeen. Good examples of the distinctly military-looking *hôtels* erected during that era, built unusually high to maximise space within the confines of the walls, can be seen in the place Châteaubriand and the rue de Chartres, alongside the ramparts near the Grande Porte.

Old St-Malo today, though, is not really as the 18th-century architects left it. Look twice at many of the buildings in the Intra-Muros and you see that the stone is too clean, the edges too sharp, for them to be that old. The modern walled city is, in fact, a very clever replica. In August 1944, when General Patton's army broke out from Avranches across Brittany to the Loire, several thousand German soldiers retreated into St-Malo, determined to deny the allies the use of the port. They were led by one Andreas von Aulock, a caricature of a Prussian general complete with monocle, who alternately infuriated and astonished his American opponents with his supercilious manner and habit of being immaculately turned out even at moments of ultimate crisis. He did have the good grace to order the civilian population out of the city, saying, 'I prefer to have my enemies in front of me'; this, though, only encouraged the US commanders to try and batter their way in with all the means at their disposal, with bombardments from artillery, aircraft and ships offshore. It still took two weeks of ferocious street-by-street fighting before von Aulock finally gave up resistance, in suitably Wagnerian style, in the castle of the old city. By then, an estimated 80 per cent of Intra-Muros St-Malo had been destroyed and the port so comprehensively sabotaged by the Germans that it would still be unusable for months —though Vauban's ramparts withstood 20th-century technology as they once had withstood cannonballs. Photos in the Castle museum show the extent of the devastation.

Post-war, the city fathers of St-Malo did not tinker with any modernistic reconstruction plans but with great determination set about getting their city back as they remembered it. Any buildings that could be were painstakingly restored; others, irredeemably lost, were replaced with new creations in matching style and materials. The resulting restoration is remarkably successful, and a model of its kind. Its cobbled streets remain atmospheric and engaging to wander around, and you will discover corners such as the Cour de la Houssaye, very near to rue de la Corne-de-Cerf and the Marco Polo, where there's a relic of St-Malo from before Vauban's time, the **Maison**

Saint Malo

de la Duchesse Anne, a fine example of a 15th-century Breton stone townhouse. They also attract thousands of visitors, which can make the main squares overpowering in high summer, but other streets stay much more tranquil. Place du Marché (of course) hosts a vigorous **market** every Tuesday and Friday morning that's a great place to stock up on every kind of food (there are also markets in districts outside the walls, on every day except Sunday). Non-market shopping is concentrated around place du Pilori, where there are some elegant fashion shops, and plenty of opportunities to buy Breton-y knick-knacks and other souvenirs.

Here and there in the old town there are sections that retain a raffish, port-city air, such as the line of bars and restaurants, now touristified, set into the ramparts along rue d'Orleans, or waterfrontish dives like the Midnight Café on rue de Chartres. The main social focus of old St-Malo, however, is the **place Châteaubriand** by the Porte St-Vincent, site of a clutch of admittedly expensive grand cafés which have famous turn-of-the-century interiors restored more lovingly than the city's cathedral. Overlooking them on one side of the *place* is the castle, now housing the **Musée d'Histoire de la Ville** (*open Oct–Easter, Mon, Wed–Sun, 10am–noon, 2–6pm; closed Tues and holidays; Easter–Sept, 10am–noon, 2–6pm daily; adm 19F; 9F under-16s*). A visit to the museum allows you to explore the inside of the drum-towered castle, first built in the 1420s, and take in the great views from the top ramparts, with their low galleried roofs. The museum collection itself makes scarcely any concessions to progressive notions of history or modern museum techniques, and is for the most part an unabashedly old-fashioned and gung-ho celebration of local heroes, especially mariners and pirates. Piracy had long been practised by the seamen of St-Malo, but it was not until the 1660s that Louis XIV's minister Colbert followed England and Holland in authorising French captains to engage in privateering attacks on ships so long as they belonged only to the country's enemies, and a portion of the booty was passed on to the state. For much of the 18th century, privateering employed as many men in St-Malo as did conventional trade, and its profits did much to build the post-Vauban city. The legendary Corsair captains are fully commemorated in the museum: there's Duguay-Trouin, who plundered Rio de Janeiro in 1711 and ended up as one of the town's wealthiest citizens; La Bourdonnais, taking Madras from the British in 1746; and Robert Surcouf, who privateered for Napoleon and seized HMS Kent in 1803. Needless to say, these Gallic sea-dogs have never rated much of a mention in standard British history books, but then, one man's dashing pirate hero was always another's seaborne hooligan. Also present in the museum are less martial heroes such as the explorer Cartier, Châteaubriand and the Catholic writer Lamennais, and a mixed bag of displays on aspects of St-Malo's history.

There are also attractive parts of St-Malo outside the walls. From any of the gates on the harbour side of the ramparts, turn right and walk around the quays, past the ferry terminal, from where boats also depart on excursions around the Rance and the bay of Mont St-Michel. Cut right at rue Clémenceau and rue Dauphine, and you will come to the **plage des Sablons**, a sheltered beach on a neatly arc-shaped cove that's now full of yachts and dinghies. Beyond it, clad in trees and standing out into the estuary, is the promontory of **Cité d'Aleth**. This was actually the site of the first city of St-Malo, a Gallo-Roman and then an early Breton settlement; however, the erosion of the peninsula led to the main community's transferring to the Intra-Muros area in 1146. There is a beautiful walk on the Corniche path around the Aleth peninsula, with great views of Dinard and the Rance. On the other side, winding, narrow streets and snug, rocky inlets with shingle beaches much used by dinghy sailors have the feel of a small harbour town rather than part of a city, probably because this, like several other outlying parts of town, was only incorporated into St-Malo in 1967. On a spit of rock stands the **Tour Solidor**, a 14th-century fortress that now contains St-Malo's other main museum, the **Musée International des Cap-Horniers** (*open Oct–Easter, Mon, Wed–Sun, 10am–noon, 2–5pm; closed Tues & holidays; Easter–Sept, daily, 10am–noon, 2–6pm; adm 19F; 9F under-16s*), dedicated to post-pirate maritime traditions, the sailing ships that went to fish the Newfoundland banks and, especially, around Cape Horn.

St-Malo also has another nautical attraction that's potentially of much wider interest, the **Manoir de Jacques Cartier** (*open Oct–Mar, 10am–3pm; June–Sept, 10–11.30am, 2.30–6pm; Sept–June, Mon–Fri only; July–Aug, daily; adm 20F, 15F 5–10s*) at Limoëlou, away on the eastern edge of the city in the suburb of Rotheneuf. Cartier discovered the St Lawrence river and founded Montreal, and so French Canada; his house is actually the only home of any of the voyagers of the great age of exploration, of any country, that still exists and is open to view. It's quite hard to find—the best way to get there is probably to follow the beach road and avenue Kennedy straight out of St-Malo, and then look for signs when you get to Rotheneuf—but this plain little Breton manor house, in its drains, marriage chests, and simple kitchen, gives a fascinating insight into the life of a none-too-prosperous gentleman of the time. This is despite the fact that none of the articles at the house actually belonged to Cartier, for the manor-farm had been through many owners before its restoration by a Canadian foundation in the seventies. Cartier first sailed to Canada in 1534, and then again the next year, when he discovered the Canadian winter and lost most of his crew to cold or scurvy. Before his third voyage in 1542 he was told by King François Ier that, as a commoner, he had to go as second-in-command to a nobleman; the irascible Cartier refused to accept this and sailed off in his own ship, hoping to reinstate himself with the King by returning with some gold given to him by Indians. However, this turned out to be no more than iron pyrites or 'fool's gold', and Cartier retired to his basic house disgraced and unthanked. He died of the plague in 1557; it has been believed that he was buried in the cathedral in St-Malo, although during restoration of the house an unidentified body was discovered buried beneath the kitchen.

If you are continuing east from St-Malo, be sure to go on from Rotheneuf directly on to the coast road, the D201. This will take you past headlands, lighthouses, and a succession of beautiful coves with open seas and scudding surf to the fishing harbour of **Cancale**, one of Colette's favourite holiday towns, and famous throughout France for its oysters. On a good day, there are also views all the way across to Mont St-Michel.

A Culinary Glossary

The full French culinary vocabulary is enormous, and several pocket guides are available that give extensive lists of the many terms and phrases. The following should, though, provide some of the necessary basics.

Useful Phrases

I'd like to book a table (for two/at 12.30pm)	*Je voudrais réserver une table (pour deux personnes/à midi et demie)*
lunch/dinner	*le déjeuner/le dîner*
Is it necessary to book for lunch/dinner today?	*Est-ce qu'il faut réserver pour déjeuner/dîner aujourd'hui?*
Waiter/Waitress! (to attract their attention)	*Monsieur/Madame/Mademoiselle! S'il vous plaît*
The 130F menu, please	*Le menu à centtrente francs, s'il vous plaît*
Which are your specialities?	*Quelles sont les specialités de la maison?*
What is (this dish), exactly?	*Qu'est-ce que c'est exactement, (ce plat)?*
The wine list, please	*La carte des vins, s'il vous plaît*
Another bottle of wine, please	*Une autre bouteille, s'il vous plaît*
water (from the tap, perfectly good in France, and usually given as a matter of course)	*une carafe d'eau*
mineral water/fizzy/still	*eau minérale/gazeuse/plate*
coffee (espresso)	*café*
white coffee	*café au lait /café crème*
That was wonderful	*C'était formidable/délicieux*
We've enjoyed the meal very much, thank you	*Nous avons très bien mangé, merci*
The bill, please	*L'addition, s'il vous plaît*

Some Northern and Norman Specialities

barbue à l'oseille	brill in a sorrel sauce (Norman)
canard, caneton rouennais	duck or duckling lightly roasted and served with a wine and cognac sauce thickened with blood and juices
carbonnade	beef braised in beer with onions, typical of Flanders
caudière	fish stew with mussels, from the coast of the Pas-de-Calais
coq à la bière	chicken cooked in beer with mushrooms
ficelle picarde	crêpe filled with ham, mushrooms and onions and covered in a cheese sauce
flamiche/tarte flamiche	tart, like a quiche, filled with leeks, cream and cheese; Picardy and the north
jambon au cidre	ham baked in cider
marmite dieppoise	fish and shellfish stew with white wine, leeks and cream
moules à la crème (normande)	mussels cooked in white wine, onions and cream, sometimes a touch of cider
moules marinière	mussels cooked in white wine with onions, shallots, butter and parsley
poulet, veau, etc, Vallée d'Auge	served with a crème fraîche, Calvados and onion sauce, with sautéd apples and mushrooms
sauce normande	sauce with a base of cider and crème fraîche
sole normande	sole poached in cider and cream, served with apples
soupe maraîchère/des Hortillons	fresh garden vegetable soup (Amiens)
tarte au Maroilles	rich flan made with Maroilles cheese
teurgoule	Norman rice pudding with thick cinnamon-flavoured crust
tripes à la mode de Caen	classic Norman dish of beef tripe, onions, other vegetables and spices cooked in water, cider and Calvados
Waterzooi	chicken or river fish stewed with vegetables (Flanders)

Poissons et Coquillages (Fish and Shellfish)

bar	sea bass	*lieu*	pollack or ling
barbue	brill	*lotte*	monkfish
bigorneau	winkle, sea snail	*loup de mer*	sea bass
bulot	whelk, large sea snail	*maquereau*	mackerel
		merlan	whiting
cabillaud	fresh cod	*morue*	salt cod
calamar	squid	*moules*	mussels
colin	hake	*mulet*	grey mullet
coques	cockles	*ombre*	grayling
coquilles St-Jacques	large scallops	*oursin*	sea urchin
		palourde	clam
crabe	crab	*pétoncle*	small scallop
crevettes grises	shrimps	*poulpe*	octopus
crevettes roses	prawns	*raie*	skate
daurade	sea bream	*rascasse*	scorpion-fish
écrevisses	freshwater crayfish	*rouget*	red mullet
escargots	snails	*St-Pierre*	John Dory
espadon	swordfish	*saumon*	salmon
flétan	halibut	*saumonette*	dogfish
fruits de mer	seafood	*sauterelles*	shrimps in Picardy
gambas	large prawns	*sole*	sole
hareng	herring	*thon*	tuna
homard	lobster	*tortue*	turtle
huîtres	oysters	*tourteau*	large crab
langouste	spiny lobster or crawfish	*truite*	trout
		truite saumonée	sea/salmon trout
langoustine	Dublin Bay prawn	*turbot*	turbot

Viandes, Volaille, Charcuterie (Meat, Poultry, Charcuterie)

abattis/abats	giblets/offal	*andouille*	large sausage made from offal, served cold
agneau (de pré-salé)	lamb (raised on salt marshes)		

andouillette	smaller than an *andouille*, eaten hot	*lapereau*	young rabbit
ballotine	boned, stuffed and rolled meat (cold)	*lapin*	rabbit
		lard (lardons)	bacon (diced)
biftek, bifteck	steak	*lièvre*	hare
bœuf	beef	*marcassin*	young wild boar
boudin blanc	white pudding, a sausage made with veal, chicken, pork	*merguez*	spicy red sausage, (North African)
		moëlle	beef marrow
boudin noir	black pudding	*navarin (d'agneau)*	lamb stew with spring vegetables
caille	quail		
canard, caneton	duck, duckling	*oie*	goose
cervelas	garlic pork sausage	*os*	bone
cervelles	brains	*perdreau*	young partridge
chapon	capon	*perdrix*	partridge
chevreau	kid	*petit salé*	salt pork
chevreuil	roe deer; also venison in general	*pintade*	guinea fowl
		pintadeau	young guinea fowl
civet	stew (rabbit or hare)		
colvert	mallard	*porc*	pork
daguet	young venison	*poularde*	fattened chicken
dinde, dindon	turkey	*poulet*	chicken
dindonneau	young turkey	*poussin*	spring chicken
estouffade	braised meat stew		
faisan	pheasant	*queue de bœuf*	oxtail
foie	liver	*rillettes*	potted meats (duck, goose, pork, rabbit)
foie gras	fattened goose or duck liver		
		ris (de veau)	sweetbreads (veal)
galantine	meat stuffed, rolled, set in its own jelly	*rognons*	kidneys
		sanglier	wild boar
gésier	gizzard	*saucisses*	sausages
gibiers	game	*saucisson*	salami-type sausages, cold
grive	thrush		
jambon	ham	*tête (de veau)*	head (of veal)
jambon cru	salt-cured, raw ham	*tripes*	tripe
langue (de veau, de bœuf)	tongue (veal, ox)	*veau*	veal
		venaison	venison

Meat Cuts

aiguillette	long, thin slice	magret, maigret (de canard)	breast (of duck)
carré (d'agneau)	rack (of lamb)	noisette (d'agneau)	small round cut (of lamb)
Châteaubriand	double fillet steak, usually with a béarnaise sauce	onglet	flank of beef
contre-filet, faux-filet	sirloin steak	pavé	thick, square fillet
		pieds	trotters
côte, côtelette	chop, cutlet	râble (de lièvre, de lapin)	saddle (of hare, rabbit)
cuisse	leg or thigh		
entrecôte	rib steak	rôti	roast
épaule	shoulder	selle (d'agneau)	saddle (of lamb)
escalope	thin fillet	tournedos	thick round slices of steak
gigot (d'agneau)	leg (of lamb)		
jarret	shin or knuckle	travers de porc	pork spareribs

Cooking Terms for Steaks and Grills

bleu	very rare	à point	medium rare
saignant	rare	bien cuit	well done

Légumes, Herbes, Épices (Vegetables, Herbs, Spices)

ail	garlic	betterave	beetroot
algue	seaweed	blette	swiss chard
aneth	dill	cannelle	cinnamon
aromates	aromatic herbs	carotte	carrot
artichaut	artichoke	céleri	celery
asperges	asparagus	céleri-rave	celeriac
aubergine	aubergine	cèpes	wild, large, brown, fleshy mushrooms
avocat	avocado		
avoine	oats	cerfeuil	chervil
badiane	star anise	champignons	mushrooms
baies roses	pink peppercorns	chanterelles	wild, yellowish mushrooms (girolles)
basilic	basil		

chicorée frisée	curly endive lettuce	*morilles*	morel mushrooms
chou	cabbage	*muscade*	nutmeg
chou-fleur	cauliflower	*navet*	turnip
chou-frisé	kale	*oignons*	onions
chou de mer	seakale	*oseille*	sorrel
choux de Bruxelles	Brussels sprouts	*panais*	parsnip
		persil	parsley
ciboulette	chives	*petits-pois*	peas
citrouille	pumpkin	*piment*	pimento, hot red pepper
cœur de palmier	palm hearts	*piment doux*	sweet red or green pepper (*poivron*)
concombre	cucumber		
coriandre	coriander	*pissenlit*	dandelion
cornichons	gherkins	*pleurotes*	soft-fleshed wild mushrooms
courge	pumpkin		
cresson	watercress	*poireau*	leek
échalote	shallot	*pois chiche*	chickpea
endive	chicory	*poivron*	sweet red or green pepper
épinards	spinach		
estragon	tarragon	*pomme de terre*	potato
fenouil	fennel	*radis*	radish
fèves	broad beans	*raifort*	horseradish
flageolets	white, dried beans	*riz*	rice
frites	chips	*romarin*	rosemary
genièvre	juniper	*safran*	saffron
gingembre	ginger	*salade*	salad
girofle	clove	*salade verte*	green salad
girolles	same as *chanterelles*	*salsifis*	salsify
haricots (rouge, blanc, vert)	beans (kidney, white, green)	*sarriette*	savoury (the herb)
		sarrasin	buckwheat
laitue	lettuce	*sauge*	sage
laurier	bay leaf	*scarole*	escarole
lentilles	lentils	*seigle*	rye
maïs (épis de)	sweet corn (on the cob)	*thym*	thyme
		tomate	tomato
marjolaine	marjoram	*truffes*	truffles
menthe	mint		

Fromages (Cheeses)

Affinage is one of the greatest of French inventions, the delicate process by which cheeses are aged by being washed in different liquids—eau-de-vie, brine, beer—in special cellars to create subtle flavours. A craft cheese merchant who does this on his or her own premises is identified as a *Maître Fromager Affineur*. Any good *fromager* will have a choice of cheeses from all over the country, but the following are the most commonly seen local cheeses in Normandy and northern France.

Cheeses are always *affinés* to reach their best at a certain time, and when buying you will almost certainly be asked when you intend to eat the cheese that's caught your eye. Most of the cheeses below, being soft, have a fairly short life, and after about two weeks from purchasing are liable to become pretty odorous and acidic.

brebis	sheep's-milk cheese
chèvre	goats'-milk cheese
Camembert	Camembert can now be made virtually anywhere, but the authentic local product is identified as 'Camembert de Normandie'. In good Camembert the rind but should have some browny-red colour in it, and it should have a noticeable but not over-strong smell.
Livarot	Norman cow's milk cheese always made in round disks wrapped in five strips of paper, with a thick yellowy-orange rind. Quite pungent, the strongest of the Normandy cheeses.
Maroilles	the classic cheese of northern France, with variants found from Picardy to Flanders. It's a strong cow's milk cheese with a dark reddy-brown rind, a soft texture and (sometimes) a powerful smell. Some Maroilles is washed in beer during affinage, which gives it extra strength in taste and odour.
Neufchâtel	from the Pays de Bray (*see* p.89), the only one of the main Normandy cheeses from north of the Seine, and very different from Camembert and the others from further south. It has a slightly crumbly texture, a mild but still flavoursome taste and a white, powdery rind.
Pavé d'Auge	very similar to Pont l'Evêque, but stronger, with a darker rind
Pont-l'Evêque	tender Norman cow's milk cheese, made in squares, with a whiteish-brown rind. Softer in texture than Camembert and milder in flavour, but still with a noticeable tang. Should not have a very strong smell.
Rollot	another northern cheese, strong and spicy like Maroilles, with a lighter, yellower rind. It is often made in round- or heart-shapes.

Fruits, Noix, Desserts (Fruits, Nuts, Desserts)

abricot	apricot	groseilles	red currants
amande	almond	macarons	macaroons
ananas	pineapple	madeleine	small sponge cake
banane	banana	mandarine	tangerine
bavarois	made with whipped cream, egg custard	mangue	mango
		marrons	chestnuts
bombe	ice-cream dessert in a round mould	miel	honey
		mirabelles	small yellow plums
brugnon	nectarine	mûres	mulberries, blackberries
cacahouètes	peanuts		
cajou	cashew nut	myrtilles	bilberries
cassis	blackcurrant	noisette	hazelnut
cerise	cherry	noix	walnut
charlotte	dessert in a mould with ladies' fingers	œufs à la neige	light meringue in a vanilla custard
citron/citron vert	lemon/lime	pamplemousse	grapefruit
clafoutis	black-cherry tart	parfait	Chilled mousse
coing	quince	pastèque	watermelon
corbeille de fruits	basket of fruits	pêche	peach
coupe	ice-cream cup	pignons	pine nuts
crème anglaise	very light custard	pistache	pistachio
crème Chantilly	sweet whipped cream	poire	pear
crème fleurette	double cream	pomme	apple
crème fraîche	sour cream	prune	plum
crème pâtissière	custard filling	pruneau	prune
dattes	dates	reine Claude	greengage
figues	figs	raisin	grapes
figue de Barbarie	prickly pear	raisins secs	raisins
fraises (des bois)	strawberries (wild)	sablé	shortbread biscuit
framboises	raspberries	savarin	ring-shaped cake, in rum- or kirsch-flavoured syrup
fruit de la passion	passion fruit		
génoise	sponge cake		
glace	ice cream	tarte Tatin	caramelised apple pie, upside-down
grenade	pomegranate		
		truffes	chocolate truffles

General Terminology

aigre-doux	sweet and sour	*confit*	meat preserves
allumettes	strips of puff pastry or potatoes	*confiture*	jam
		coulis	thick sauce, purée
amuse-gueules	appetisers	*court-bouillon*	stock
(à l') anglaise	plain boiled	*croustade*	savoury pastry case
barquette	small pastry boat	*(en) croûte*	in a pastry crust
béarnaise	classic sauce of egg yolks, white wine shallots, butter, tarragon	*cru*	raw
		crudités	raw vegetables
		cuit	cooked
béchamel	white sauce of butter, flour, milk	*demi-glace*	basic brown sauce, reduced meat stock
beignets	fritters	*diable*	peppery sauce: mustard, vinegar, shallots
Bercy	similar to a *beurre blanc*, but thicker		
		Duxelles	mushrooms and shallots sautéd in butter and cream
beurre blanc	reduced sauce of butter, white wine, vinegar, shallots		
		émincé	thinly sliced
beurre noir	browned butter, lemon juice, capers and parsley	*épices*	spices
		farci	stuffed
		(au feu de bois)	cooked over a wood fire
bisque	thick soup, usually of seafood		
		feuilleté	flaky pastry leaves
blanquette	thick creamy stew	*forestière*	with mushrooms bacon and potatoes
bouchée	tiny mouthful, or vol-au-vent		
		(au) four	oven-baked
bouillon	stock or broth	*fourré*	filled or stuffed, usually sweets
braisé	braised		
brioche	sweet bread or roll	*frappé*	with crushed ice
(à la) broche	spit-roasted	*fricassé*	braised in sauce of white wine, butter, and cream
brouillé	scrambled		
brûlé	caramelised ('burnt)		
chasseur	white wine sauce, mushrooms, shallots	*frit*	fried
		friture	mixed platter of small fried fish
chausson	pastry turnover		
cocotte	round ceramic dish	*fumé*	smoked
		galette	buckwheat pancake

garni	garnished; served with vegetables	*poché*	poached
		poêlé	pan-fried
gelée	aspic	*poivrade*	peppery sauce: a demi-glace, wine, vinegar, vegetables
glacé	iced		
grillade	mixed grill		
hachis	minced or chopped	*poivre*	pepper
hollandaise	sauce of egg yolks, butter, lemon juice	*potage*	thick soup
		primeurs	early-season vegetables
jardinière	with diced garden vegetables		
		printanière	garnish of spring vegetables
marmite	small casserole		
matelote	fish stew	*quenelles*	dumplings made with fish or meat
meunière	fish: floured, fried in butter, with lemon and parsley		
		râpé	grated, shredded
		rémoulade	mayonnaise with capers, mustard, gherkins, herbs; also shredded celery
mijoté	simmered		
Mornay	cheesy béchamel		
mousseline	hollandaise sauce with egg whites and whipped cream		
		roulade	rolled meat or fish, often stuffed
moutarde	mustard		
(à la) nage	poached in an aromatic broth (fish)	*sabayon*	whipped up wine, egg-yolks and sugar (*zabaglione*)
nature, au naturel	simple, plain	*salé*	salted, spicy
panaché	mixed, a mixture	*sauvage*	wild
pané	breaded	*Soubise*	white onion sauce
(en) papillote	baked in buttered paper or foil	*sucré*	sweet, sugared
		suprême	boned breast of poultry; fish fillet; a creamy sauce
Parmentier	with potatoes		
pâte	pastry, dough		
pâte à chou	choux pastry	*tiède*	lukewarm
pâte brisée	shortcrust pastry	*timbale*	small pie cooked in dome-shaped mould
paupiettes	thin slices of fish or meat filled, rolled, wrapped to cook		
		tranche	slice
		(à la) vapeur	steamed
paysan, paysanne	country-style; with bacon, potato, carrot, onion, turnip	*velouté*	white sauce flavoured with stock
		Véronique	garnished with grapes